MAKE TRAX

WESTPRINT Nhill

AUSTRALIA
4WD • OUTBACK • COUNTRY • STATE • TRAVEL
ATLAS

AFN FISHING & OUTDOORS

First published 2015
Reprinted 2016, 2019
Updated 2024

Published and distributed by
Australian Fishing & Outdoors
PO Box 544 Croydon, Victoria 3136
Telephone: (03) 9729 8788
Email: sales@afn.com.au Website: www.afn.com.au

ISBN: 9781 8651 32952
J1045

KEY MAP AND CONTENTS

MAP SYMBOLS

	Freeway or expressway
118	Major highway; Distance between major features (km)
	Major road, sealed; Unsealed; Bridge
45	Minor road, sealed; Unsealed; Minor distance (km)
	Station track (private); Grid; 4WD track; Gate
	Suggested Outback Track or Trip (see list below)
1 1 20 D96	National highway number; National route; State routes
■ □ ●	Homestead; Ruin; Landmark or tourist feature
	Pastoral Lease or Aboriginal Land boundary
	Railway line and station
	Bore or well; Spring; Tank or dam
	Watercourse; Waterhole; Fishing spot
	Perennial lake; Mainly dry or salt lake
	Sandridges
	National or conservation park
	Regional or other reserve
	Military training or prohibited area (restricted access)
	Aboriginal land (permit may be required to enter)
� · ↓VHU8 P	Windmill; Yard; Tower (with UHF callsign); Parking bay
	Roadside rest area; Airport or airstrip; Fuel supplies
A ⌂ A	Camping; Caravan park; All services

NOTES FOR THE MAP USER

1. Map reliability and content

Westprint Maps have specialised in publishing maps of the inland deserts and Outback regions of Australia for many years. All care has been taken to ensure the most accurate and up to date information has been used in the preparation of the map pages covering the Outback. Data has been sourced from local authorities and agencies, and in many cases, personally checked in the field by Westprint Maps to provide greater reliability however, no guarantee of absolute accuracy can be made.

Some map pages contain significantly more Geoscience Australia data than others and much of this has not been verified in the field by Westprint Maps. The affected maps are identified by a warning note as they may contain less detail than may be found elsewhere. Many of these pages occur in the east of Australia, outside of Westprint's area of specialty.

2. Gates

Leave all gates as you find them and treat station owners and their property with respect. They are not there to provide services for travellers (tourist enterprises excepted).

3. Station tracks

Do not use station tracks as shown on these maps without prior permission. Many private properties and areas subject to petroleum exploration contain a maze of tracks which may cause disorientation to some travellers.

4. Road and track conditions

The condition of some roads shown on this map can change dramatically after rain. Average condition only is shown.

All maps in this atlas are supplied by **Westprint Maps** Pty Ltd,
6 Park St Nhill, Victoria 3418
Web: www.westprint.com.au Email: info@westprint.com.au
Ph: 03 5391 1466 Fax: 03 5391 1473
Maps contain base data that is © copyright
Geoscience Australia 2022.
All maps are © copyright Westprint Maps 2022.
Cartography and book design by John Frith,
flatEARTHmapping.com.au

Geographic projection based on WGS 84 datum.
See individual map pages for scale information.

WESTPRINT
OUTBACK MAPS

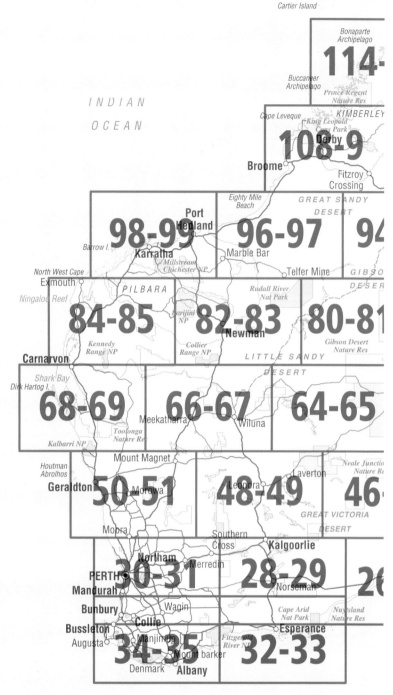

OUTBACK TRACKS AND TRIPS

*The suggested 4WD tracks and trips listed below are all clearly highlighted and labelled on
the atlas maps. To locate a track, simply refer to the page numbers shown.*

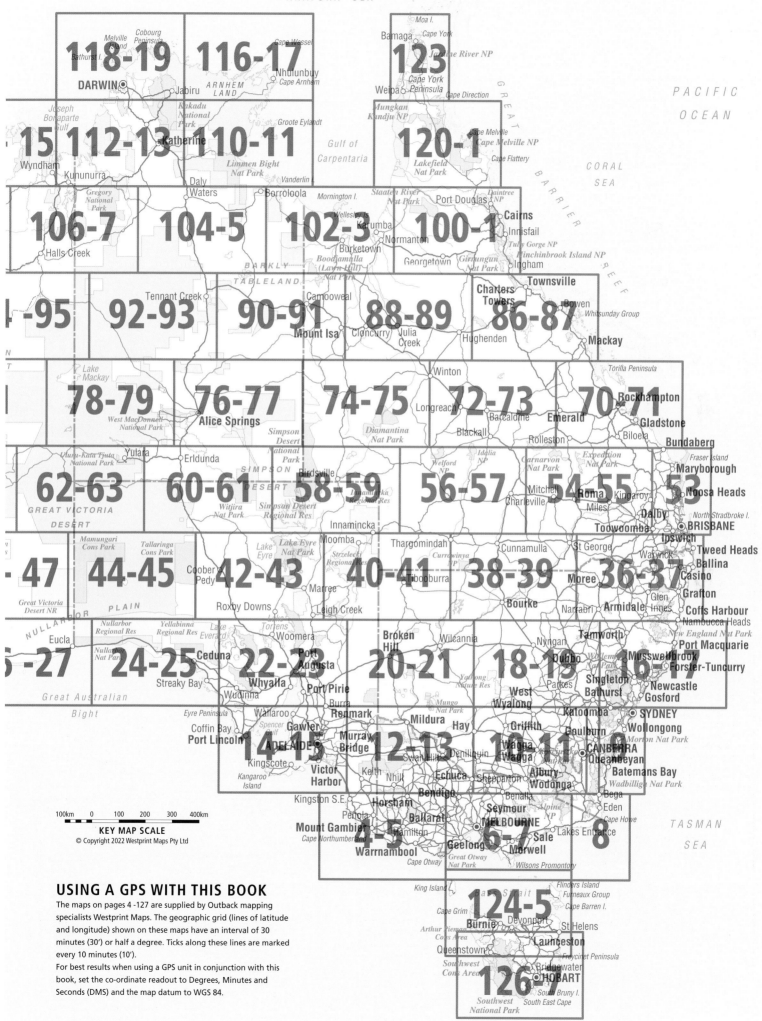

ARAFURA SEA

PACIFIC OCEAN

118-19 DARWIN

116-17 ARNHEM LAND

123

15 **112-13** Katherine **110-11**

120-1

Gulf of Carpentaria

CORAL SEA

106-7 Halls Creek

104-5

102-3

100-1 Cairns

Townsville

-95

92-93 Tennant Creek

90-91 Mount Isa

88-89 Cloncurry Julia Creek

Charters Towers

86-87 Mackay

78-79 Alice Springs

76-77

74-75

72-73

70-71 Rockhampton Gladstone

Bundaberg

62-63 GREAT VICTORIA DESERT

60-61

58-59

56-57

54-55 Roma

53 Maryborough Noosa Heads

BRISBANE

-47

44-45 Coober Pedy

42-43 Roxby Downs

40-41 Tibooburra

38-39 Moree

36-37 Grafton Coffs Harbour

-27 Eucla

24-25 Ceduna Streaky Bay

22-23 Whyalla Port Pirie

20-21 Broken Hill

18-19 Dubbo Bathurst

16-17 Newcastle Gosford

Port Lincoln

14-15 ADELAIDE

12-13 Mildura Hay

10-11 Wagga Wagga

8 CANBERRA Batemans Bay

4-5 Warrnambool

6-7 MELBOURNE Sale

TASMAN SEA

124-5 Burnie Devonport Launceston

126 HOBART

100km 0 100 200 300 400km
KEY MAP SCALE
© Copyright 2022 Westprint Maps Pty Ltd

USING A GPS WITH THIS BOOK

The maps on pages 4 -127 are supplied by Outback mapping specialists Westprint Maps. The geographic grid (lines of latitude and longitude) shown on these maps have an interval of 30 minutes (30') or half a degree. Ticks along these lines are marked every 10 minutes (10').

For best results when using a GPS unit in conjunction with this book, set the co-ordinate readout to Degrees, Minutes and Seconds (DMS) and the map datum to WGS 84.

40'   50'   **139°**   10'   20'   30'   40'   50'   **140°**   10'   20'   30'   40'   50'   **141°**   10'

12

108

Upper South East
Marine Park

Padthaway   Padthaway
Cons Park

Bangham
Cons Park

Bangham

Little Desert
National Park

66

112

Lake Nadzab

Lacepede
Bay

Keppoch

40

Frances   Minimay

Lake Cadnite

Neurapurr

RIDDOCH

Binnum

Kingston S.E.

19

B1

Mount
Scott CP

Avenue
Range

Fairview
Cons Park

28

A66

Kybybolite

Talageira
Mullinger Swamp

Lake
Bringalbert

Bringalbert
Benayeo

Cape Jaffa
Cape Jaffa
Lighthouse

B101

48

Lucindale

Naracoorte

Hynam

32   Apsley

37°

Wright Bay

44

• Mt Benson

48

34

23

Boatswain Point

Southern

Lake
Hawdon
North

Bool
Lagoon

Naracoorte Caves
Cons Park

Joanna

Langkoop

Upper South East
Marine Park

Guichen
Bay

Robe

Lake Robe

Lake Hawdon
South

Greenways

**Big Heath
Cons Park**

Maaoope

Struan

50   **Glen Roy**
Cons Park

Bool Lagoon
Game Reserve

Father
Woods

Wrattonbully

Poolaijelo

Lake Eliza

Ports

42

Reedy

Glenroy

Bailey's
Rocks

Little Dip CP

46

M

Coonawarra

Nora Creina

Lake St Clair

Drain

Woakwine
Cutting

B1

62

Penola
Cons Park

Penola

Dorodong

Lake George

B101

172

38

HWY

Furner

Netherley

Ktongart

101

Lake
Mundi

Beachport CP

Beachport

Ck

Hatherleigh

52

Penola
Forest

Lake Mundi

Highway

Rendelsham

Nangwarry

A66

Rivoli Bay

Southend

32

Mount
Burr

Kalangadoo

Wepar

51

Tarpeena

Lindsay

Millicent

Oil Rig Square

Tantanoola

Glencoe
Woolshed

Wandilo

Mt Gambier
Airport

Ardno

GLENELG

Strathdownie

Canunda
National Park

PRINCES

50

B1

Mil-Lel

Lower South East
Marine Park

Lake
Bonney

Compton

Myora

Forest

Rennick

Puralka

A1

Number Two
Rocks

▲MOUNT GAMBIER

Glenburnie

Caroline
Forest

50

HWY

Carpenter Rocks

Kongorong

Bellum Bellum

B66

Caveton

Caroline

Princess Margaret
Rose Caves

Blackfellows Caves

28   •Mt
Schank

Caveton

36

Nene Valley
Cons Park

Allendale East

Donovans
Nelson

G192

38°

Port
MacDonnell

Stony
Point

Piccaninnie
Ponds CP

Lower Glenelg
National Park

Discovery
Bay

10'

20'

30'

NT

QLD

WA

SA

NSW

39°

VIC

TAS

10'

▲
NORTH

20'

10km   0   10   20   30   40km

© Copyright Westprint Maps Pty Ltd 2022

30'

40'   50'   **139°**   10'   20'   30'   40'   50'   **140°**   10'   20'   30'   40'   50'   **141°**   10'

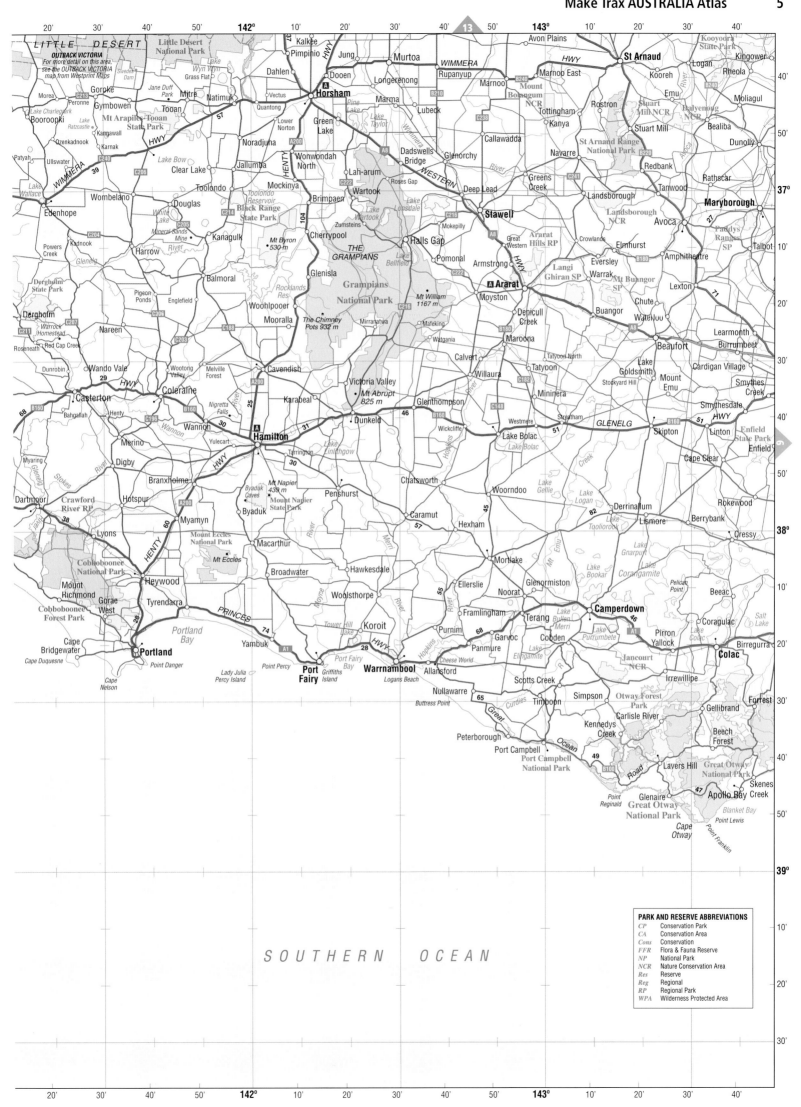

LITTLE   DESERT
OUTBACK VICTORIA
For more detail on this area,
see the Outback Victoria
map from Westprint Maps

Little Desert
National Park

Kooyoora
State Park

Kalkee
Pimpinio   Jung   Murtoa   Avon Plains
Morea   Gorake   WIMMERA   Kingower
Peronne C213   Rupanyup   Marnoo East   St Arnaud   Logan   Rheola
Gymbowen   Dahlen   Dooen Longerenong   Marnoo   B240 Mount   Kooreh   Moliagul
Booroopki   Mitre Natimuk Vectus   B210   Bolangum   Rostron Emu
Swede's   Jane Duff   Lubeck   C238   NCR   Tottingham   Kanya   Stuart   Balyenong
Dam   Park   Tooan   Quantong   Horsham   Marma   Mill NCR   NCR
Lake   HWY   Green   Lower   Callawadda   Navarre Redbank   Bealiba
Charlegark Mt Arapiles-Tooan   Noradjuha Norton Lake   River Greens   Landsborough
Patyah Lake   State Park   Wonwondah   Roses Gap Glenorchy   Creek C241 NCR   Dunolly
Ozenkadnook Ratzcastle Kangawall Karnak   North Lah-arum   Deep Lead   Landsborough Tanwood
Ullswater   Clear Lake   Mockinya   Wartook   Lake   Stawell   NCR   Avoca Maryborough
WIMMERA C240   Jallumba   Brimpaen   Zumsteins Lonsdale Mokepilly   Crowlands Elmhurst
39   C206 Toolondo   Black Range   Halls Gap   Great   Langi   Eversley Amphitheatre
Lake   Douglas   State Park   Cherrypool   THE   Lake Pomonal Western Ararat Ghiran SP Warrak Talbot
Wallace Edenhope   Kanagulk   GRAMPIANS Bellfield   Hills RP   Mt Buangor
Powers   Kadnook Harrow   Mt Byron   Glenisla   Grampians   Armstrong HWY   SP Lexton 71
Creek C204   Balmoral 530 m   Rocklands National Park Mt William   Denicull Chute
Dergholm C207   Woohlpooer Reservoir 1167 m   Moyston   Creek Waterloo
State Park Nareen   Mooralla   Englefield C216 Mafeking B180 Maroona Buangor Beaufort Learmonth
Dergholm C211 Pigeon   C203   The Chimney   Mirranatwa   Calvert Maroona   Burrumbeet
Warrock Ponds   C188   Pots 932 m   Watgania   Tatyoon North Cardigan Village
Homestead   Cavendish Victoria Valley Willaura Tatyoon   Lake Smythes
Roseneath Red Cap Creek   Mt Abrupt   Glenthompson C182   Goldsmith Mount Creek
Dunrobin Wando Vale   Wootong 825 m   Karabeal   Stockyard Hill Emu Smythesdale
29 HWY Vale Melville A200 Nigretta   Dunkeld 46 B160 Westmere Mininera C148 Skipton HWY Linton Enfield
Casterton Coleraine Forest Falls 25   Wickcliffe   Stretham   B160 51   State
68 B160   31   Lake Bolac   GLENELG Cape Clear Park
Bahgallah Henty C195 B160   Yulecart   Lake Linlithgow Lake Bolac 51   Enfield SP
Merino C196 Wannon 30 Hamilton Tarrington Lake Hopkins Lake Bolac   Smythesdale
Myaring   Digby   A 30 Bolac   Creek Woorndoo   Rokewood
Dartmoor Crawford   Branxholme   Mt Napier Chatsworth   Lake Berrybank Cressy
River RP 38 Hotspur   Byaduk 439 m Penshurst   Gellie Lismore
Lyons   Myamyn   Byaduk Mount Napier   Caramut Hexham   Logan 82
Mount 60 Macarthur Caves State Park   57   45   Lake Tooliorook
Eccles   Heywood   Mt Eccles   Hawkesdale   Mortlake Lake Glenormiston
Cobboboonee National Park Broadwater   Ellerslie Gnarput Bookar Beeac
Mount National Park   Woolsthorpe   55 Noorat Lake Lake Pelican
Richmond Gorae Tyrendarra   Tower Hill Koroit Framlingham Merri Corangamite Point
Cobboboonee West 28 PRINCES Lake   Purnim 68 Terang   Camperdown Coragulac
Forest Park   74   Yambuk   Moyne HWY   Garvoc Bullen A1 Pirron Lake 46 Birregurra
Cape Portland Portland Point Percy A1 Port Fairy Warrnambool Panmure Cobden Purrumbete Yallock Colac
Bridgewater Bay   Lady Julia Port Bay Cheese World Elingamite Jancourt Irrewillipe Salt
Cape Duquesne   Percy Island Fairy Griffiths Allansford   NCR   Lake
Cape   Point Danger   Point Percy Island Logans Beach   Scotts Creek   Forrest
Nelson   Nullawarre 65   Simpson Otway Forest
Buttress Point Curdies Timboon   Park Gellibrand
Great   Kennedys   Carlisle River Beech
Peterborough   Creek   Forest
Port Campbell 49   Lavers Hill Great Otway
Port Campbell B100   Road   National Park Skenes
National Park   Glenaire 47 Apollo Bay Creek
Point Great Otway Blanket Bay
Reginald National Park Point Lewis
Cape Point Franklin
Otway

PARK AND RESERVE ABBREVIATIONS

CP	Conservation Park
CA	Conservation Area
Cons	Conservation
FFR	Flora & Fauna Reserve
NP	National Park
NCR	Nature Conservation Area
Res	Reserve
Reg	Regional
RP	Regional Park
WPA	Wilderness Protected Area

S O U T H E R N   O C E A N

BENDIGO
MARYBOROUGH
Castlemaine
BALLART
MELBOURNE
Geelong
Seymour
Euroa
Benalla
Mansfield
Healesville
Dandenong
Cranbourne
Frankston
Mornington
Werribee
Bacchus Marsh
Melton
Sunbury
Craigieburn
Woodend
Macedon
Warragul
Trafalgar
Leongatha
Korumburra
Wonthaggi
Apollo Bay
Lorne

Port Phillip

B A S S   S T R A I T

King Island

Please Note:
Many features on this map have
been derived from Australian Government
digital data and have not been thoroughly
checked in the field by Westprint Maps.

Great Otway
National Park

Mornington Peninsula
National Park

French Island
National Park

Lake Eildon
National Park

Kinglake
National Park

Yarra Ranges
National Park

20' 30' 40' 50' **147°** 10' 20' 30' 40' 11 50' **148°** 10' 20' 30' 40'

Moyhu
Myrtleford
Ovens
Mitta Mitta
Lake Dartmouth
Tom Groggin
Ingebyra
Numbla Vale

King Valley
Alpine
Eurobin
Alpine National Park
Granite Peak 1393 m
Buckwong Creek
Mt Pilot 1831 m
Mulligans Mtn 922 m

Whitfield
Mount Buffalo Nat Park
Porepunkah
Tawonga
Mt Bogong 1984 m
Kosciuszko National Park

Cheshunt
The Horn 1723 m
Bright
Mount Beauty
Bogong
Suggan Buggan
NSW VIC

Dandongadale
Harrietville
Mt Feathertop 1922 m
Falls Creek
Glen Valley
Alpine National Park
Corrowong

Tolmie
Lake Buffalo
Bogong High Plains
Rocky Valley Reservoir
Benambra
Lake Omeo

Merrijig
Mt Hotham 1868 m
Hotham Heights
Omeo
Marble Gully Mount Tambo NCR
Delegate River

Mirimbah
Mt Buller 1805 m
Mount Buller Alpine Village
Mt Murray 1640 m
Cobungra
Great
Bindi
Dellicknora

The Viking 1508 m
Alpine
Mt Richardson 1250 m

The Governor 1446 m
Alpine National Park
Swifts Creek
Gelantipy

GREAT
Mt Reynard 1710 m
The Pinnacles 1445 m
Ensay
Snowy River National Park

Woods Point
Mt Wellington 1635 m
Tambo Crossing
Murrindal
Martins Creek FFR
Errinundra Nat Park

Licola
Avon Wilderness Park
Castleburn
Dargo
Mount Elizabeth NCR
Buchan

Aberfeldy
Mitchell River National Park
Bullumwaal
Brodribb FFR

Mt Baw Baw 1565 m
Melwood
Wiseleigh
Sarsfield
Nowa Nowa
Newmerella
Orbost
Cabbage Tree Creek

Beardmore
Lindenow
Nicholson
Colquhoun Reg Park
Tostaree
Lake Curlip

Baw Baw Alpine Village
Glenmaggie
Briagolong
Bairnsdale
Swan Reach
Lake Tyers
Marlo

Walhalla
Glenmaggie Reservoir
Newry
Boisdale
Lakes Entrance
Cape Conran

Erica
Maffra
Paynesville
Metung
Kalimna

Moondarra
Heyfield
Tinamba
Stratford
Bengworden
Meerlieu
Point Wilson

Moondarra State Park
Cowwarr
Bundalaguah
Nambrok
The Lakes National Park

Glengarry
Toongabbie
Winnindoo
Loch Sport

Moe
Traralgon
PRINCES
Sale
Lake Wellington

Yallourn
Morwell
Rosedale
Longford
Lake Coleman

Narracan East
Flynns Creek Upper
Holey Plains SP
Paradise Beach

Yinnar
Churchill
Traralgon South
Gormandale
Golden Beach

Boolarra
Balook
Carrajung
Stradbroke FFR
Seaspray

Tarra-Bulga National Park
Blackwarry
Darriman
Woodside

Womerah
Devon
Woodside Beach

Binginwarri
Yarram
Hunterston

Toora
Hedley
Alberton
St Margaret Island

Port Franklin
Welshpool
Port Albert
Sunday Island
Clonmel Island

Port Welshpool
Shallow Inlet
Snake Island

Corner Inlet
Duck Point
Lighthouse Point

Wilsons Promontory
Monkey Point
Rabbit Island

Mt La Trobe 755 m
Wilsons Promontory National Park

Oberon Bay
Sealers Cove

Tidal River
Cape Wellington
Waterloo Bay

Anser I.
South East Point
South Point

Rodondo Island
Hogan Island

Erith Island
Kent Group
Curtis Island
Dover Island
Deal Island

PARK AND RESERVE ABBREVIATIONS

CP	Conservation Park
CA	Conservation Area
Cons	Conservation
FFR	Flora & Fauna Reserve
NP	National Park
NCR	Nature Conservation Area
Res	Reserve
Reg	Regional
RP	Regional Park
WPA	Wilderness Protected Area

NORTH
10km 0 10 20 30 40km

© Copyright Westprint Maps Pty Ltd 2022

40' | 50' | **149°** | 10' | 20' | 30' | 40' | **9** | 50' | **150°** | 10' | 20' | 30' | 40' | 50' | **151°**

Numbla Vale

Jimenbuen

River

111

Pigeon Box Mtn
1080 m

Brogo

**Biamanga
NP**

66

99

41

Bemboka

B72

Bega

Tanja

Mimosa Rocks National Park

**South East Forest
National Park**

Bimbaya

Kameruka

Candelo

Tathra

Bournda National Park

Bibbenluke

51

Wolumla

Wallagoot Lake

**Merriangaah
Nature Reserve**

B23

Cathcart

Bournda Nature Reserve

Merimbula

Corrowong

Bombala

Coolangubra Mtn
1093 m

Wyndham

Lochiel

Pambula

Pambula Beach

37°

Delegate

River

HWY

Delegate
River

Mila

27

37°

Delegate

Craigie

Towamba

Eden

**N S W
V I C**

**South East Forest
National Park**

**Mount Imlay
National
Park**

Kiah

East Boyd

Dellicknora

Bendoc

Queensborough

Nungatta Mtn
939 m

A1

**Ben Boyd
National Park**

**Errinundra
Nat Park**

Buldah

58

**Coopracambra
National Park**

**South East
Forest
Nat Park**

Wonboyn
Lake

Green Cape

Disaster
Bay

Weeragua

River

River

Genoa

PRINCES

61

Combienbar

Benn

**Nadgee
Nature Reserve**

Genoa

R

Nadgee Point

Club Terrace

Noorinbee

River

47

A1

*Mallacoota
Inlet*

Cape Howe

Cann River

HWY

Thurra

Betka R

Mallacoota

Gabo Island

PRINCES

76

River

Cann

Mueller River

**Alfred
NP**

Wingan R

Little Rame Head

Cabbage Tree
Creek

Bemm
River

*Swan
Lake*

**Croajingolong
National Park**

Wingan Point

Rame Head

Sandpatch Point

*Cape
Conran*

*Pearl
Point*

*Sydenham
Inlet*

*Tamboon
Inlet*

*Cape
Everard*

*Petrel
Point*

38°

T A S M A N   S E A

39°

© Copyright Westprint Maps Pty Ltd 2022

NORTH

10km | 0 | 10 | 20 | 30 | 40km

*Please Note:
Many features on this map have
been derived from Australian Government
digital data and have not been thoroughly
checked in the field by Westprint Maps.*

NT

QLD

WA

SA

NSW

VIC

TAS

PARK AND RESERVE ABBREVIATIONS
CP   Conservation Park
CA   Conservation Area
Cons   Conservation
FFR   Flora & Fauna Reserve
NP   National Park
NCR   Nature Conservation Area
Res   Reserve
Reg   Regional
RP   Regional Park
WPA   Wilderness Protected Area

© Copyright Westprint Maps Pty Ltd 2022

NORTH

10km   0   10   20   30   40km

Please Note:
Many features on this map have
been derived from Australian Government
digital data and have not been thoroughly
checked in the field by Westprint Maps.

NORTH

10km 0 10 20 30 40km

© Copyright 2014 Westprint Maps Pty Ltd

Please Note:
Many features on this map have been derived from Australian Government digital data and have not been thoroughly checked in the field by Westprint Maps.

145°　10'　20'　30'　40'　**18**　50'　146°　10'　20'　30'　40'　50'　147°　10'

Merungle　Cowl Cowl　63　Coondaloo　Monia Gap　Naradhan　Kikoira　Ungarie　Malvena

Inverness　Yarranholm　Gibsonvale　Yalgogrin

Natue　Belmore　Rankins Springs　Weethalle　**West Wyalong**

Booligal　Merriwagga　HIGHWAY　143　B64　Wyalong

Gunbar　Avondale　Goolgowi　Wandella　Stackpoole　Buralyang　Tallimba

34°　Gunbar　Berngarrie　Cocopara Nature Reserve

80　Wyoming　WESTERN　110　Tabbita　49　Cocoparra National Park　70　Wargin

Tarana　Days　Warburn　Beelbangera　Yenda　Binya　86　Barellan　Moombooldool　Mirrool　Ariah Park

MID　Yeadon　Beckom

Bagomba　Carrathool　**Griffith**　Yoogali　Kamarah　Ardlethan　68

36　Hanwood　Murrami

Hay　Illiliwa　Wahwoon　117　Willbriggie　Whitton　67

MURRUMBIDGEE　STURT　Leeton　NEWELL

Oolambeyan National Park　RIVER　57　Yanco

Braemar　Elginbah　Oolambeyan　Coleambally　Way　Lake Coolah　Grong Grong

Singorimbah　Way　Narrandera　Matong　Ganmain

Eurolie　96　Morundah　Afton　Coolamon

Booroorban　Golden Bays　Corobimilla　HIGHWAY　Galore

127　Oak Vale　91　Currawarna

WA　NT　QLD　Sanside　98　Collingullie

SA　NSW　Goree　Boree Creek

VIC　Broome　Uranquinty

TAS　Wood Park　HWY　Lake Urana　Lockhart　Milbrulong　French Park

Wanganella　Lake Cullivel

Moulamein　Creek　Jerilderie　Urana　Mangoplah

Conargo　51　Urangeline　Yerong Creek

Redbank　Boongara　Pleasant Hills

NEWELL　Oaklands　Urangeline East　Henty　Cookardinia

Naringal　Mayrung　Ferndale　OLYMPIC

Deniliquin　B58　RIVERINA　Rand

Blighty　62　B58　HWY　Daysdale　Bulgandra　Culcairn　Morven

Finley　Berrigan　Walbundrie

77　Edward River　40　Savernake　Coreen　Walla Walla

Mathoura　A39　104　Rennie　Brocklesby　Woomargama

Barmah State Park　MURRAY　Barooga　Buraja　Baldale　Burrumbuttock　Gerogery

Moira Lake　Barmah State Park　Strathmerton　15　Yarroweyah　Cobram　MURRAY RIVER　Mulwala　Lake Mulwala　Corowa　53　Howlong　Jindera　Mullengandra

Barmah Lake　38　Katunga　Yarrawonga　Wahgunyah　Lavington　Woomargama SCA

Echuca　Barmah　Nathalia　Waaia　A39　Numurkah　Katamatite　Bundalong　Esmond　VALLEY　**Rutherglen**　**Albury**　Jarvis Creek Plateau RP

Koyuga　Wyuna　55　Wunghnu　Tungamah　Wilby　Chiltern　Barnawatha　Bethanga

Tongala　Goulburn River　Katandra West　St James　Warby Range State Park　52　Springhurst　**Wodonga**　Lake Hume

Strathallan　**Kyabram**　Undera　Congupna　Dookie　Chiltern-Mt Pilot NP　Baranduda RP　Kiewa　Tallangatta

Girgarre　MIDLAND　Tallygaroopna　Cosgrove　Thoona　Boorhaman　Wooragee　Tangambalanga

Corop　74　Mooroopna　**Shepparton**　Devenish　Waranga Basin　Eldorado　**Beechworth**　Yackandandah

Carag Carag　Tatura　Kialla West　Goorambat　Tarrawingee　Noorongong

Lake Cooper　Arcadia　62　A300　**Wangaratta**　Oxley　Stanley　Glen Creek　Tallandoon

Rushworth　HWY　Lake Mokoan　Glenrowan　Milawa　Murmungee　Mudgeegonga　Dederang

Colbinabbin　Whroo NCR　Murchison　43　Baddaginnie　Moyhu　**Myrtleford**　Ovens　Eurobin

Violet Town　54　Reef Hills State Park　**Benalla**　49　Gapsted　B500　29

145°　50'　10'　20'　30'　**6**　40'　146°　10'　20'　30'　40'　50'　147°　10'

Lake Cowal

20' 30' 40' 148° 10' 20' 30' 40' 19 50' 149° 10' 20' 30' 40' 50'

Gooloogong
Wirrinya
Billimari
33
Mandurama Carcoar Newbridge
Barry
Marsden
Westfield
MID
Conimbla National Park
WWII POW Camp
A41 104 Lyndhurst Neville Rockley Oberon
Woodstock
Holmwood
Copperhannia Nature Reserve
Mount David
Lake Oberon
Eurowie
B64 B64
Caragabal
123
Yambira Mtn 774 m
Cowra
Moonbinna
Trunkey
Burraga
Black Springs
A39 38
Grenfell
B64
WESTERN
Bumbaldry
Wattamondara
Darbys Falls
Wyangala
Razorback Nature Reserve
Abercrombie River NP
34°
Quandialla
Bimbi
Greenethorpe
HWY
Koorawatha
Lake Wyangala
Bigga
Peelwood
Barmedman
Bribbaree
Thuddungra
A41
Monteagle
Bendick Murrell
Reids Flat
Tuena
68
Dananbilla Nature Reserve
Glenbrook
Binda
10'
Trungley Hall
Milvale
OLYMPIC
Young
Young Chinese Garden
Murringo
Frogmore
Laggan
Taralga
Temora
Combaning
62
Wombat
Kingsvale
137
Boorowa
Rugby
Abbeyvale
Grabben Gullen
Crookwell
Springdale
Stockinbingal
Wallendbeen
Damondrille
VALLEY
Rye Park
30'
Ingalba Nature Reserve
Murrumburrah
Galong
Kangiara
Dalton
Towrang
Cootamundra
112
Binalong
WAY
Jerrawa
Gunning
Breadalbane
Goulburn
40'
HWY
Bethungra
Muttama
HUME
Bookham
Bowning
M31
80
Old Junee
Illabo
Jugiong
Yass
HWY
Collector
Allawah
Marrar
Marinna
Coolac
141
Burrinjuck Nature Reserve
A25
Murrumbateman
92
Lake Bathurst
50'
Junee
A41
Burrinjuck
BARTON HWY
70
Gundaroo
Tarago
Lake Bathurst
Downside
Harefield
Nangus
Gundagai
Lake Burrinjuck
Wee Jasper
35°
Wantabadgery
MURRUMBIDGEE
RIVER
Tumblong
Brungle
Hall Sutton
Mitchell
Lake George
Nadjigomar NR
Wagga Wagga
Forest Hill
A20
Mount Horeb
Brindabella National Park
Brindabella SCA
Belconnen
Braddon
CANBERRA
Bungendore
KINGS
81
10'
50
Ladysmith
SNOWY
Tumut
Argalong
Kingston
Fyshwick
Queanbeyan
Tallaganda NP
Tarcutta
B72
Adelong
Gilmore
147
Brindabella
Weston Creek
Woden
Hoskinstown
Tallaganda SCA
Braidwood
20'
M31
HUME
Wondalga
Wereboldera
Blowering Reservoir
Kosciuszko National Park
Bimberi Nature Reserve
Corin Dam
Tuggeranong
Royalla
Yanununbeyan SCA
Yanununbeyan NP
Majors Creek
144
Humula
Batlow
Talbingo
MOUNTAINS
Bimberi Peak 1912 m
Namadgi National Park
Tharwa
Captains Flat
Tinderry NR
Araluen
Monga Nat Park
30'
Kunama
Laurel Hill
Bendora Dam
Michelago
Wyanbene Caves Mtn 1058 m
Fairfield
Rosewood
Talbingo Reservoir
Yarrangobilly
Tantangara Reservoir
Scabby Range NR
Yaouk
Gourock National Park
Holbrook
Mannus
Tumbarumba
Yaouk NR
119
Jerangle
Deua National Park
40'
Woomargama National Park
Bogandyera NR
Kiandra
Bredbo
GREAT
50'
Talmalmo
Jingellic
Burrowa Pine Mountain National Park
Cabramurra
Tumut Pond Reserve
Adaminaby
Numeralla
Peakview
Jillicambra Mtn 1052 m
36°
Granya
Mt Lawson State Park
Burrowye
Walwa
Tintaldra
Greg Greg
Tooma
Lake Eucumbene
89
Eucumbene
B23
Kybeyan SCA
Nerrigundah
10'
Koetong
Cudgewa North
Mt Burrowa 1300 m
Bullioh
Berringama
Cudgewa
Hwy
B400
Towong
Khancoban
Kosciuszko National Park
Numeralla
Rock Flat
Kybeyan
Cobargo
20'
Lucyvale
Corryong
Biggara
Khancoban Pondage
Geehi Reservoir
Lake Jindabyne
Berridale
Dangelong Nature Res
Wadbilliga National Park
79
Quaama
Wabba Wilderness Park
Nariel Creek
MURRAY RIVER
Perisher Valley
Snowy River
Cooma
Mt Kosciuszko 2228 m
Jindabyne
Alpine Way
Dalgety
Pigeon Box Mtn 1080 m
30'
Mitta Mitta
Dartmouth
Alpine National Park
Tom Groggin
Thredbo Village
Numbla Vale
Ingebyra
Nimmitabel
66
South East Forest National Park
111
99
Bemboka
Bega
A1
Granite Peak 1393 m
Lake Dartmouth

20' 30' 40' 7 50' 148° 10' 20' 30' 40' 8 50'

NORTH

Please Note:
Many features on this map have been derived from Australian Government digital data and have not been thoroughly checked in the field by Westprint Maps.

10km   0   10   20   30   40km

© Copyright Westprint Maps Pty Ltd 2022

PAR02   PARCOOLA

WA   NT   QLD   SA   NSW   VIC   TAS

Chowilla Regional Reserve
Bookmark Biosphere Reserve
CALPERUM
HAWKS NEST
Chowilla Game Res

Coleraine
Bunnerungee
Burtundy
RIVER
Glen Esk
DARLING
Narweena
Nulla
Warrananga
Fletchers Lake
Dareton
Lake Gol Gol
Border Cliffs
Customs House
Cal Lal
Lake Victoria
Rufus River
Wentworth
Buronga
Lock 6
Cooltong
Murtho Forest Res
100m Step
Murray River NP (Bulyong I.)
Lindsay Point
State Forest
Lindsay Point
Kulnine East
Merbein
MILDURA
Renmark North
Paringa
Renmark
Cooltong Cons Park
Loch Luna Game Res
Pooginook Cons Park
Goyder Hwy
Cadell
Waikerie
Kingston-on-Murray
Lock 5
Berri
Barmera
Glossop
Lyrup
Yamba
Neds Corner
Kulnine
Meringur North
Merbein South
Irymple
Red Cliffs
STURT HWY
Murray River NP (Katarapko)
Lexton
Taldra
Kopi Plains
Ingalta
Noora
Noora Gate
Morkalla
Karween
Meringur
Millewa
Bambill
Carwarp
Tarrango
Callaghan Plain
Benetook
Carwarp
Myrla
Gerard
Wunkar
Taplan
Nangari
Taplan Gate
Shearers Quarters
Settlement
Bakara Cons Reserve
Pata
Veitch
Trig
Nadda
Meribah Gate
SUNSET COUNTRY
Rocket Lake
Raak Plain
Nowingi
Mercunda
Bakara
Meribah
Cobera
Alawoona
Paruna
Millewa South Bore
Aboriginal Rock Holes
Pheenys
Last Hope
Hope
Last
One Tree Plain
Copeville
Mindarie
Wanbi
COX PLAIN
Murray-Sunset National Park
Mopoke Hut
Mt Crozier 111 m
Mt Cowra
Kalyan
Halidon
Sandalwood
Berrook State Forest
Berrook
Underbool
Wymlet Tank
Perponda
Lowaldie
Borrika
Billiat Conservation Park
Butchers Soak
Peebinga
Karte
Peebinga Cons Park
Boltons Soak
Sunset
Green Opal Mine
Linga State Forest
Pink Lakes
Lake Becking
Mt Jess 126 m
Mt Gray
Paignie
Galah
Karoonda
Wynarka
Marama
Mulpata
Smithville
Claypan Bore
Goongee
Manya
Pallarang
Linga
HIGHWAY
Walpeup
Underbool
Timberoo South
Pinnaroo
Panitya
Carina
MALLEE
Cowangie
Tutye
Bolnka
Murrayville
Danyo
Kow Plains
Big Desert State Forest
Mt Observatory 111 m
Patchewollock
MALLEE HIGHWAY
Buccleuch
Sherlock
Peake
Jabuk
Geranium
Parrakie
Wilkawatt
Lameroo
Parilla
Scorpion Springs
Fruit Fly Inspection
Ngallo
Firebreak
Lone Pine
White Springs
Murrayville
O'Sullivan's Lookout & Nature Walk
12 Mile Patch
Baring
Willa
Coomandook
Yumali
Ki Ki
Netherton
One Tree Hill Soak
One Tree Hill 114 m
Baan Hill Picnic Area
Pine Hut Soak
Alcharinga Airstrip
Nanam Well
Pines Camp
Cactus Bore
Coburns Pines
Sim Perry's Bore
Big Dune
Big Billy Bore
Snow Drift
Lake Agnes
Casuarina
Carcuma Cons Park
Box Flat
Hensley Trig Lookout & The Gums Camp
BIG DESERT
Wyperfeld National Park
Hopping Mouse Hill
Lake Brambruk
Eastern Lookout
Wonga
Coonalpyn
Ngarkat Conservation Park
Pertendi Hut
Little Doughboy Mount
Milmed
Milmed Rock
Rock
Milmed Swamp
Trig Pt Hill
Hopetoun West
Mount Boothby Cons Park
Mt Boothby 128 m
Culburra
Comet Bore
Doggers Hut
Big Desert Wilderness Park
Moonlight Tank
Chinaman
Round Swamp
Lake Albacutya
Western Beach
Yaapeet
Yaapeet Beach
Boothby Rocks
Tolmer Rocks
Tintinara
Rabbit Island Soak
Gosse Hill
Mt Rescue 129 m
South Boundary Rd
Mt Shaugh
Gum Tree Well
Red Bluff
Southern Firebreak Track
Wagon Flat Tank
Chinaman Well
Big Desert State Forest
Hopevale
Albacutya
Pella
Rainbow
Kenmare
Bucks Camp Soak
Coombe
Red Bluff Flora & Fauna Reserve
Sanders
Broken Bucket Tank
Williamson's Beach
Outlet Creek
Werrap
Pullut
Messent Cons Park
Martin Washpool CP
Bunbury CP
Blackett Scrub CP
Keith
Brimbago
Wirrega
Cannawigara
Emu Flat Road
Lowan Vale
Karnangook Flora & Fauna Res
Telopea Downs
Old vermin proof fence
Broughton
Yanac
Yanac South
Yanac Swamp
Shultzes Beach
Perenna
Netherby
Lake Hindmarsh
Four Mile Beach
Willenabrina
Jeparit
Peppers Plains
Angip
Gum Lagoon Cons Park
Tilley Swamp CP
Willalooka
Mundulla
Wolseley
Bordertown
Serviceton Reservoir
Yarrock
Ullimur
Kaniva
Miram
Diapur
Boyeo
Nhill
Lorquon
Detpa
Woorak
Traeger Memorial
Tarranyurk
Glenlee
Antwerp
28 Mile Crossing
Coola Coola Swamp
Cesert Camp Cons Reserve
Padthaway
Padthaway Cons Park
Bangham Cons Park
Little Desert National Park
Serviceton
Custon
Western Flat
Three Chain Rd
Yanipy
Miram South
Kinimakatka
Browns Dam
Lawloit
Salisbury
Kiata
Gerang Gerung
WESTERN HWY
Kalkee
Pimpinio
Dopen
Dimboola
Murra Warra
Wail
Mt Moffat 135 m
LITTLE DESERT
Stans Camp
Little Desert National Park
Little Desert Lodge
Bangham
OUTBACK VICTORIA
For more detail on this area, see the OUTBACK VICTORIA map from Westprint Maps.
Swedes Dam
Lake Wyn Wyn
Grass Flat
Dahlen
Wimmera River

20' 30' 40' 50' 143° 10' 20' 30' 40' 21 50' 144° 10' 20' 30' 40' 50'

40'

B&W Camp 30 (Burke's Gambala)
Top 46 Hut Rd
B&W Camp 29 (Becker's Gambala)
Cavan 33
Jamesville
Orange Grove
Murrungrung
Culpataro
Mutherumbung
Top Hut
Tourtmundo Tank
Junction Tank
B&W Camp 29 (McPherson's)
Old Arumpo Station
14
Mungo
Lake Mungo
The Walls of China
Boree Plains
The Vale
Alma
Natue

50'

Joulni
Mungo National Park
Marona
Hatfield

20
39
Arumpo
14
Chibnalwood Lakes
Wampo
Glen Alvie
Oxley
Corrong
Ulonga
80

34°

13
39
16
Turlee
B&W Camp 28 (Kormpang)
Bindura
B&W Camp 23
Lachlan River
Ita Lake
Kalyarr SCA
Tarana

10'

27
Banoon
22
B&W Camp 27 (Linklinkwhoo)
Cole Lagoon
B&W Camp 26 (Goowall)
Road sign at Paika calls this track 'Bourke and Wills Road'
Great Cumbungi Swamp
Kalyarr National Park
Darcoola
Bagomba

A
Mallee Cliffs National Park (No public access)
Prungle
Gullalby Tank
Prungle Lakes
Prungle Hills
B&W Camp 25 (Engin)
Pyong Tank
10
Tin Tin Lake
Tin Tin
B&W Camp 22 (Tinn)
Pilarpunga Lake
Ganaway Lake
Tori Lake
Toopuntul
Newmarket

Monak
A20
Karadoc
83
Prungle
28
Bramah
Muckee Lake
22
Penarie
Nap Nap
Maude
Hay

30'

Murray River
Nangiloc
Colignan
160
Euston
Robinvale
Dry Lake Benanee
Lake Behanee
STURT
58
Road
25
Paika Lake
Paika
B&W Camp 21
B&W Camp 20
Yanga National Park
Lake Tala
Torry Plain
Ravensworth
Booroorban
127

40'

Hattah-Kulkyne National Park
Kulkyne
NSW VIC
B400
MURRAY
19
A20
HWY
Balranald
Yanga Nature Reserve
Yanga SCA
Yanga Lake
131
Warwaegae
Glenhope

Hattah Lakes
Murray-Kulkyne NP
Bannerton
MURRAY
Boundary Bend
92
MURRUMBIDGEE
22
Piamble
Tchelery
Miegunyah

50'

Hattah
35
C252
Wemen
Annuello
C251
Kooloonong
MURRAY VALLEY RIVER
Wakool River
B&W Camp 19 (near Coniston HS Gate)
15

Annuello Flora and Fauna Reserve
Koimbo
Bolton
Natya
B&W Camp 18
Kyalite
Edward River
Moulamein
Wanganella

35°

Trinita
Kiamal
20
18
110

10'

HWY
Nunga
MALLEE
55
Wagant
Manangatang
B12
43
HIGHWAY
Piangil
Tooleybuc
Lake Poon Boon
12
Dilpurra

Ouyen
Mittyack
A79
Chinkapook
Cocamba
HWY
B400
9
Nyah
43
Lake Poomah
Speewa
B&W Camp 17
12
11

20'

Gypsum
67
SUNRAYSIA
Pier Milan
Lake Wahpool
Chillingollah
Lake Timboram
Swan Hill
B&W Camp 16
B&W Camp 15 (Swan Hill riverside park)
Noorong
River
Wakool
Edward River

Tempy
Speed
C248
Nandaly
Lake Tyrrell
Tyrrell Downs
C261
Lake Boga
Fish Point
B&W Camp 14 (The Clump)

30'

Yarto
B220
Nyarrin
119
Long Plains
C246
Ultima
Goschen
Tresco
Lake Boga
Benjeroop
Murrabit
Wakool

Turriff
Gama
Sea Level
Boigbeat
CALDER
Meatian
Tyrrell
Lalbert
Mystic Park
Lake Tutchewop
57
B400

40'

C247
Lascelles
Woomelang
A79
Berriwillock
Lake Lalbert
Lalbert
Beauchamp
Kangaroo Lake
Lake Cullen
Lake Charm
B&W Camp 13 (estimated)
Barham
Koondrook
Thule

Hopetoun
Lake Lacelles
Lake Coorong
Goyura
Watchupga
C244
Culgoa
Cokum
Tittybong
The Marsh
Lake Bael Bael
Kerang
Duck Lake
Reedy Lake
Kerang East
NSW VIC
Bunnaloo

50'

Rosebery
Yarriambiack
Rosebery East
Sutton
Towaninny
Quambatook
C262
Dingwall
C266
Kerang South
48
Cohuna
Womboota

Beulah
C243
Reedy Dam
Curyo
44
Nullawil
Oakvale
Leaghur
B260
Horfield
Leitchville
Gunbower

36°

Galaquil
B200
Kinnabulla
Whirily
Dumosa
Barraport
LODDON
Macorna
B&W Camp 11
Kow Swamp
Patho
RIVER

10'

Brim
Lah
C242
Birchip
B220
Narraport
Wycheproof
C267
Bunguluke
Boort
Durham Ox
Mt Hope
Cairn
Pyramid Hill
Terrick Terrick National Park
Mt Terrick Terrick
B&W Camp 10
Torrumbarry
50
B400

Batchica
Watchem
Morton Plains
Thalia
Corack East
Teddywaddy
Woolshed Swamp
Lake Boort
Mitiamo
Kotta

20'

Warracknabeal
Homecroft
Massey
Banyenong
Wooroonook
Charlton
C273
Wychitella
Wychitella NCR
Borung
Jarklin
Calivil
Prairie
Milloo
Rochester
55

Kellalac
B210
Sheep Hills
Lawler
Litchfield
Wooroonook Lakes
C271
C272
Wychitella
Korong Vale
Serpentine
A79
CALDER
Dingee
B&W Camp 9

30'

Mihyip
C236
Donald
Dooboobetic
Yeungroon
Wedderburn
Glenalbyn
B82 HWY
Raywood
Elmore
A300
Lake Cooper
Colbinabbin

Jung
Murtoa
SUNRAYSIA
Rich Avon
Avon Plains
31
Kurnwill West
Kingower
Inglewood
Greater Bendigo NP
Campbells Forest
Goornong
Bagshot
Green Lake
Corop

40'

B200
WIMMERA
Rupanyup
Marnoo
Cope Cope
Coonooer Bridge
Kooyoora State Park
Logan
Bridgewater
B260
Huntly
B&W Camp 8
Cairn
52

20' 30' 40' 50' 143° 10' 5 20' 30' 40' 50' 144° 10' 20' 30' 6 40' 50'

PARK AND RESERVE ABBREVIATIONS
CP — Conservation Park
CA — Conservation Area
Cons — Conservation
FFR — Flora & Fauna Reserve
NP — National Park
NCR — Nature Conservation Area
Res — Reserve
Reg — Regional
RP — Regional Park
WPA — Wilderness Protected Area

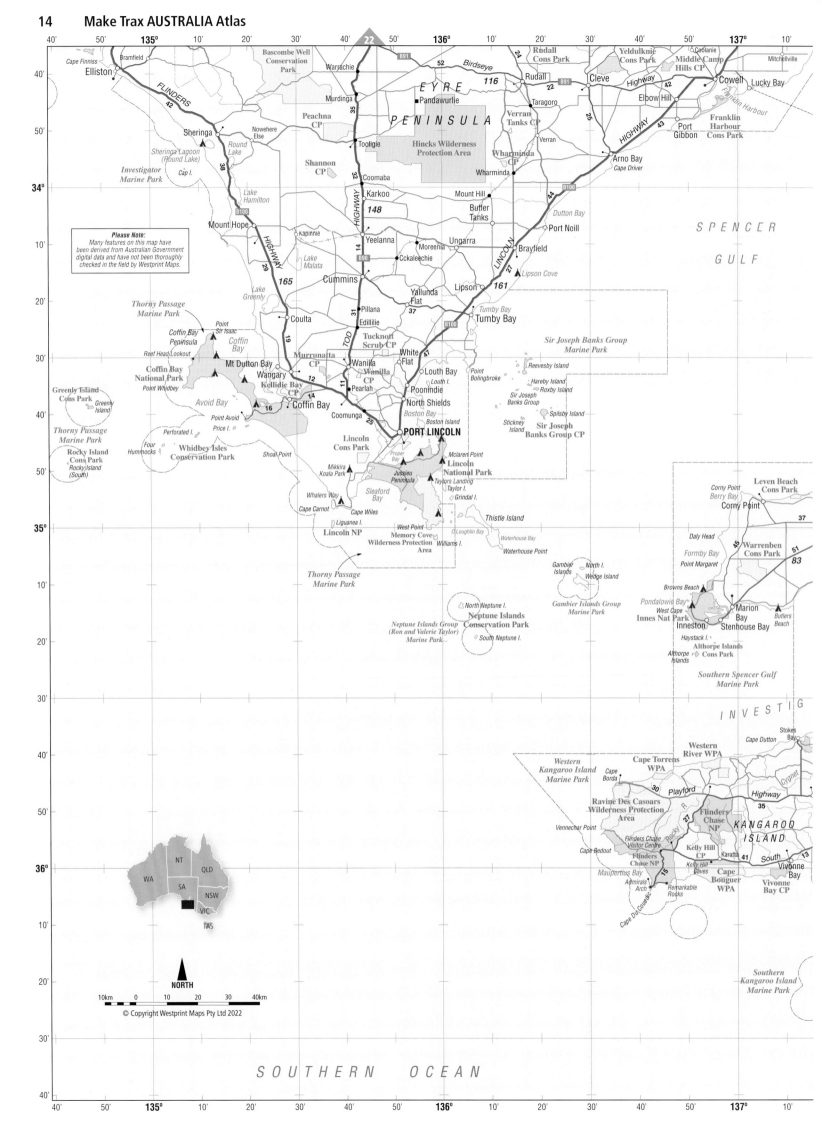

EYRE PENINSULA

SPENCER GULF

Cape Finniss
Elliston
Bramfield
FLINDERS
42
Sheringa
Nowehere Else
Round Lake
Sheringa Lagoon (Round Lake)
Cap I.
38
Investigator Marine Park
Lake Hamilton
Mount Hope
Kapinnie
Lake Malata
HIGHWAY
29
165
Lake Greenly
Coulta
19
Point Sir Isaac
Coffin Bay Peninsula
Reef Head Lookout
Coffin Bay
Mt Dutton Bay
Wangary
Kellidie Bay CP
Murrunatta CP
12
14
16
Coffin Bay
Coomunga
Point Whidbey
Avoid Bay
Point Avoid
Price I.
Perforated I.
Four Hummocks
Whidbey Isles Conservation Park
Shoal Point
Greenly Island Cons Park
Greenly Island
Thorny Passage Marine Park
Rocky Island Cons Park
Rocky Island (South)
Thorny Passage Marine Park
Coffin Bay National Park
Point Whidbey
Mikkira Koala Park
Whalers Way
Cape Carnot
Liguanea I.
Cape Wiles
Lincoln NP
West Point
Memory Cove Wilderness Protection Area
Williams I.
O'Loughlin Bay
Thorny Passage Marine Park

Warrachie
Murdinga
Bascombe Well Conservation Park
52
Birdseye
116
Peachna CP
35
Tooligie
32
Coomaba
Shannon CP
Karkoo
HIGHWAY
148
Yeelanna
14
Cckaleechie
B90
Cummins
Pillana
31
Edililie
TOD
11
Murrunatta CP
Wanilla
Wanilla CP
Pearlah
Tucknott Scrub CP
White Flat
Yallunda Flat
37
B100
Louth Bay
Louth I.
Poonindie
North Shields
Boston Bay
Boston Island
PORT LINCOLN
Proper Bay
Lincoln Cons Park
Jussieu Peninsula
Mclaren Point
Taylors Landing
Taylor I.
Lincoln National Park
Grindal I.
Sleaford Bay
Pandawurlie
Hincks Wilderness Protection Area
Verran Tanks CP
Wharminda CP
Wharminda
Mount Hill
Butler Tanks
Moreenia
Ungarra
Brayfield
LINCOLN
27
Lipson
161
Tumby Bay
Lipson Cove
Dutton Bay
Port Noill

Rudall Cons Park
24
B91
Rudall
22
Taragoro
25
Verran
44
B100
Yeldulknie Cons Park
Cleve
Highway
42
Elbow Hill
Port Gibbon
HIGHWAY
43
Arno Bay
Cape Driver
Middle Camp Hills CP
Coolanie
Cowell
Lucky Bay
Franklin Harbour
Franklin Harbour Cons Park

Point Bolingbroke
Reevesby Island
Hareby Island
Roxby Island
Sir Joseph Banks Group
Stickney Island
Spilsby Island
Sir Joseph Banks Group CP
Sir Joseph Banks Group Marine Park

Thistle Island
Waterhouse Bay
Waterhouse Point
Gambier Islands
North I.
Wedge Island
Gambier Islands Group Marine Park
North Neptune I.
Neptune Islands Conservation Park
Neptune Islands Group (Ron and Valerie Taylor) Marine Park
South Neptune I.

Leven Beach Cons Park
Corny Point
Berry Bay
Corny Point
Daly Head
Formby Bay
Point Margaret
Warrenben Cons Park
45
37
51
83
Browns Beach
Pondalowie Bay
West Cape
Innes Nat Park
Inneston
Marion Bay
Stenhouse Bay
Butlers Beach
Haystack I.
Althorpe Islands
Althorpe Islands Cons Park
Southern Spencer Gulf Marine Park

INVESTIG

Cape Dutton
Stokes Bay
Western River WPA
Cape Torrens WPA
Cape Borda
Playford
30
Cygnet
Highway
35
Western Kangaroo Island Marine Park
Ravine Des Casoars Wilderness Protection Area
Vennechar Point
Flinders Chase NP
Rocky R.
27
Flinders Chase Visitor Centre
Cape Bedout
Flinders Chase NP
15
Maupertius Bay
Admirals Arch
Cape Du Couedic
Remarkable Rocks
KANGAROO ISLAND
Kelly Hill CP
Kelly Hill Caves
Karatta
Cape Bouguer WPA
41
South
13
Vivonne Bay
Vivonne Bay CP

NORTH

10km 0 10 20 30 40km

© Copyright Westprint Maps Pty Ltd 2022

WA
NT
QLD
SA
NSW
VIC
TAS

SOUTHERN OCEAN

Southern Kangaroo Island Marine Park

Franklin Harbor Marine Park

Port Broughton
Mundoora
Lake View
Koolunga
Andrews
Hilltown
Burra
Redcliff

Wokurna
Brinkworth
37
Goyder
Samson Well

29
Tickera Bay
108
Snowtown
Burra Creek Gorge Reserve
B64

Tickera
Alford
25
Blyth
Clare
Farrell Flat
Emuville
Creek
88

North Beach
Bute
Lochiel
24
Mintaro
Waterloo
Robertstown
Morgan
Cadell

Wallaroo
Kadina
9
23
38
Watervale
A32
52
Emuville

Warburto Point
17
19
Paskeville
13
Auburn
Waterloo
Mount Mary
34

Moonta
Cunliffe
Melton
Halbury
11
Saddleworth
Marrabel
Eudunda
57

Port Hughes
Tiparra Bay
35
Agery
36
A1
Clinton CP
8
Bowmans
Balaklava
55
Rhynie
Riverton
Hamilton
Robertstown
Blanchetown

Cape Elizabeth
Weetulta
18
Port Clinton
Erith
HWY
25
153
34
28
Brookfield Cons Park
40

Eastern Spencer Gulf Marine Park
14
Arthurton
25
Price
Sandy Point
37
Avon
Owen
Alma
Tarlee
Kapunda
STURT
130
24
A20
HIGHWAY

Balgowan
Petersville
29
Ardrossan
Tiddy Widdy Beach
Parham
Pinery
Hamley Bridge
34
Freeling
Greenock
15
Truro
22
Mount Pleasant

Chinaman Wells Reef Point
Maitland
30
101
12
Dublin
98
Wasleys
27
Nuriootpa
Angaston
23
Swan Reach

Point Pearce
South Kilkerran
22
Sandilands
Upper Gulf St Vincent Marine Park
22
Roseworthy
A20
Tanunda
Sedan
33
Swan Reach Cons Park

Port Victoria
Urania
Pine Point
Two Wells
Kangaroo Flat
GAWLER
Lyndoch
Eden Valley
Cambrai
Nildottie
Bakara

Wardang Island
YORKE
Black Point
Angle Vale
16
Williamstown
50
Marne
River
Black Hill
31
Walker Flat

Port Rickaby
PENINSULA
Sheoak Flat
Virginia
Para Wirra Rec Park
Springton
Caurnamont
Purnong

Curramulka
38
Port Julia
St Kilda
Barker Inlet
A1
Elizabeth
44
Kersbrook
Mount Pleasant
Birdwood
Palmer
32
Younghusband
Pellaring Flat

Bluff Beach
Minlaton
42
Port Vincent
Torrens Island Cons Park
39
Salisbury
26
Modbury
Gumeracha
Mannum
Cowirra
Coolcha
Bowhill
Kalyan

Hardwicke Bay
32
24
Port Adelaide
Gepps Cross
Morialta Cons Park
Lobethal
32
Perponda

Point Hardwicke Bay
Brentwood
30
Stansbury
Wool Bay
Henley Beach
ADELAIDE
Uraidla
Cleland CP
Woodside
Mannum
35

Point Souttar
Point Turton
21
Yorketown
18
Coobowie
Adelaide Airport
Glenelg
Cleland CP
32
Hahndorf
Nairne
Mypolonga

Warooka
34
Edithburgh
Sultana Point
Brighton
Blackwood
Stirling
21
Callington
A20
Murray Bridge
Army Field Firing Range
Chapman Bore
Wynarka

Sturt Bay
Troubridge Island
GULF ST VINCENT
M2
Mount Barker
Echunga
96
M1
FWY
18
25
Kulde

Point Davenport Cons Park
Troubridge Point
Noarlunga
34
Onkaparinga River NP
Macclesfield
Hartley
Tailem Bend
Naturi
B12
70

Foul Bay
Lower Yorke Peninsula Marine Park
Seaford
Maslin Beach
Meadows
Strathalbyn
Langhorne Creek
Jervois
Moorlands
Sherlock

McLaren Vale
Port Willunga
Willunga
25
27
Ashbourne
Finniss
Wellington
A8
B1
Cooke Plains
Coomandook

Sellicks Beach
Mypongo Reservoir
16
Myponga
A13
Mount Compass
Milang
Lake Alexandrina
B1
51
DUKES
64
Yumali
135

Carrickalinga Normanville
Yankalilla
Goolwa
Clayton
Narrung
Lake Albert
Ashville
Two Sisters 79 m
HIGHWAY

Yankalilla Bay
B23
Rapid Bay
34
Fleurieu Peninsula
Inman Valley
Port Elliot
17
Middleton
Sturt Monument
Hindmarsh Island
Pink Lake
Waltowa Swamp
Binnie Lookout
Ki

Cape Jervis
Delamere
Victor Harbor
Rosetta Head
Encounter Bay
Murray Mouth
Meningie
Mount Boothby Cons Park

ENCOUNTER STRAIT
Backstairs Passage
Deep Creek Cons Park
Waitpinga Beach
Newland Head Cons Park
Encounter Marine Park
Younghusband
Field
Mt Boothby 128 m
Boothby Rocks

Cape Cassini
Emu Bay
Point Marsden
Encounter Marine Park
SeaLink Ferry
Coorong National Park
Magrath Flat

Lathami CP
Cygnet River
Bay of Shoals
Penneshaw
American River
43
Princes
191

Parndana CP
Kingscote
Nepean Bay
B23
28
Dudley Peninsula
Woods Well
B1
Messent Cons Park

Parndana
39
Beyaria CP
32
30
Dudley CP
Cape Willoughby
18

49
Cape Gantheaume CP
Salt Lagoon
Simpson Cons Reserve
Lesueur CP
Salt Creek
Martin Washpool CP

Seal Bay CP
Pennington Bay
False Cape
Cape Gantheaume WPA
D'Estrees Bay
Point Tinline

Seal Bay
Cape Gantheaume
Southern Kangaroo Island Marine Park
42 Mile Crossing
Coorong National Park

28 Mile Crossing
79

PARK AND RESERVE ABBREVIATIONS

CP	Conservation Park
CA	Conservation Area
Cons	Conservation
FFR	Flora & Fauna Reserve
NP	National Park
NCR	Nature Conservation Area
Res	Reserve
Reg	Regional
RP	Regional Park
WPA	Wilderness Protected Area

Upper South East Marine Park

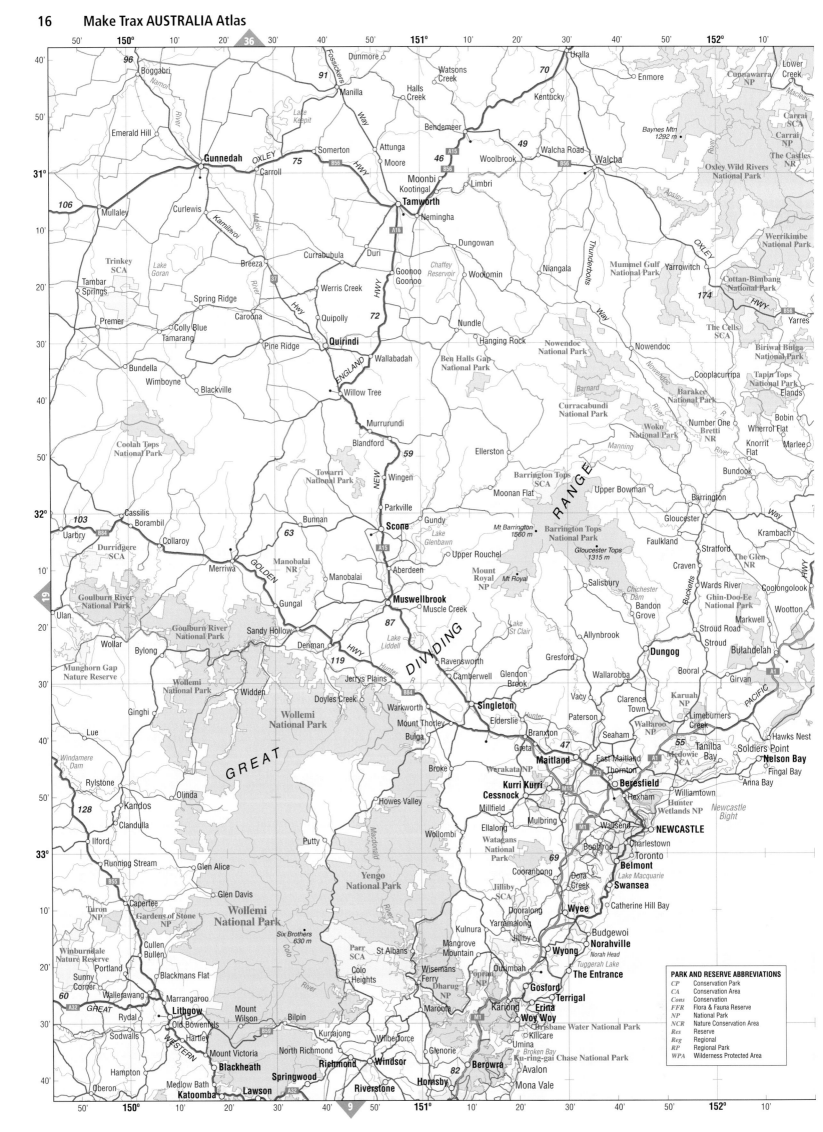

PARK AND RESERVE ABBREVIATIONS

CP	Conservation Park
CA	Conservation Area
Cons	Conservation
FFR	Flora & Fauna Reserve
NP	National Park
NCR	Nature Conservation Area
Res	Reserve
Reg	Regional
RP	Regional Park
WPA	Wilderness Protected Area

30'   40'   50'   **153°**   10'   20'   30'   37   40'   50'   **154°**   10'   20'   30'   40'   50'

Bowraville
Nambucca Heads
Macksville
Burrapine
Upper
Taylors Arm
Scotts Head
Comara
Donnellyville
Bellbrook
Ngambaa
NR
Stuarts Point
Millbank
Eungai
Creek
Trial Bay
Willawarrin
South West Rocks
Smoky Cape
Smithtown
Frederickton
Hat Head
Willi Willi
NP
Korogoro Point
Kempsey
Mt Banda Banda
1258 m
Hat Head
National Park
Boonanghi
NR
Kumbatine
NP
Crescent Head
HIGHWAY
45
Kundabung
Rollands
Plains
Telegraph
Point
Limeburners Creek
Nature Reserve
Point Plomer
Birdwood
Bellangry
Saltwater Lake
Pappinbarra
Pembrooke
M1
Ellenborough
Beechwood
Port Macquarie
Wauchope
Tacking Point
Byabarra
Lake Innes Nature Reserve
Bago
Bluff
NP
Herons
Creek
Lake Cathie
Comboyne
73
Bonny Hills
Kendall
Kew
Queens Lake
Lorne
Camden Haven
Killabakh
NR
Hannam
Vale
Watson Taylor Lake
Johns River
Lansdowne
Crowdy Bay
National Park
Coopernook
Moorland
Wingham
Croki
Taree
Harrington
Tinonee
Farquhar Inlet
Old Bar
Talawahl
NR
M1
Khappinghat
Nature Reserve
Nabiac
Failford
Hallidays Point
72
Tuncurry
Forster
Wallis
Lake
Elizabeth Bay
Wallingat National Park
Blueys Beach
Smiths Lake
Myall
Lake
Sugarloaf Bay
Myall Lakes
National Park
Boolambayte Lake
The Broadwater
Broughton Island

PACIFIC

River

87

T A S M A N   S E A

NORTH

10km   0   10   20   30   40km

© Copyright Westprint Maps Pty Ltd 2022

NT
QLD
WA
SA
NSW
VIC
TAS

Please Note:
Many features on this map have
been derived from Australian Government
digital data and have not been thoroughly
checked in the field by Westprint Maps.

40'
50'
31°
10'
20'
30'
40'
50'
32°
10'
20'
30'
40'
50'
33°
10'
20'
30'
40'

145° 50' 10' 20' 38 30' 40' 50' 146° 10' 20' 30' 40' 50' 147° 10'

Trilby
Station stay
Winbar
Idalia
Deerina
Wee Toura
Curraweena
Byrock
Nemeena
Branglebar
Mulgawarrina
Kimbriki
Wamboin
Wongowal
Coronga
Peak
Glenariff
Tubbavilla
Mundadoo
Bellsgrove
Koonawarra
Wilgareena
Wilga Downs
Oakvale
Bunyarra
Colossal
Iona
Tundulya
Landsdowne
Wilgaroon
Lyndhurst
Cooneybar
Boorara
Newhaven
Narwarre
Yandilla
Bald Hills
Woodlands
Coolabah
Colly Burl
Gambolalley
Karoo

31°
Wyoming
Darling Downs
Windera
El Trune
Coolabah
Karingal
Murrawombie
Burnamwood
Gidgee
Poon Boon
Tindarey
Tanbar
Kergunyah
Berwick
Windella
Carlton
Wuttagoona
Elura
Mine
Mount
Drysdale
Coronga
Downs
Girilambone
Colane
Yimkin
Booroomagga
Glenhope
Moonagee
Moquilambo
Mt Gap
Mount
Grenfell
Maryvale
CSA
Mines
Sussex
Wilgalong
Wilga Downs
Birrimba
Fairview

Pinchinara
Tambua
Buckwaroon
Jersey
Windara
Nullogoola
Meadow Glen
BARRIER
Cobar
HIGHWAY
Florida
Budgery
Thorndale
Miandetta
Nynga
Lilyvale
Korreo
Barnato
Stansfield
158
Meryula
Narri
Canbelego
Hermidale
133
Warri
Boulkra
Broadmeadows
Elliston
Bel-Air
The Meadows
Lerida
Brura
The Rookery
Urunda
Auroa
Clareview
The Plains
Kia-Ora
Double Gates
Nullawarra
Koree
Mount Lewis
Quanda
Nature Reserve
Mudall
Kaleno
Bulgoo
Rosevale
Rainbow Ridge
Creeper Gate
Poplar
Grove
Everdale
Bundycoola
Killala
Nymagee
Babinda
Buddabaddah
Bloomfield
Widgeland

32°
Belarabon
Bindi
Lachlan
Downs
Shuttleton
Nymagee
Homeville
Euambeline
Kulwin
Yarranvale
Avonmore
Willow Glen
Koonaburra
Kiama
Taringo Downs
Glenwood
Four Corners
Delby
Kiaora
Lansdale
Overflow
Wiralong
Ettawanda
Balowra
Bobadah
Bombah
Millridge
Berangabah
Karwarn
Warbraccan
Iris Vale
Nangerybone
Walkers Hill
The
Bluff
Inveralla
Ballatta
Yallock
W-Tree
Red Tank
Irymple
254
Moothumbil
Eremaran
Glenkerry
Minnalong
Ashleigh
Downs
Stanifords
Wirchilleba
Burthong
Tara
Vermont Hill
Wing Ding
Yathong
Nature
Reserve
Yathong
Black
Range
Kerein Hills
Melrose
Kajuligah
Nature Reserve
Moolah
Nombiginni
Redluom
Tallebung
Palistan
Tollingo
Nature Reserve
Murtonga
Tiarri
Vivigani
Flamingo
Woggoon
Nature Reserve
Marlow
Coombie
Bundure
Penshurst
Roma
Conoble
Mount Hope
Yara
Yarto
Derrida
Bimbella
Lockerbie
Conoble
Mylone
Round Hill
Nature Reserve

33°
Trida
Nombinnie
State Conservation
Area
Euabalong
West
Euabalong
Condobolin
Roto
Nombinnie
Nature
Reserve
Warraway Mtn
273 m
Euabalong
Willandra
Creek
Willandra
Lysmoyle
Euabalong
Murrin Bridge
Wardry
South
Milby
Willandra
National Park
Gunniguldrie
Lake Cargelligo
Bogandillon
Swamp
Moolbong
Hunthawang
Valroona
Wallanthery
Currawong
Manies
Lake
Tullibigeal
Wilga
Plains
Euglo
Banar
Lake
Moolbong
Creek
Ballatherie
Kidman
Ballyrogan
Merri
Merrigal
Lake
Brewster
Burcher
Yarto
Hillston
Yarran Park
Tullibigeal
Ungarie
Malven
NORTH
Monia Gap
Naradhan
Kikoira
10km 0 10 20 30 40km
Merungle
Coondaloo
Inverness
63
Gibsonvale
© Copyright Westprint Maps Pty Ltd 2022

Please Note:
Many features on this map have
been derived from Australian Government
digital data and have not been thoroughly
checked in the field by Westprint Maps.

148° 149°

Bora · The Myalls · Gunyillah · Yugilbar · Kenebri · 119
Edale · Wycombe · Gilgooma · Oaklahoma · Timallallie National Park · Piliga East State Conservation Area
Macquarie Marshes Nature Reserve · Kilree · Youie · Teridgerie · Piliga Nature Reserve
Fairholme · Sandy Camp · Nelgowrie · Narraway · Baradine · Pilliga Nature Reserve
Quambone · Macquarie Marshes · Coonamble · Wilgadeen · Calga · Yarragin NP
Buckiinguy · Oxley · Gerwa · Carwell · Kuringai · Combara · Nyora · Warrumbungle National Park · Bugaldie · OXLEY · HWY · 106
Ilabunda · Mount Foster · Gradgery · Athlone · Eulalia · Coonabarabran · Ulamambri · Purlewaugh · Tambar Springs
Emby West · Yarramundi · NEWELL · 95
Merryanbone · Bealbah · Bourbah · Gulargambone · Binnaway Nature Reserve
Reedy Corner · Mumblebone · Earlside · Yarran · Armatree · Tooraweenah
Eenaweenah · Bellvue · New Merrigal · Curban · Biddon
Whitewood · Glencoe · Collie · Biddon SCA · Greenwood Vale · Weetaliba
Mullengudgery · OXLEY · HWY · 105 · Ashgrove · Gilgandra · Mendooran · Merrygoen · Coolah
Gunningbar · Warren · Bundemar · Breelong National Park · 92 · Dunedoo · Leadville · 103
Belaringar · Nevertire · Gin Gin · Warriston · Goonoo SCA · Cobbora · Uarbry · Durridgere SCA
Wahroonga · 93 · HIGHWAY · 61 · Eumungerie · GOLDEN · 89 · Goulburn River National Park
Gobabla · Trangie · Goonoo NP · Mogriguy · Ballimore · Goolma · Ulan
Werombie · A32 · 34 · Mungeribar · Brocklehurst · Hillcroft · Gulgong
Wyoming · Meringo · 40 · Narromine · Dubbo · MITCHELL · Wongarbon · Geurie · 50 · Home Rule · Munghorn Gap Nature Reserve
Burdenda · Dandaloo · Waterloo · 53 · A39 · 51 · Wellington · Narbethong · Mudgee
Tottenham · Albert · Kolonga · Warranmunga · NEWELL · Tomingley · Gullengamble · Dripstone · Hillgrove · Lue
Lorraine · Glenaren · Goobang National Park · Wandoo · Yeoval · Neurea · 63 · Allambi · Windeyer · Windamere Dam
Berillee · Tullamore · Hyrock · Dunmore · Peak Hill · 65 · Burrabadine Peak 749 m · Croyden · Mumbil · Gundowda · Hargraves · 128
Fifield · Trewilga · Stuart Town · Triamble · Pyramul · Ilford
Brooklyn · Trundle · Woolgar · Alectown · Cumnock · Larras Lee · Kerrs Creek · Dalmeny · Hill End · Sofala
Derriwong · Byong · Goobang National Park · Wolabler Mtn 790 m · Molong · Garra · Clergate · Wattle Flat
Ootha · Bogan Gate · Gunningbland · Manildra · Borenore · Mullion Creek · Winburndale Nature Reserve
Glencoe · Yarrabandai · Parkes · Cookamidgera · Cudal · MITCHELL · 34 · Orange · Lucknow
Wheatlands · Murga · Toogong · 58 · Spring Hill · A32 · 54 · HWY · BATHURST · Kelso · Sunny Corner · 60
Pine Hill · 34 · Daroobalgie · Four Ways · Eugowra · Mt Nangar 650 m · Cargo · Millthorpe · Perthville · Oconnell
Bedgerebong · Nangar Nat Park · Murga · Georges Plains · The Lagoon · A32
Forbes · 69 · Goologong · Canowindra · Manildara · Blayney · Newbridge · Raglan
Garema · Wirrinya · Billimari · 33 · Carcoar · Barry · Rockley · Oberon
Lake Cowal · Nalleen · NEWELL · HIGHWAY · A39 · A41 · 104 · Lyndhurst · Neville

148° 149°

LAKE FROME

Lake Frome National Park

Lake Elder
Lake Maljanapa
Lake Kuturu
Lake Karpi
Lake Moko
Lake Millyera
Lake Tarkarooloo
Lake Namba

FROME DOWNS
Eurnilla
Billeroo Creek

Frome Downs
16

BILLEROO WEST

MULYUNGARIE

STRZELECKI DESERT

Mingary Creek

Benagerie
Mulyungarie

YARRAMBA

NT
QLD
WA
SA
NSW
VIC
TAS

Mooleulooloo

MOOLEULOOLOO

Yarramba

Strathearn

Oonartra Creek

Kalkaroo

KALKAROO

BOOLCOOMATTA

Boolcoomata

KALABITY

Spring Hill

Kalabity

MOUNT VICTOR

Mt Victoria 457 m

Bimbowrie Conservation Park

Bimbowrie

BINDARRAH

PLUMBAGO

Plumbago

Binberrie Hill 500 m

Ameroo Hill 495 m

Bulloo Creek

Oonartra Ck

HIGHWAY

Cockburn

A32

Mingary

27

Cutana

Pine Creek

Tepco

Corella

Four Brothers

OUTALPA

Outalpa

Weekeroo Hill 540 m

King Bluff 400 m

YLC3

Olary

A2

198

Olary Creek

TIKALINA

Ballara

Quartz Hill 272 m

Marialpa

FLORINA

37

Weekeroo

OULNINA

Maldorky Hill 413 m

Mutooroo

Altandee Hill 561 m

Manna Hill

Wadnaminga

Maldorky

Devonborough Downs

Duffields

MUTOOROO

BARRIER

44

Taltabooka

Giles Nob 329 m

West Creek

Oulnina Hill 705 m

Oulnina Park

Benda Range

BENDA

Dlorah Downs

Tiverton

Netley Gap

Munda Creek

Mununda

MANUNDA

LILYDALE

OAKVALE

Lilydale

QUONDONG

Oakvale

Oakbank

VLF3

STURT VALE

Sturt Vale

Morgan Vale

Pine Valley

PINE VALLEY

Fords Lagoon

Lords Well

OLD KOOMOOLOO

BALAH

Danggali Conservation Park
Bookmark Bioshpere Reserve

Canopus

Hypurna

Chowilla Regional Reserve
Bookmark Biosphere Reserve

NORTH
10km 0 10 20 30 40km

© Copyright Westprint Maps Pty Ltd 2022

SOUTH AUSTRALIA
NEW SOUTH WALES
(follows border)
Dog Fence

Brougham Gate
8
Avenel
Tielta
Teilta
27
Morphetts Ck

Pine View

Yellow Waterhole

Westwood Downs

Joulnie
40
16

The Veldt

Nundora

Kara

Bancannia Lake

B&W Camp 42 (Teltawongee Creek)

Nundooka

B&W Camp 41

Noonthorangee Creek

Floods Creek

Fowlers Gap Research Station

Fowlers Creek

SILVER CITY HWY
14
24

McDougalls Well

14
19

Mount Woowoolahra

17

14

Kantappa

Willewurrawa

Corona

177

Caloola Creek

Sturts Meadows

B&W Camp 40 (Bengora Creek)

Old Rowena

53

Campbells Creek

Willangee

Tarrawingee Lime Quarry

Tarrawingee Spring

Wendalpa

Mount Gipps

Tramway

Treloar Creek

46

23

Gairdners Creek

Eldee

53

Purnamoota

Yanco Glen

Mundi Mundi Plain

MUNDI MUNDI

Umberumberka Reservoir

16

Stephens Creek

Little Topar Roadhouse

Meltool

Silverton

Sculpture site

21

15

Stephens Creek Reservoir

A32

BROKEN HILL
A

A32

48

Farmcote

Huonville

31

Redan

22

Quandong

Wirryilka

Ascot Vale

SILVER CITY

50

127

Kars

47

B79

35

Burta

Wonga

Netley

Wendi

Middle Camp

Tandou

Lake Tandou

Nettlegoe Lake

Leonora Downs

KINCHEGA National Park

Cawndilla Lake

South Ita

42

HIGHWAY

Kimberley Plain

Harriedale

Woolcunda

Coombah Lake

Coombah Roadhouse

Double Yards

Tor Downs

Packers Lake

Loch Lilly

Popilta Rest Area (toilets)

Popio

Cuthero

Cuthero Lake

B79

80

Popiltah Lake

Popio Lake

Little Lake

Lake Mindona

Ennisvale

Nanya

Tarrara

Belvedere

Nialia Lake

Yelta Lake

Nearie Lake Nature Res

Warrawenia Lake

Milkengay Lake

Travellers Lake

Yarlta Lake

178

Bunnerungee

Huntingfield

Coleraine

TARRAWI Nature Reserve

20'   30'   40'   50'   **143°**   10'   **41**   20'   30'   40'   50'   **144°**   10'   20'   30'   **38**   40'   50'

Wonnaminta
Kayrunnera
Oak Vale
Caradoc
Carney
Idalia
Bellsgrove
Goodwood
Poloko Lake
Gilpoko Lake
Green Lake
River
Myall
Polocara
Tara
Nuntherungie
Glen Hope
Peery
Mandalay
Paroo-Darling National Park
Peri Lake
Paroo
Kallara
Curranyalpa
Morambie
Whipstick
Polpah
White Cliffs
Talalara
Coolibah Lodge Caravan Park
Tilpa
Wertago
Creek
Arrow Bar
Momba
Mount Jack
Mount Pleasant
Koonawarra
Mutawintji Nature Reserve
Tarella
Mount Pleasant
Nangara
Wyoming
Gnalta
Mutawintji National Park
Glen Gowrie
Coona Coona
Mooratchia Lake
Wild Duck
Kalkaroo
Marra
Cairo
Buckanbe
Burnamwood
Mt Wright 349 m
Duntroon
Ulalie
Cobrilla
Dunoak
Innesowen
Daubeny
93
Copago
Paroo-Darling National Park
Tilpilly
Tiltagoonah
Cymbric Vale
Wilandra
Moona Vale
Paroo-Darling State Conservation Area
Trevallyn
Thackomble
Manara
Mootwingee
B&W Camp 39 (Langawirra Gully)
Lake Dick
Darling
Tilpilly Lake
Pinchinara
Grasmere
Mena Murtee
Netallie
Capon
Mount Murchison
Bonview
Wongalara Lake
Musheroo
Waterbag
Boorungie
Comarto
Paroo-Darling National Park
B&W Camp 38 (Botoja)
Wilcannia
Murtee
Poopelloe Lake
Cultowa
Bulla Park
Lilyvale
Glenora
Devon
Cawkers Well
The Strip
Gunyulka Lake
Volo
Alma Park
258
A32
Korreo
Koralta
HIGHWAY
Churinga
Culpaulin
Ellendale
Goonalga
92
Wongalara
Emmdale Roadhouse
Boulkra
BARRIER
197
A32
Bilpa
Carmarla
Billilla
Goonoolchrach
Bulla Bulla
B&W Camp 37
Allambie
Fairmount
Coomeratta
Broughton Vale
B&W Camp 36 (Kokriega)
Barraroo
B75
Kewell East
Everdale
Byrnedale
Cowary
Burndoo
Yelta
Beechworth
Teryawynia
Moira Plains
Please Note:
Many features on this map have been derived from Australian Government digital data and have not been thoroughly checked in the field by Westprint Maps.
Balaka
Viewmont
COBB
Rosewood
Burwood
Corinya
Koonaburra
B&W Camp 35 (Totoynya)
Binnie Lake
Bushley
188
Kerpa Outstation
Capt Hollow
Pamamaroo Lake
Tandure Lake
Windalle
Blantyre
Nyngynderry
Teryaweynya Lake
Glen Albyn
Bambilla
Berangabah
Sunset Strip
Dry Lake
Denian
HIGHWAY
Yallock
Menindee Lake
B&W Camp 36 (Depot Camp)
Avon
Dead Horse Lake
Talyawalka
Glen Ora
Manara
Menindee
Anabranch
North Lake
Ratcatchers Lake
Marfield
Wallangarra
Bootingee
Larloona
Ashmont
Wallace Lake
Albemarle
Victoria Lake
Burtundy
Gypsum Palace
Kajuligah
Bono
B&W Camp 34
Keiara
Boolaboolka Lake
Boola Boolka
Brummeys Lake
Rose Hill
Bonton
Bonuna
Wilga Valley
Kajuligah Nature Reserve
RIVER
23
Nelia Outstation
Stirling Vale
Sayers Lake
Surveyors Lake
Monivea
Moondene
Bindara
Tolarno
Blackfellows
Gum Lake
Orana
B75
Marlow
18
B&W Camp 33
Dalmorino
Darnick
Quamby
Ivandale
Waiko
Conoble
Peppora
Bellpajah
Ivanhoe
Karoola
Cooyarunda
Karpa Kora
Overnewton
El Dorado
Beilpajah
Abbotsford
Conoble
Wyarama
19
Wyoming
Wilkurra
Girrawheen
Moornanyah Lake
Kilfera
Strathavon
Mossgiel
B&W Camp 32 Cuthero Point
Chalkey Well
C Lake
Peneena
COBB
Coona Point
Bulgamurra
Mulurulu Lake
Melton Grove
Clarebank
Barneys Lake
Bellevue
Polia
Manfred
Willandra
Moorara
Clare
Kinross
34
Ringwood
Mungo National Park
Mulurulu
Mandleman
Clare Corner
Stanbridge
Clearview
134
B&W Camp 31 (Bilbarka)
Pooncarie
Birdwood
Garnpung Lake
Gol Gol
Rosalind Park
Moangul
Tarcoola
29
Dugout Tank
Balranald Gate Tank
Garnpung
Lake Leaghur
Binda
Murrungrung
Culpataro
Yarto
HIGHWAY
B&W Camp 30 (Burke's Gambala)
Top
46
Hut
Rd
Top Hut
14
Lake Mungo
Stitzs Hut
Orange Grove
The Vale
Cavan
B&W Camp 29 (Becker's Gambala)
Tourtmundo Tank
Boree Plains
Mutherumbung

20'   30'   40'   **143°**   10'   **13**   20'   30'   40'   50'   **144°**   10'   20'   30'   40'   50'

Burke & Wills party may have followed more than one track between Tourtmundo Tank and Tarcoola.

Burke rides back from Bilbarka to Gambanna on 29/9

135°   42   136°   137°

WOOMERA PROHIBITED AREA
Roxby Downs
ROXBY DOWNS
Andamooka
Lake Parakylia
Lake Reynolds
Lake Younghusband
Purple Downs
PURPLE DOWNS
Shell Lagoon
Hardy Hill 183 m
WLG 06
Wilgena Hill 258 m
Mt Eba 228 m
VLA4
Rocky Hill 178 m
Lake Labyrinth
Lake Moolkra
Wilgena
Ferguson
North Well
Kingoonya
Renton Hill 165 m
Kingoonya Hill 178 m
Glendambo
VLE3
Coondambo
East Well Outstation
Lake Patricia
Lake Ross
Beggy Lake
COONDAMBO
Arcoona
ARCOONA
Lake Mary
Lake Richardson
Red Lake
Bulpara Hill 244 m
New Year Hill 181 m
Yerda
Stony Top Hill 165 m
Kultanaby
Relief Hill 182 m
113
Wirramina
Wirramina
Lake Hanson
Lake Hart
MNT05
VLF7
Lookout
Woomera
Pimba
Intercept Hill 223 m
Emmie New 240 m
Chitaniga Hill 317 m
Kokatha
VLF2
Lake Gairdner National Park
Heim Tank
KOKATHA
Lake Johnston
WIRRAMINNA
WOOMERA PROHIBITED AREA
Island Lagoon Tracking Station (abandoned)
Lookout
Lake Windabout
Mt Gunson 233 m
Wirrappa
Mt Gunson Mine
Lake Everard
Middle Tanks
LAKE GAIRDNER
Island Lagoon
OAKDEN HILLS
Oakden Hills
McLeay
Glyde Hill 188 m
Skull Camp Tanks
Lake Gairdner National Park
MAHANEWO
Lake Finniss
Old clay mine
167
73
Nuckulla Hill 255 m
Lake Everard
LAKE EVERARD
Grant Well
Kangaroo Hut
VNO07
Belt Hill 332 m
MOONAREE
Mahanewo
Yalymboo
YALYMBOO
Lake Blyth
Lake Dutton
KONDOOLKA
Kondoolka
Waverley Hill 385 m
UNO03
Lake Acraman
Kangaroo Bluff 188 m
Lake MacFarlane
YUDNAPINNA
PINJARRA
YARNA
Mt St Mungo 359 m
Moonaree
Beacon Hill 175 m
NONNING
Yudnapinna
Koolgera Conservation Reserve
Mt Hiltaba 450 m
Hiltaba
Ilkina Hill 175 m
Mt Friday 390 m
GAWLER RANGES
Hiltaba Nature Reserve
Hiltaba is a Nature Foundation SA managed reserve
Public Access Route to lakeside lookout and campground
Old Waltumba Tank
Lookout
Pondanna Dam
GAWLER RANGES
KOLENDO
BAXTER RANGE
SIAM RANGE
Low Hills Woolshed
Scrubby Point 230 m
Carriewerloo
Wallala Hill 168 m
Gawler Ranges
Rd
YAR01
Yardea
Yardea Dam
Mount Ive
Kolendo
Barkers Hill 294 m
Reid Lookout 240 m
WARTAKA
Wartaka
Dog Fence
Ford Ck
YARDEA
Thurlga
Edward John Eyre's Camp No. 6
UNO07
Edward John Eyre's Camp No. 7
Mt Micollo 359 m
Nonning
Siam
Koorinja Hill 321 m
West End Hill 333 m
Gawler Ranges Cons Reserve
Kododo Hill
Scrubby Peak
Organ Pipes
Yandinga
Mattera
Mt Nott 429 m
Kolay Hut
Kolay Mirica Falls
Spring Hill 377 m
MOUNT IVE
Stringer
NON06
Boundary Dam
22
Uno
Lake Gilles Tank
COR02
Corunna
A1
Cungena
Capietha
Poochera
Karcultaby
Chandada
Parla Peak 160 m
Inkster
Scrubby Peak
Gawler Ranges National Park
Old Paney
VL50C
Paney (Ranger Station)
The track to Paney is a Public Access Route (PAR)
BUCKLEBOO
Wilcherry Hill 346 m
Lake Gilles Conservation Reserve
UNO
Harris Bluff 395 m
Gilles Downs
Iron Knob Mine
Iron Knob
EYRE HWY
Stone Dam
Pildappa Rock
HIGHWAY
Condada
Minnipa
Tcharkuldu Hill
Poldinna
Waganny
Barns Rd
Pinkawillinie Conservation Park
Stock Route 22
Buckleboo
Wirriganda Hill 430 m
Yeltanna Hill 424 m
Wilcherry
Iron Prince Mine
Iron Baron Mine
Kalliparu Cons Res
Carina
Lake Yaninee
Yaninee
Corrobinnie Hill 210 m
Peella Rocks
Buckleboo Rd
Moongi CR
Moongi
Buckleboo CR
Buckleboo Hall
Bascombe Rocks Lookout
Mootra Cons Res
Lake Gilles Cons Park
Carradoo Tanks Site
South Dam
Iron Duke and Iron Duchess Mine
Port Kenny
Kalliparu Cons Park
Pygery
Moonlight Flat
Port Kenny Rd
Wudinna
Lake Wannamana
Kyancutta
Goyders Monument
Koongawa
Darkes Memorial
Stringer Hwy
Cortlinye Cons Res
Kimba
Barna
COOYERDOO
Refuge Rocks (Secret Rocks)
Iron Knight Mine
Venus Bay
Coodlie Park Farm Retreat
COURTABIE
Mount Damper
Cocata Cons Res
Warramboo
87
Caralue Bluff Cons Res
A1
Sheoak Hill Cons Res
LINCOLN
Granite Hill 255 m
Midgee
105
Woolshed Cave, Talia Caves
Lake Newland
Talia
Mt Wedge Road
Cocata Conservation Park
Barwell Cons Res
53
Hambidge Wilderness Protection Area
Caralue
Carappee Hill CP
Heggarton Cons Res
The Plug Range Cons Res
Mt Geharty 279 m
Lake Newland Cons Park
Mount Wedge
Birdseye Highway
93
60
Evelyn Downs
Lock
Darke Peak
Mangalo
Yeldulknie Cons Park
Middle Camp Hills CP
Walkers Rock
Colton
Bramfield
Bascombe Well Conservation Park
Warrachie
Birdseye Highway
116
Murdinga
Warrachie
52
Rudall Cons Park
Rudall
Cleve
Cowell
Lucky Bay
Cape Finniss
Elliston
Mitchellville
Coalanie

Island Lagoon Tracking Station
The huge white 'Golf Ball' structure that can be seen from the highway is the only remaining part of the Joint Defence Facility Nurrungar. It was one of the deep space tracking stations constructed and administered by NASA as part of its Mariner Space Project. Nurrungar was operational from 1968 to 1999 and was directly involved in monitoring nuclear explosions and space exploration. Nurrungar was one of three Joint Defence Facilities in Australia which included Pine Gap near Alice Springs and North West Cape in Western Australia. Most of the Nurrungar facility has been removed and the area rehabilitated.

Mount Ive Station
Mount Ive Stn provides an ideal outback base with shearers quarters accom. (BYO food for self catering) or camping, incl. some powered sites and bush camping. A kiosk, liquor store, fuel and EFTPOS available. Mud maps to scenic self drive private station tracks incl. Organ Pipe' rocks, Ridge Tops and Lake Gairdner. Other attractions incl. bird watching, photography and bush walking. Ph. 08 86 481817 email: info@mtive.com.au

NORTH FLINDERS RANGES

SOUTH FLINDERS RANGES

Lake Torrens National Park

LAKE TORRENS

LAKE FROME

Lake Frome National Park

ANGEPENA

NANTAWARRINA ABORIGINAL LAND

Ikara-Flinders Ranges National Park

BELTANA

NILPENA

Nilpena Ediacra National Park

MOTPENA

WINTABATINYANA

PERNATTY

SOUTH GAP

YADLAMALKA

KOOTABERRA

CARRIEWERLOO

WERTALOONA

WIRREALPA

ERUDINA

CURNAMONA

WILLIPPA

BARATTA

KOONAMORE

MOUNT VICTOR

MINBURRA

MELTON

Place names and features:

Mt Deception 687 m
Puttapa
Beltana
Beltana Roadhouse
Warraweena 1087 m · Mt Hack
Nantawarrina
Mulga View
Teatree OS
Wertaloona
Moro Gorge
Mt Brooke 680 m
Mt Chambers 409 m
Mt Frome 393 m
Wirrealpa
Angorichina
Blinman
Alpana
Angorichina Village
Parachilna
Mount Falkland
Mt Samuel
Nilpena
Moolooloo
Narrina
Frome Downs
Motpena
Commodore
Brachina
Oraparinna
Willow Springs
Bunkers Cons Reserve
Edeowie
St Mary Pk 1168 m
Martins Well
Erudina
Merna Mora
Moralana
Upalinna
Wilpena
Wilpena Pound
Artipena Hill 228 m
Curnamona
Lake Torrens
Mernmerna
Cotabena
Rawnsley Park
Arkapena
Chace Range
Willippa
Spring Hill
Wonaka Historic Site
Arkaba
Warcowie
Mt Davidson 610 m
Wallerberdina
Neuroodla (Abandoned)
Mt Plantagenet 952 m
Holowilena
Willipa
Hawker
Mt Victor 465 m
Mount Victor
Yadlamulka
Cradock
Yednalue
Old Baratta
Baratta
Koonamore
Hesso
Uro Bluff 279 m
Wilkatana
Argadells
Mt Arden 845 m
Bagalowie
Belton
Four Brothers
Altandee Hill 561 m
Clifden
Glenroy
Montana
Marchant Hill 803 m
Melton
The Dutchmans Stern 837 m
Uroonda Hill 640 m
Price Hill 760 m
Boolcunda
Stoke Hill 779 m
Carrieton
Minburra
Quorn
Mt Brown Cons Park
Hammond Historic Town
Eurelia
Johnburgh
Port Augusta
Illeroo
Corraberra Hill 315 m
Stirling North
Mt Brown 969 m
Lavington
Waroonee Hill 591 m
Yunta
Oulnina Hill 705 m
Myall Creek
Woolshed Flat
Horrocks Pass
Wilmington
Willowie
Morchard
Orroroo
McCoys Well
Mergenia
Nackara
Oak Park
Winninowie
Nectar Brook
Mt Remarkable National Park
Black Rock
Depot Hill 789 m
Parkvilla
Paratoo
Tiverton
Sunset Hill 297 m
Mt Whyalla 233 m
Mt Remarkable 963 m
Melrose
Booleroo Centre
Pekina
Dawson (ruins)
Hillgrave
Oodla Wirra
Mununda
Mambray Creek
Pt Douglas
Murray Town
Tarcowie
Peterborough
Ucolta
Whyalla
Port Germein
Wirrabara
Appila
Yongala
Mannanarie
Pandappa
Pine Creek
Braemar
Port Pirie
Napperby
Laura
Jamestown
Terowie
Whyte Yarcowie
Mallett
Pulpara
Bendigo
Port Davis
Warnertown
Gladstone
Georgetown
Whyte Yarcowie
Wilkins
Kia Ora
Crystal Brook
Narridy
Spalding
Hallett
Caroona
Redhill
Merriton
Gulnare
Pandappa
Fisherman Bay
Mundoora
Lake View
Yacka
Booborowie
Mount Bryan
Port Broughton
Koolunga
Andrews
Wokurna
Brinkworth
Hilltown
Burra
Redcliff

© Copyright Westprint Maps Pty Ltd 2022

NORTH

10km 0 10 20 30 40km

Nullarbor Regional Reserve

46
Trans Australian
Railway Access Road
For more information on this
route, refer to the Trans Australian
Railway map-on-demand from
Westprint Maps

Denman

42

58

Blow hole

31

98

20

Pidinga
Rockhole

Lake
Ifould

31°

Diprose Cave No 3
Diprose Cave No 1
Diprose Cave No 2

36

94

The
Catacombs
Knowles Cave

No 5 Bore

No 6
Bore

Disappointment
Cave

Lake
Tallacootra

10'

38

Eyre

Highway

**Nullarbor
National Park**

Jimmies
Cave

Biduna
Blowhole

Ivy Tank

Old

EYRE

P

45

Emergency
telephone

Monburu
Tank

20'

Koonalda Cave

7

Koonalda

Old

Eyre

Hwy

Murrawijinia
Caves

Ivy
Cave

Nullarbor Roadhouse

14

P

12

Yalata Swamp

White Well
Ranger Station

**YALATA
ABORIGINAL
LAND**

148

HIGHWAY

33

VLA7

Ooldea

Road

Oodea

30'

13

7

Mallabie
Tank

42

A1

Whale Watching
Lookout

Head
of Bight

Yalata Roadhouse
(closed indefinitely)

Yalata (No public access)

26

Black Hill
85 m

77

28 P

HIGHWAY

185

Bunda

RFDS airstrip
on highway

46 P

Lookout

Cliffs

Emergency
telephone

10

9

P

Gilgarrabie
Bore

Great Australian Bight
Marine Park Whale Sanctuary

Dog Fence

P

Colona

A1

Lookout

Wigunda
Cave

**Great Australian
Bight Marine Park
(Commonwealth Waters)**

VLA1

P

**Far West Coast
Marine Park**

**Wagunyah
Conservation
Reserve**

40'

Dog Fence Beach

**Far West Coast
Marine Park**

50'

GREAT AUSTRALIAN

BIGHT

Cape Adieu

Cheetima Beach

Nuyts Reef
**Nuyts Reef
Conservation Park**

32°

Bunda Cliffs, Great Australian Bight

The Dog Fence meets the sea

NT

QLD

WA

SA

NSW

VIC

TAS

NORTH

10km   0   10   20   30   40km

SOUTHERN   OCEAN

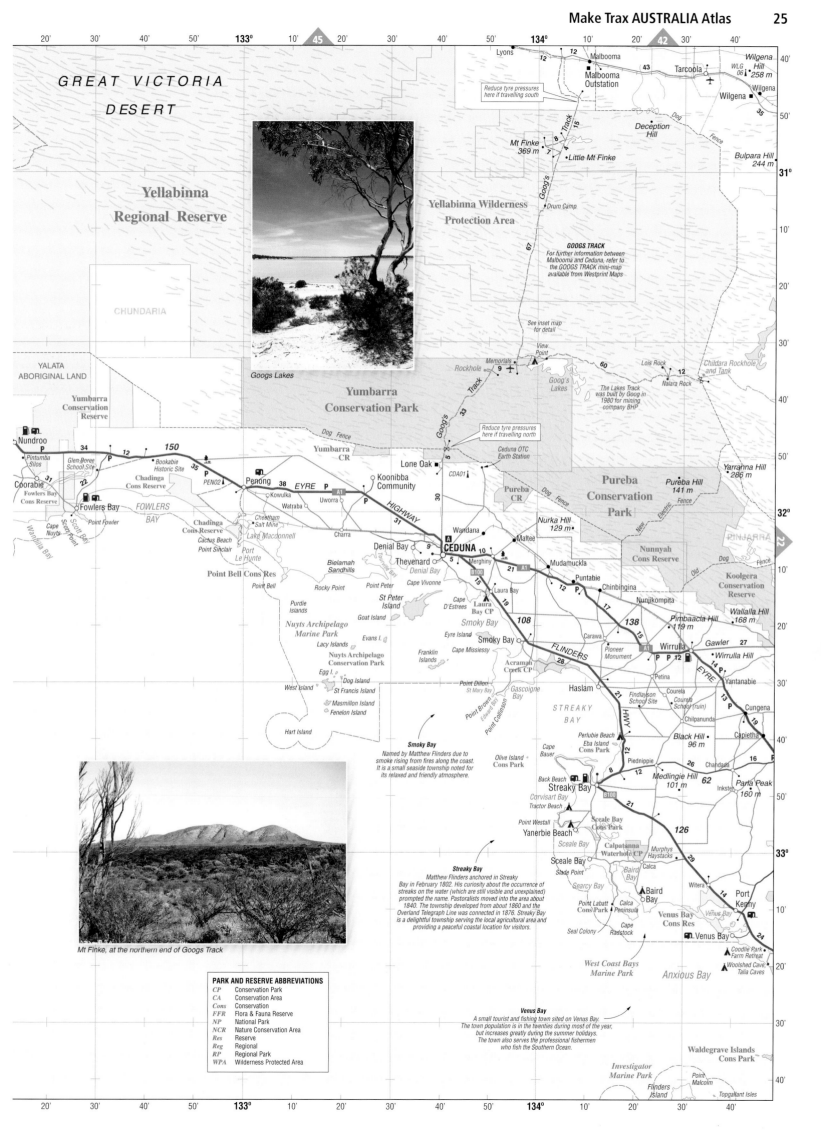

GREAT VICTORIA DESERT

Yellabinna Regional Reserve

CHUNDARIA

Googs Lakes

Lyons

Malbooma

12
12

43
Tarcoola

Wilgena Hill 258 m
WLG 06

Wilgena
35

Wilgena

Reduce tyre pressures here if travelling south

Deception Hill

Dog Fence

Bulpara Hill 244 m

31º

Mt Finke 369 m
Little Mt Finke
8
7
4
Goog's Track

67
Drum Camp

Yellabinna Wilderness Protection Area

GOOGS TRACK
For further information between Malbooma and Ceduna, refer to the GOOGS TRACK mini-map available from Westprint Maps

See inset map for detail

10'

20'

30'

View Point

Memorials
9
Rockhole

60

Lois Rock
Nalara Rock
12

Childara Rockhole and Tank

Goog's Lakes

The Lakes Track was built by Goog in 1980 for mining company BHP

Yumbarra Conservation Park

Goog's Track
33

YALATA ABORIGINAL LAND

Yumbarra Conservation Reserve

Reduce tyre pressures here if travelling north

40'

Ceduna OTC Earth Station

Pureba CR

Pureba Conservation Park

Yarranna Hill 286 m

Pureba Hill 141 m

Yumbarra CR

Lone Oak
CDA01

5

30

Nundroo
Pintumba Silos
34
12
150

Glen Boree School Site
P
PEN02
35
Bookabie Historic Site

Koonibba Community

Dog Fence

New Electric Fence

Old

RINJARRA
22

Coorabie
31

22

Penong
38
EYRE
A1
P

Kowulka
Watraba
Uworra
HIGHWAY
31

Denial Bay
9

CEDUNA
10
Merghiny
Maltee

Wandana

Nurka Hill 129 m

Nunnyah Cons Reserve

Koolgera Conservation Reserve

Fowlers Bay Cons Reserve
Fowlers Bay
Point Fowler

FOWLERS BAY

Chadinga Cons Reserve
Cheetham Salt Mine
Cactus Beach
Point Sinclair

Lake Macdonnell

Charra

Thevenard
5
B100
21
A1

Mudamuckla

Dog Fence

Wallalla Hill 168 m

Cape Nuyts
Scott Point
Waripilla Bay

Port Le Hunte

Point Bell Cons Res
Point Bell

Bielamah Sandhills
Rocky Point
Point Peter

Touronne Bay
Denial Bay
Cape Vivonne

15

Laura Bay
19

Puntabie
12
P
Chinbingina
Nunjikompita
17

138
15

Pimbaacla Hill 119 m

32º

Purdie Islands

St Peter Island
Goat Island

Cape D'Estrees
Laura Bay CP

Smoky Bay

108

Carawa

Wirrulla
A1
Gawler
27
Wirrulla Hill

10'

Nuyts Archipelago Marine Park

Lacy Islands

Evans I.

Eyre Island
Cape Missiessy
Smoky Bay

28

Pioneer Monument

FLINDERS

P P 12

EYRE
14
P

Yantanabie

20'

Nuyts Archipelago Conservation Park

Egg I.
West Island
Dog Island
St Francis Island
Masmillon Island
Fenelon Island

Franklin Islands

Acraman Creek CP

Petina

Findlayson School Site
Courela
Courela School (ruin)
Chilpanunda

13
P
Cungena
19
Capietha

30'

Hart Island

Point Dillon
St Mary Bay
Point Brown
Edward Bay
Point Collinson

Gascoigne Bay

Haslam
21

STREAKY BAY

Black Hill 96 m

16
Chandada
Parla Peak 160 m

40'

Smoky Bay
Named by Matthew Flinders due to smoke rising from fires along the coast. It is a small seaside township noted for its relaxed and friendly atmosphere.

Perlubie Beach
12
Eba Island Cons Park
8
Piednippie
12

Olive Island Cons Park
Cape Bauer

Back Beach
Streaky Bay
B100

Medlingie Hill 101 m

62
Inkster

26

Corvisart Bay
Tractor Beach

21

50'

Point Westall
Yanerbie Beach

Scale Bay

Scale Bay Cons Park

Calpatanna Waterhole CP
Murphys Haystacks

126

Scale Bay
Slade Point
Calca

33º

Streaky Bay
Matthew Flinders anchored in Streaky Bay in February 1802. His curiosity about the occurrence of streaks on the water (which are still visible and unexplained) prompted the name. Pastoralists moved into the area about 1840. The township developed from about 1860 and the Overland Telegraph Line was connected in 1876. Streaky Bay is a delightful township serving the local agricultural area and providing a peaceful coastal location for visitors.

Searcy Bay

Point Labatt Cons Park
Calca Peninsula

Baird Bay

Baird Bay

Witera
14
Port Kenny

10'

Cape Radstock

Venus Bay Cons Res

Venus Bay

Seal Colony

West Coast Bays Marine Park

Anxious Bay

Venus Bay
24

Coodlie Park Farm Retreat
Woolshed Cave, Talia Caves

20'

Venus Bay
A small tourist and fishing town sited on Venus Bay. The town population is in the twenties during most of the year, but increases greatly during the summer holidays. The town also serves the professional fishermen who fish the Southern Ocean.

PARK AND RESERVE ABBREVIATIONS
CP	Conservation Park
CA	Conservation Area
Cons	Conservation
FFR	Flora & Fauna Reserve
NP	National Park
NCR	Nature Conservation Area
Res	Reserve
Reg	Regional
RP	Regional Park
WPA	Wilderness Protected Area

Googs Lakes

Mt Finke, at the northern end of Googs Track

Waldegrave Islands Cons Park

Investigator Marine Park

Point Malcolm
Flinders Island
Topgallant Isles

40' 50' **125°** 10' 20' 30' 40' 46 50' **126°** 10' 20' 30' 40' 50' **127°** 10'

Rawlinna
The Rawlinna community is no longer involved in maintaining the Trans Australian Railway facilities for the area. The only industry is a mine that produces lime for the gold mines at Kalgoorlie. Rawlinna is also the start of the Connie Sue Highway, an outback track that leads to Warburton. There are no tourist services at Rawlinna.

Numerous small shallow depressions

Railway Sidings
Many of the old, original railway sidings have now been removed. Few traces remain at these sites.

Seymore Downs

Connie

Connie Sue Highway Detail
Fence   Connie Sue Hwy   Old car wreck
Connie Sue Hwy   Bore

Kinclaven

Kanandah

Rail crossing and gate indicate the southern end of the Connie Sue Highway

Old car wreck
Bore   Bore

Loongana   Railway

Lynch Cave

31°   35   Naretha   Nurina   Trans-Australian   48   10

913 Mile   48   Rawlinna (No services)   31   Trans   Access   42   Haig   Road   44   Nurina   45

Rawlinna   WWII Prisoner of War Camp   Kybo

Balgair   WWII Prisoner of War Camp

Recommended route to Eyre Highway follows vermin proof fence.

46

Carlisle   Loongana   Road

125   100

Madura Road

Track   57

All tracks in this area traverse private pastoral land. Permission to travel should be requested. Leave all gates as they are found. Slow travelling.

Ruins of the WWII prisoner of war camp near Nurina siding

Depot

Firestick Cave   Walpet Cave

Arubiddy   Madura Pass

Madura

Road (Private track)

Cocklebiddy Cave   29   Cocklebiddy   Moonera Tank Cave   HIGHWAY   P   P   Madura   RFDS airstrip on highway

10   12   EYRE   157   HAMPTON

32°   1   P   P   17   75   Olwolgin Bluff 102 m

Wool   53   Tommy Graham's Cave   Emergency telephone

Burnabbie   Graham Tank

Straight Road
At 146.6 kilometres, this part of the Eyre Highway is the longest straight stretch in Australia

P   Caiguna   Nuytsland Nature Reserve   Eyre   Nuytsland Nature Reserve

29   50   HIGHWAY   P   17   Eyre Bird Observatory   Burramul Sandpatch

EYRE   P   Kanidal Beach

5   Baxter (toilets)   Toilets & water   Twilight Cove camping area   Twilight Cove   Scorpion Bight

Tower (emergency telephone)

John Baxter Memorial

Point Dover

B A X T E R   C L I F F S

Toolinna Rockhole
Toolinna Cove

Point Culver

Memorial to John Baxter, a member of Edward John Eyre's exploration party to cross the Nullarbor Plain

Trans Australian Railway
More information about the railway line track is shown on the TRANS AUSTRALIAN RAILWAY map available in both paper and digital form from Westprint.

Deakin

Deakin Obelisk

Trans-Australian Railway

Hughes 46

53

Reid

56

59

Mundrabilla

Trans

Access

Road

56

Forrest

32

8

Road

104

50

51

WESTERN AUSTRALIA

SOUTH AUSTRALIA

Anketell

31°

115

Numerous small shallow depressions

Eucla

10'

Numerous small shallow depressions

N U L L A R B O R   P L A I N

Forrest Road

91

Road

62

20'

All tracks in this area traverse private pastoral land. Permission to travel should be requested. Leave all gates as they are found. Slow travelling.

Eyre   Hwy

Warbla Cave

Bunabie Tank

Old

Koomooloobooka Cave

Roaches Rest Cave

Mundrabilla Road

Bunabie Blowhole

Coompana Tank

30'

Old

Wileura Rockhole

Coach

90

Road

Eucla Pass

7

14

12

12

Eucla Nat Park

WA-SA Border Village

30

Lookout

A1

EYRE

30

Emergency telephone

28 p

Lookout

Mullamullang Cave

58

Kuthala Pass

Abrakurrie Cave
Kutowall Doline
Winbirra Cave

Moopina

Eucla
A

Far West Coast Marine Park

T A B L E L A N D

30

Drinking water

Mundrabilla Motel

66

Wilson Bluff

Merdayerrah Sandpatch

48

P

P

P

HIGHWAY

RFDS airstrip on highway

E J Eyre and Border Survey Memorials

27

Moodini Pass

P

53

Mundrabilla

P

1

193

EYRE

35

P

RFDS airstrip on highway

G R E A T   A U S T R A L I A N

32°

R O E   P L A I N S

B I G H T

10'

Noonaera

Low Point

Red Rocks Point

Middini Beach

Deakin Obelisk on the Trans Australian Railway near the border of SA and WA

Old Telegraph Repeater Station ruins at Eucla

S O U T H E R N   O C E A N

NT

QLD

WA

SA

NSW

VIC

TAS

NORTH

10km   0   10   20   30   40km

© Copyright Westprint Maps Pty Ltd 2022

Dunnsville

Kunanalling

KALGOORLIE BOULDER

Kundana Mine

Bush Two-up School
Power station

Bulong Nickel Project

Bulong Nickel Mines

Lake Yindarlgooda

Super Pit Mine

Hampton Hill

Mt Burges 554 m
Mount Burges

Kurrawang

Bonnie Vale

Lakeside Timber Res

Golden Ridge

Stoneville

Curtin
Trans

Stewart

Coolgardie

Kangaroo Hills Timber Reserve

Red Lake

White Lake

Brown Lake

Duplex Hill 421 m

Mount Monger

Darrine

Proposed Conservation Area (formerly Jaurdi Station)

(Camping and accommodation)

Jaurdi Nature Stay

Jaurdi

Wallaroo

Wallaroo Rock Conservation Park

Bulla Bulling

GOLDFIELDS

New Celebration Mines

Granite Hill

Weowanie Rock

Lake Seabrook

Lake Walton

Lake Eva

Yellowdine Nature Res

Boorabbin National Park

Goldfields Woodland CP

Yerdani Well

Bulla Bulling Mines

Gibralter Mines

Gnarlbine Rock

Nepean Mine

Seahill Timber Reserve

Yallari Timber Reserve

Woolibar

Karalee Rock

GREAT

EASTERN

Boorabbin

184

Nalarine Rock

Goldfields Woodlands National Park

Goldfields Woodland Management Area

Victoria Rock

Toilets

Quairnie Rock

Durgulyie Rock

Goldfields Woodland CP

Kambalda Nature Reserve

Victor Mine

Kambalda

Kambalda West

LAKE LEFROY

Saint Ives Mines

Yellowdine
Yellowdine Nature Res

Koorarawalyee

Victoria Rocks Nature Reserve

Burra Rock

Burra Rock Nature Reserve

Roysalt

Saint Ives Mining Centre

Pigeon Hole

Thursday Rock

Holland Track
More information about the Holland Track is available on the HOLLAND TRACK map available on CD from Westprint.

Widgiemooltha

Mt Morgan 408 m

Binneringie

Mareil

Nevoria Mine

Yilgarn Star Mine

Toomey Hills

Parker Range Mine

Olga Rocks

Jilbadji Nature Reserve

Agnes Gnamma Hole

Diamond Rock

Krackouer Rocks

Barker Lake

Lake Percy

Cat Camp

Drilling Site

View Point

Cave Hill 456 m

Cave Hill Nature Reserve
Toilets

Sandalwood Camp

Binaronca Nature Res

Poseidon South Mine

Higginsville

LAKE COWAN

Split Rocks

Sandalwood Rocks

Toovey Claypan

Banks Rock 382 m

Old

Hyden

Road

Hayes Hill 345 m

Pioneer

Bounty Gold Mine

The Banker Mt Day Road appeared to be in fair condition but rarely used in 2004

McDermid Rock 373 m

Lookout

Toilet

Scamp Rock

Knapp Rock

Disappointment Rock 403 m

Toilet

Norseman

Mt Thirsty

North Royal Mine

Theatre Rocks 382 m

Lake Cowan

Buldania Rocks

Dundas Hills

Rockholes

Mt Holland 478 m

Mine

Wattle Rocks

Mt Day 498 m

Maggie Hays Mine

Thiel Rock

Alice Rock

Taylor Rock

Road

Lookout

Norseman

Lake Cronin Nature Reserve

Lake Cronin

Norseman

Maggie Hays Hill 368 m

Lake Johnston

Dundas Heritage Trail
Old Coach Road follows the route taken by Cobb & Co coaches, passing through the original town of Dundas.

Picnic Lake

Jyndabinbin Rocks

Mt Stewart 434 m

Digger Rocks

View Point

Lake Johnston

Mt Gordon 457 m

Lake Hope

Red Lake

Lake Medcalf

Bremer Range

View Point

Difficult when wet

Bromus

Numerous small claypans

Lake Dundas

Jackson Nature Reserve

Hatter Hill Remote Mining Locality

Ninety Mile Tank

Claypan

Stennet Rock

Daniell

Gilmore Rocks

Lake Gilmore

Beete

Numerous small salt lakes

Frank Hann National Park

Lake Kathleen

Lake Ace Nature Res

Lake Ace

Three Star Lake

Lake Tay

Lake Sharpe

Peak Charles National Park

Peak Charles 651 m

Dog Rock 299 m

Peak Eleanora 501 m

Kumarl

Dowak

Salmon Gums

Salmon Gums Nature Reserve

Lilian Stokes Rock

Lake King

Lake

King

Swallow Rock

Lake Tay

Lake Mends

Circle Valley

Dingo Rock

Pallarup Nature Res

Lake Pallarup

Lake Milarup

Mt Madden 387 m

Stennetts Lake

Cascades

Peters Soak

Pyramid Lake

Red Lake

Grass Patch

Mt Ridley

Ravensthorpe

BEWARE
Numerous cleared lines in this area make navigation hazards

Chedanup Nature Reserve

Truslove Townsite Nature Reserve

Scaddan

James Dunn Mine

Lookout

Kundip Nature Res

SOUTH   **COAST**

Munglinup

Boydells

Gibson

Dalyup

Map coordinates (top)

20'   30'   40'   50'   **123°**   10'   **49**   20'   30'   40'   50'   **124°**   10'   20'   **46**   30'   40'

Mt Charnleigh
389 m

Lake Roe

Lake Yindana

Kalin Granite Rock
364 m

CUNDEELEE
Aboriginal Community

40'

Wallaby Rocks
Timber Reserve

Coonana
Timber Reserve

Emu Rocks

CUNDEELEE
ABORIGINAL LAND

50'

Hampton
Plains

Emu Rocks
Timber Reserve

Randell   Avoca
Downs   Karonie   Bronco Plains

Ponton

65

52

Access   30   Road   Chifley   34   Railway   Coonana   Zanthus   Trans-Australian   Railway   **31°**

Trans-Australian

Kitchener   29   Boonderoo   35   913 Mile

*Trans Australian
Railway Access Road*
For more information between
Kalgoorlie and Kingoonya, refer to the
Trans Australian Railway map-on-
demand from Westprint Maps

Upurl Upurlila
Ngurratja   42

28   Balladonia

Lake
Boonderoo

The Elder Scientific Exploration Expedition
Led by David Lindsay, the expedition left Warrina (on the
Oodnadatta Track) for a known point in the Everard Ranges
(north-west of Marla). The exploration then extended west through
the Great Victoria Desert toward what is now Kalgoorlie and then
on to settled areas near Geraldton.

Lake
Rivers

Harris Lake   Zanthus

20'

Cherternerlynyer
Lagoon

34   Road

Madoonia
Downs

Salt   Ck

30'

121   33   61   125

Yardina
Soak

Moochabinna
Rockhole

Symons Hill
394 m

Zanthus

50

Pioneer Tank   Ruin   Emu Point Tank

50'

Sinclair
Soak

All tracks in this area traverse
private pastoral land. Permission
to travel should be requested. Leave
all gates as they are found.
Slow travelling.

New Pioneer
Tank   Goorlitharina Tank

McPhersons
No 1 Dam

Walogerina
Soak

32°

P   *EYRE*   Ten Mile
85   Rocks   Emergency
telephone

20   Fraser Range
Station Stay
(Accommodation,
nature walks)   *HIGHWAY*

Zanthus   Road

P   193   **1**   **P**   38   **P**   **P**   Newman
Rock   75   97   *Straight Road*
At 146.6 kilometres, this part
of the Eyre Highway is the longest
straight stretch in Australia

Heartbreak Ridge
(Tower and
emergency
telephone)   Ten Mile
Rocks   23   **P**   **P**   Balladonia   **26**

Southern Hills
Mt Malcom
425 m   Harms Lake   27   **P**   Harms
Lake   **10'**

Noondoonia   15   **P**

Balladonia Roadhouse   **P**   5   12   Afghan Rock   RFDS
Airstrip   Woorlba   *EYRE*   **P**   **P**   **1**   Tower
(emergency
telephone)   **20'**

Dundas   Old   Telegraph   Line   Track   Yadadinia
Rockhole   23   22   **P**   60   **P**   **P**

Fraser   Range   Road   23   Balladonia   182

Nature Reserve   **30'**

Woorlba
(Toilets &
emergency
telephone)

Wonberna
Granite Rock   **40'**

Nanambinia

Old Telegraph Station ruins at Israelite Bay

Balladonia

50'

Mt Willgonarinya
237 m   Wylie Scarp

33°

Ruin   Rays Rock
Bills   Balbinya
Paddock
corner   Heinsman
Rock   Wylie Scarp   **10'**

Juranda Rockhole   Wattle Camp

Pine Hill Dam   Mt Dean
467 m   **20'**

Kau Rock
Nature Reserve   Beaumont
Nature
Reserve   Tower Peak
593 m
Mt Ragged   *Nuytsland
Nature
Reserve*   NT   QLD

Parmango   WA   SA   NSW

Muntz
Nature
Reserve   VIC   **30'**

Burdett South
Nature
Reserve   16   Road   Gora   *Cape Arid
National Park*   Old Telegraph
Station (ruins)   Israelite Bay   TAS

Balladonia   Point Dempster   **NORTH**

Lake
Daringdella   © Copyright Westprint Maps Pty Ltd 2022

10km   0   10   20   30   40km   **40'**

20'   30'   40'   **123°**   10'   **33**   20'   30'   40'   50'   **124°**   10'   20'   30'   40'

NORTH

10km 0 10 20 30 40km

© Copyright Westprint Maps Pty Ltd 2022

Please Note:
Many features on this map have been derived from Australian Government digital data and have not been thoroughly checked in the field by Westprint Maps.

INDIAN OCEAN

Geographe
Bay

WA NT QLD SA NSW VIC TAS

Grey
Cooljarloo Mine
Billinue
Dandaragan
Jurien Bay Marine Park
Wanagarren Nature Reserve
Lancelin Military Training Area
Moora
Bindi Bindi
Walebing
Kondut
Jam Hill Nature Reserve
Wedge Island
Piawaning
Lake Hinds Nature Reserve
Wongan Hills Nature Reserve
Rogers Nature Reserve
Eneminga Nature Res
Pindaree
Gillingarra
Yerecoin
Wongan Hills
Manmanning Nature Reserve
Nilgen Nature Reserve
Nanming Nature Reserve
Mogumber West NR
New Norcia
Lake Ninan Nature Reserve
Gathercole NR
Lancelin
River
Mogumber
Calingiri
Konnongorring
Ledge Point
Lake Wannamal NR
Burabadji
Walyormouring Nature Res
Dowerin
Karakin Lakes
Wannamal
Moore River National Park
Bolgart
Goomalling
Seabird
Boonanarring Nature Res
Camerer NR
Drummond
Beejoording
Rossmore
Hingmarsh Nature Res
Guilderton
Gingin
Flat Rock Gully NR
Jennacubbine
Moore River Nature Res
Bindoon
Chittering
Rugged Hills NR
Wongamine NR
West Toodyay
Jennapullin
Yeal Nature Res
Two Rocks
Moondyne Nature Res
Avon
Toodyay
Yanchep
Muchea
Avon Valley NP
Clackline NR
Northam
Grass Valley
Meckering
Yanchep National Park
Bullsbrook
Walyunga NP
Morangup NR
EASTERN
Neerabup National Park
Quinns Rocks
Nature Res
Lake Joondalup
Wanneroo
Wundowie
Bakers Hill
Spring Hill
Mortlock
Burns Beach
Upper Swan
John Forrest NP
Kwolyinine NR
Mokine NR
Mullaloo
West Swan
Herne Hill
Gidgegannup
Inkpen Road NR
Wootating NR
York
North Beach
Midland
Mount Helena
Chidlow
Greenhills
Scarborough
Mundaring
The Lakes
Kalamunda NP
PERTH
Kalamunda
Helena River Reservoir
Wandoo National Park
Rottnest Island
Cottesloe
Como
Helena National Park
Cape Vlamingh
Phillip Point
Korung Nat Park
Punine
Fremantle
Gosnells
Beverley
Coogee
Jandakot
Roleystone
Mount Kokeby
Garden Island
Armadale
Canning Reservoir
Annandale
Brookton
Rockingham
Kwinana
Byford
Monadnocks Cons Park
Gleneagle
Westdale
Brookton Highway NR
Shoalwater Islands Marine Park
Mundijong
Gooralong Cons Park
HIGHWAY
Becher Point
Serpentine
Jarrahdale
Serpentine Nat Park
Boyagarring Cons Park
Lupton Conservation Park
Boyagin NR
Golden Bay
Singleton
Goegrup Lake Nature Res
Serpentine Dam
Dattening NR
Pingelly
Madora
North Dandalup
ALBANY
Mandurah
Barragup
Furnissdale
North Bannister
Falcon
North Pinjarra
Wandering
Popanyinning
Wannanup
Pinjarra
Bannister
Austin Bay Nature Reserve
Peel Inlet
Dwellingup
Harvey Estuary
Coolup
Yalgorup National Park
Kooljerrenup NR
Boddington
Crossman
Lake Clifton
Lake Banksiadale
Lane Poole Reserve
Mooradung Nature Res
Buller NR
Waroona
Marradong
Preston Beach
Hamel
Lake Kabbamup
Lavender Nature Reserve
Wagerup
Lake Preston
Yarloop
Quindanning
Williams Nature Reserve
Williams
Cookernup
Josbury
Harvey Dam
Falls Brook Nature Res
Myalup
Harvey
Tallanalla
Binningup
Benger Swamp NR
Benger
Stirling Dam
Lane Poole Reserve
Leschenault Peninsula Conservation Park
Leschenault Inlet
Lake Balingall
Brunswick Junction
Boolading Nature Reserve
Hillman Nature Res
Darkan
Arthur River
Australind
Harris Dam
Eaton
Koombana Bay
Burekup
Allanson
Bunbury
Waterloo
Collie
Wollaston
Dardanup
Shotts
Bowelling
Beaufort Bridge NR
Cape Naturaliste
Lighthouse and Museum
Boyanup
Dardanup Cons Park
Collie Cardiff
Muja Cons Park
Capercup Road North Nature Res
Sugarloaf Rock Nature Reserve
Eagle Bay
Wellington Dam
Wellington National Park
Dunsborough
Tuart Forest National Park
Capel
Mumballup
Greater Preston NP
Haddleton Nature Res
Yallingup
Busselton
Donnybrook
Greater Preston NP
Moodiarrup
Towerrinning Nature Res
Cape Clairault
Vasse
Yelverton Nat Park
Carbunup River
Yoongarillup
Paynedale
Kirup
Grimwade
Wilga
Bindaree
Muja Cons Park
Wild Horse Swamp NR

Map Labels

Top border (longitude/latitude markers): 10' 20' 30' 40' 50' 118° 10' 51 20' 30' 40' 50' 119° 10' 20' 48 30' 40'

Right border: 40' 50' 31° 10' 20' 30' 50' 32° 10' 28 20' 30' 40' 50' 33° 10' 20' 30' 40'

Towns and features:

Cadoux
Koorda
Bencubbin
Mukinbudin
Walyahmoning Nature Reserve
3 Mile Rocks
Lake Deborah East
Chiddarcooping Nature Reserve
Lake Deborah West
Golden Valley Homestead
Koolyanobbing
Koolyanobbing Mine
Nature Reserve
Baladjie Lake Nature Reserve
Hughes Hill
Baladjie Rock
Lake Seabrook
Billyacatting Hill 417 m
Billyacatting Hill NR
Lake Brown
Lake Campion
Warralakin
Bullfinch
Copperhead Mine
Lake Baladjie
Lake Deborah East
Duladgin Nature Reserve
Trayning
Wyalkatchem
Nungarin
Lake Campion Nature Reserve
Sandford Rocks
Moorine Rocks
Hopes Hill Mine
Yellowdine Nature Reserve
Southern Cross
Lake Julia
Nukarni
Westonia
Elouera Farmstay
Noongar
Moorine Rock
Frasers Mine
Yellowdine
Burracoppin
Walgoolan
Bodallin
Jilbadgie Rocks
Marvel Loch Supergibd Mine
EASTERN HWY
Merredin
Nature Reserve
Jilbadgie Rock Nature Reserve
Frog Rock Picnic area
Marvel Loch
Nevoria Mine
Tammin
GREAT HWY
Doodlakine
Maughan Nature Res
Nature Reserve
Mt Hampton 457 m
Hampton Nature Reserve
Great Victoria Mine
Yilgarn Star Mine
Cunderin
Kellerberrin
Cockatoo Tank
Parker Range Mine
Toomey Hills
Charles Gardner Nature Res
Olga Rocks
River
Salt
River
Bruce Rock
Shackleton Nature Res
Cairn Nature Res
Neendojer Rock Nature Reserve
Skeleton Rock 458 m
Split Rocks
Shackleton
Mokami Nature Res
Neendojer Rocks
Welsh Nature Reserve
Jilbadji Nature Reserve
Quairading
Dangin
Ardath
Wandjagill Nature Res
Narembeen
Gibb Rock
Rockholes
Yenyening Lakes Nature Reserve
Lake Mears
Boolanelling Nature Res
Seagroatt Nature Res
South Kumminin
Wave Rock
An unusually weathered, wave-shaped granite monolith, measuring 110 metres long and 15 metres high.
Yenyening Lakes
Lake Kurrenkutten Nature Reserve
Billericay
North Karlgarin Nature Reserve
The Humps
Wattle Rocks
Native Rocks
Sheoak Rock
Track
Mine
Tower
Corrigin
Hyden
Wave Rock
Hyden
Emu Rock
Norseman
Tutanning Nature Reserve
Lake Yealering
Kondinin Lake Nature Res
Kondinin
Karlgarin
Lake O'Connor
Bushfire Rock
Lake Carmody
Lake Hurlstone Nature Reserve
Mt Stewart 434 m
Yealering
Dragon Rocks Nature Reserve
Track Sign
Lake Hurlstone
Kulin
Kulin
Kulin
Holt
Rock
Road
Lake Varley Nature Res
Holt Rock
Wickepin
Jitarning
Pingaring
Track Marker
Lake Varley
Cuballing
Dudinin
Dornock
Mordetta
Dragon Rocks
Mt Vernon 449 m
Lake Gunstone
Varley
HIGHWAY
Narrogin
Highbury
White Lake
Toolibin Lake
Taarblin Lake Nature Reserve
Nomans Lake Nature Reserve
Kuender
Harris Nature Reserve
Dragon Rocks Nature Reserve
Lake Biddy
Lake Fox
Lake King Nature Reserve
Lake Camm
Lake Kathleen
Arthur River Nature Reserve
Tarin Rock Nature Res
Tarin Rock
Lake Grace
Lake Grace
Sheoak Hill
Newdegate
Newdegate
Ravensthorpe Rd
Lake King
Piesseville
Duggan
Lake Grace (North)
Newdegate
Silver Wattle Soak
Plaque
Lake Buchan
Lake King Nature Reserve
Lake King
Kukerin
Silver Wattle Hill Nature Res
Beynon Nature Res
Lake Magenta
Chinocup Nature Res
Lake Grace (South)
Holland Rocks
Dunn Rock Nature Reserve
Lake Milarup
Wagin
Lake Dumbleyung
Dumbleyung
Holland Tank
Lake Magenta Nature Reserve
Dunn Rock
Lake Magenta
Lake Dumbleyung Nature Reserve
Lefroy River
Private road, no access.
Lake Pingrup
Lake Lockhart
Lake Cobham
Lake Romani
Queerarrup Lake
Chinocup NR
Nampup Spring
Way
Chinocup Lake
Kowanup Spring
Lake Morris
Woodanilling
Mojebing
Nyabing
Pingrup
Mallee
Badgebup
Plaque
Holland
John
Coyrecup Lake
Katanning
Coblinine River
Fitzgerald
River

Please Note:
Many features on this map have been derived from Australian Government digital data and have not been thoroughly checked in the field by Westprint Maps.

Bottom border: 10' 20' 30' 118° 10' 20' 35 30' 40' 50' 119° 10' 20' 30' 40'

Digger Rocks

Jackson Nature Reserve

Hatter Hill Remote Mining Locality

Frank Hann National Park

Claypan
Ninety Mile Tank
Road

Peak Charles National Park

Lake Gilmore
Lake Dundas

Beete

Kumarl

Dowak

Numerous small salt lakes

Lake Kathleen

Lake Ace Nature Res
Lake Ace

Norseman
82

Three Star Lake

Lake Tay
Lake Sharpe

Peak Charles 651 m
Dog Rock

Peak Eleanora 501 m

COOLGARDIE

Salmon Gums

Salmon Gums Nature Reserve

33°

Lake King

Lilian Stokes Rock

Lake King

Swallow Rock

Lake Tay

Lake Mends

Circle Valley

Lake King
Lake Milarup

Ravensthorpe

Pallarup Nature Res
Lake Pallarup
Mt Madden 387 m

Stennetts Lake

Cascades

Peters Soak

Pyramid Lake

Fields

Red Lake

Grass Patch

Mt Ridley

BEWARE
Numerous cleared lines in this area make navigation hazardous

Road

Road

Road
Patch

Road

ESPERANCE
99

Truslove Townsite Nature Reserve

35°

Road

Ravensthorpe
48

Coujinup Creek

Road

Rolland

Grass

Scaddan
Scaddan

Road

West

Lookout

Chedanup Nature Reserve

Point

Young

Cascades

River

Griggs

Road

Ravensthorpe

James Dunn Mine

Lookout

Rabbit Proof Fence

West

Oldfield

Cascade
38

Road

Boydells
Road

HIGHWAY

Road

Kundip Nature Res

Jerdacuttup

Jerdacuttup River

SOUTH
34

Rd

COAST
23

Munglinup

21

Neds

Corner

33

14

Coolbidge

Dalyup

Gibson

Information Bay

Lookout

Lookout

Rabbit Proof Fence follows road

Road

Munglinup

River

186

38

HIGHWAY

18

Dalyup

Lake Gore

21

Shark Lake

12

Merivale

Mt Drummond 309 m

Hammersley Inlet

John Forrest Memorial
Culham Inlet

Springdale

Dunns Swamp

Lake Shaster Nature Reserve
Lake Shaster

Park Ranger
Yerritup

Barker Inlet

Lake Mortijinup

1
28

21

13

Pink Lake

Wind Farm

Merivale Farm Stay

Fitzgerald River National Park

Dempster Inlet

Lookout

Four Mile Beach
Barrens Beach

Hopetoun

Twelve Mile Beach

Jerdacuttup Lakes Nature Reserve

Munglinup Beach

Stokes National Park

Margaret Cove
Dunster Castle Bay
Stokes Inlet
Shoal Cape
Fanny Cove

Quag Beach

Shelly Beach

Butty Head

Observatory Island

Esperance

Esperance Bay

Woody I.

Mt Le Grand 345 m

34°

Twin Bays

Quoin Head
Whale Bone Beach
Edwards Point
Cave Point

West Channel

West Group

Sandy Hook I.
Long I.
Remark I.

Point Charles
St Marys Camping & Whale Watching
Point Ann

Figure of Eight I.

Boxer I.

Causeway Channel

Recherche Archipelago Nature Reserve

Corbett I.

MacKenzie Island

Doubtful Islands Bay

Doubtful Islands

Archipelago of the *Recherche*

Termination Island

35°

NT
QLD
WA
SA
NSW
VIC
TAS

NORTH

10km 0 10 20 30 40km

© Copyright Westprint Maps Pty Ltd 2022

20'   30'   40'   50'   **123°**   10'   20'   30'   **29**   40'   50'   **124°**   10'   20'   30'   40'

**Dundas
Nature Reserve**

■ Nanambinia

Balladonia

• Mt Willgonarinya
237 m

Wylie Scarp

• Dingo Rock

Ruin □

Rays Rock •
□ Balbinya

Road

Bills
Paddock
corner

*Heinsman
Rock*

Wylie Scarp

• Wattle Camp

Juranda Rockhole

**Kau Rock
Nature Reserve**

**Beaumont
Nature
Reserve**

Pine Hill Dam

• Mt Dean
467 m

**Nuytsland
Nature
Reserve**

Wylie Scarp

Tower Peak
593 m
• • Mt Ragged

Purmango

**Muntz
Nature
Reserve**

**Burdett South
Nature
Reserve**

Road

**Cape Arid
National Park**

Old Telegraph
Station (ruins)

Wylie Scarp

Israelite Bay
▲ • Point Dempster

Fisheries
18

22   *Road*   6

16

Balladonia

95

Road

*Lake
Daringdella*

9

40

Fisheries

Condingup

20

Road   24

Merivale

Road

▲ Point Malcolm

8

Road

12

20

11   *Merivale*
20

5

11

*Park
Ranger* ■

Thomas
River ▲

Seal
Creek
▲ Sandy Bight

• Mt Pasley
164 m

• Daw Island

17

**Cape Le Grand
National Park**

*Orleans
Bay*

*Yokinup
Bay*

Cape Pasley

9

*Dunn
Rocks*

Duke of
Orleans Bay

*Alexander
Bay*

Mart Is

• Mt Arid
357 m

Jorndee
Creek
□ Hill Springs

Arid Bay

• Pasley Island

Rossiter Bay

Helfire Bay

Cheyne Point

Hammer Head

North Twin Peak I.
South Twin Peak I.

Cape Arid

□ Gulch I.

Stanley I.

Arid Strait

Lucky Bay

• Mondrain
Island

Westall I. □

Middle Island

**Recherche Archipelago
Nature Reserve**

Archipelago   of   the   Recherche

Round Island •

34°

33°

10'

20'

30'

40'

50'

Cooper Island •

*Salisbury
Island*

10'

20'

S O U T H E R N   O C E A N

30'

35°

40'

50'

10'

20'

30'

40'

20'   30'   40'   50'   **123°**   10'   20'   30'   40'   50'   **124°**   10'   20'   30'   40'

Map Labels

INDIAN OCEAN

Geographe Bay

Longitude markers (top): 40', 50', 115°, 10', 20', 30', 40', 50', 116°, 10', 20', 30', 40', 50', 117°

Latitude markers (left): 40', 50', 33°, 10', 20', 30', 40', 50', 34°, 10', 20', 30', 40', 50', 35°, 10', 20', 30', 40'

Place names and features

Harvey Estuary, Kooljerrenup NR, Coolup, Dwellingup, Bannister, Wandering, Popanyinning, Lake Banksiadale, Yalgorup National Park, Lake Clifton, Lake Clifton, Buller NR, Waroona, Lane Poole Reserve, Boddington, Crossman, Preston Beach, Wagerup, Hamel, Marradong, Mooradung Nature Res, Lake Preston, Cookernup, Yarloop, Lake Kabbamup, Williams Nature Reserve, Williams, Harvey Dam, Falls Brook Nature Res, Quindanning, Myalup, Benger Swamp NR, Harvey, Tallanalla, Lavender Nature Reserve, Josbury, Binningup, Benger, Stirling Dam, Lane Poole Reserve, Leschenault Peninsula Conservation Park, Brunswick Junction, Lake Ballingall, Harris Dam, Hillman Nature Reserve, Darkan, Arthur River, Leschenault Inlet, Australind, Koombana Bay, Eaton, Burekup, Allanson, Collie, Boolading Nature Reserve, Bunbury, Waterloo, Wollaston, Dardanup, Shotts, Collie Cardiff, Bowelling, Muja Cons Park, Capercup Road North Nature Res, Beaufort Bridge NR, Boyanup, Dardanup Cons Park, Wellington Dam, Greater Preston NP, Haddleton Nature Res, Towerrining Nature Reserve, Mumballup, Muja Cons Park, Moodiarrup, Cape Naturaliste, Lighthouse and Museum, Eagle Bay, Capel, Donnybrook, Greater Preston NP, Wild Horse Swamp NR, Sugarloaf Rock Nature Reserve, Dunsborough, Tuart Forest National Park, Yallingup, Busselton, Vasse, Yoongarillup, Paynedale, Kirup, Grimwade, Wilga, Bindaree, Boree Park, Red Hill NR, Cape Clairault, Yelverton Nat Park, Carbunup River, Kerr Cons Park, Balingup, Moses Rocks, Leeuwin-Naturaliste National Park, Whicher Nat Park, Jarrahwood, Greenbushes Nature Reserve, Greenbushes, Powlalup Nature Reserve, Hester Cons Park, Boyup Brook, Dinninup, Qualeup, Narlingup NR, Muradup, Gracetown, Cowaramup, Wiltshire-Butler National Park, Mayanup, Ellensbrook Homestead, Mowen, Bramley Nat Park, Rapids Cons Park, Mettabinup NR, Jingalup Nature Res, Margaret River, Blackwood River National Park, Dalgarup Nat Park, Bridgetown, Greater Kingston National Park, Mininup NR, South Jingalup Nature Reserve, Prevally, Witchcliffe, Forest Grove NP, Yornup, Wheatley, Alco Nature Res, Heartlea, Mammoth Cave, Lake Cave, Cape Freycinet, Forest Grove, Brockman, Chester NR, Milyeannup National Park, Easter NP, Donnelly River NR, Manjimup, Tone-Perup Nature Res, Tonebridge, Kulunilup NR, Leeuwin-Naturaliste National Park, Boranup Lookout, Hamelin Bay, Karridale, Pagett NR, Hilliger National Park, Scott NP, D'entrecasteaux National Park, Greater Beedelup Nat Park, Nyamup, Tone-Perup Nature Reserve, Unicup NR, Quindinup NR, Frankland, Jewell Cave and Moondyne Cave, Augusta, Flinders Bay, Gingilup Swamps NR, Kodjinup Nature Res, Strachan, Tootanellup NR, Cape Leeuwin, Lighthouse, Black Point, Pemberton, Gloucester Nat Park, Greater Dordagup NP, Boyndaminup NR, Byenup Lagoon, Lake Muir, Muirs, Rocky Gully, Lake Jasper, Warren NP, Quininup, Shannon Nat Park, Lake Muir NP, D'entrecasteaux National Park, Jane NP, Northcliffe, Shannon, Mt Frankland North NP, Mount Frankland National Park, Mount Roe Nat Park, D'entrecasteaux National Park, Boorara-Gardner NP, Shannon Nat Park, Mt Frankland NP, Point D'entrecasteaux, Windy Harbour, D'entrecasteaux National Park, Mt Frankland South NP, Mt Frankland 411 m, Camfield, Kent River, Broke Inlet, Walpole, Peaceful Bay, Walpole-Nornalup National Park, Point Nuyts, Nornalup Inlet, Bellanger Beach, Walpole-Nornalup NP, Point Irwin, Irwin Inlet, Quarram Nature Reserve, Boat Harbour

Scale and legend

NORTH

10km 0 10 20 30 40km

Inset map of Australia: NT, QLD, WA, SA, NSW, VIC, TAS

Please Note:
Many features on this map have been derived from Australian Government digital data and have not been thoroughly checked in the field by Westprint Maps.

50'   **149°**   10'   54   20'   30'   40'   50'   **150°**   10'   20'   30'   55   40'   50'   **151°**   10'   20'

QLD / NSW

Wongle
Enarra
Moonie
St Hilliers
New Dunmore
Teelba
Glengarry
Southwood National Park
Kinkora
Bendee
Boondandilla
Cuppine
Millmerran
Lochnagar
Dora Park
Ulupna
Allawah
Eudoia
Mount Driven
Hollymount
Westmar
Wilga Downs
Kindon
Wondul Range National Park
Koorongara
Spring Mount
Lapunyah
Trevanna Downs
Woodlawn
Lundavra
Tarewinnabar
Chelmer
Llidem Vale
Tabaringa
Monte Cristo
Goondulla
Aurifer Downs
Eaglebar
Goodar
Nariel
Yarrandine
Minnel
Inglewood
Lake Coolmunda
Weengallon
Bundah
Bungunya
Nindigully
Lalaguli
Goondiwindi
Yelarbon
Orungal
Wolonga
Wondulla
Boggabilla
Glenarbon
Bullamon Plains
Daymar
Kulali
Willarie
Boomi
Beebo
Smithfield
Limevale
Thallon
Merriot
Claremont
Thorndale
Belara
Yetman
Texas
Gleneve
Dolgelly House
Tulloona
Dthinna Dthinnawan NP
Budelah Nature Res
Boonal West
North Star
Welbondongah
Braemar
Weemelah
Tononga
Kioma
Blue Nobby
Kwiambal National Park
Bonshaw
Mungindi
Garah
Tackenbri
Moyen
Cleveland
Rosedale
Croppa Creek
Coolatai
Wallangra
Woodland
Baroona
Talmoi
Crooble
Arakoola Nature Reserve
Ashford
Oakleigh
Colmlee
Ashley
Milguy
Billy Goat Hill 642 m
Graman
Severn River Nature Reserve
Wandoona
Caithness
Yarraman
Pallamallawa
Bukkulla
Bullarah
Moree
Biniguy
Warialda
Kings Plains National Park
Binna Bunna
Gravesend
Koloona
Delungra
Mount Russell
Nullamanna Sapphire
Merrywinebone
Woodvale
Iluka
Tycannah
Warialda SCA
Little Plain
Inverell
Rowena
Bulyeroi
Millie
Ellerslie
Gurley
Terry Hie Hie
Bingara
Gilgai
Elsmore
Thalaba
Gurley Station
Stannifer
Warriana
Bellata
Weetawah
Gwydir River National Park
Tingha
Nowley
Upper Bingara
Copeton Dam
Omeo
Boolcarrol
Upper Horton
Burren Junction
Waverley
Togo
Berragoon
Merah North
Widgen
Gulf Creek
Barlow
Bundarra
Bugilbone
Weetawaa
Wee Waa
Edgeroi
Bobbiwaa SCA
Brigalows
Cobbadah
Drildool
Mt Kaputar 1508 m
Pilliga
Narrabri
Round Mtn 1074 m
Barraba
Tregoen
Mount Kaputar National Park
Strathmore
Turrawan
Plum Pudding Mtn 890 m
Kingstown
Yarrowyck
Pilliga NP
Pilliga State Conservation Area
Mt Yarrowyck 1206 m
Gwabegar
Baan Baa
Split Rock Reservoir
Warrabah National Park
Piliga West SCA
Boggabri
Dunmore
Watsons Creek
Manilla

Highways / labels: MOONIE HWY, CARNARVON HWY, BARWON HIGHWAY, LEICHHARDT HIGHWAY, GORE HIGHWAY, CUNNINGHAM HIGHWAY, BRUXNER HWY, NEWELL HIGHWAY, GWYDIR HWY, Kamilaroi Hwy, Fossickers Way

Rivers: Moonie River, Macintyre River, Boomi River, Whalan Creek, Gil Gil Creek, Gwydir River, Namoi River, Dumaresq River, Commoron Creek, Severn River

Route numbers: 182, 94, 140, 117, 122, 109, 142, 80, 63, 97, 102, 91, 96, 119, A39, A5, A42, B85, B76, B46, B49

Pittsworth
Southbrook
Camboova
82
A39
Brookstead
Felton East
Pampas
Tummaville
Nobby
Pilton
Clifton
Talgai
84
Leyburn
Hendon
Allora
Pratten

McGrath Crossing
Warrill View
Harrisville
Purga
Peak Crossing
Roadvale
Kalbar
Boonah
Bromelton
Beaudesert
Maryvale
Aratula
Moogerah Peaks National Park
Mt Mistake 1092 m
164
CUNNINGHAM
Lake Moogerah
Main Range National Park
Rockbrae
Emu Vale
Warwick
Mt Superbus 1381 m
Tannymorel
Mount Barney National Park
Mt Barney 1359 m
Maroon
Rathdowney
Lamington
HWY

Beenleigh
Logan Village
Jimboomba
Tamborine
Plunkett CP
140
Tamborine NP
Pimpama
Sanctuary Cove
Tamborine Mtn 600 m
Eagle Heights
Nerang National Park
Southport
Surfers Paradise
Broadbeach
Burleigh Heads
Coolangatta
Tweed Heads
Banora Point
Kingscliff

Naree Budjong Djara NP
Southern Moreton Bay Islands NP
Eden Island
South Stradbroke Island CP
South Stradbroke Island

Gold Coast
28°

Canungra
Muggeeraba
Beechmont
Springbrook NP
Lamington NP
Laravale
108
Lake Leslie
42
Killarney
Legume
Koreelah NP
Dalman
Tooloom NP
Urbenville
Woodenbong
Border Ranges National Park
Lindesay View
Mt Chinghee NP
Limpinwood NR
Point Lookout 1080 m
Chillingham
Tyalgum
Wollumbin NP
Uki
Tumbulgum
Murwillumbah
Condong
Bogangar
Pottsville
Burringbar
28

Dalveen
Cotton Vale
115
Amiens
Stanthorpe
Liston
Captains Creek NR
Yabbra National Park
Old Bonalbo
Toonumbar
Capeen
Richmond Range NP
Ettrick
Mebbin NP
Kunghur
Mt Jerusalem NP
Nightcap NP
Mullumbimby
Nimbin
Ocean Shores
Brunswick Heads
79
Byron Bay
Bangalow
Suffolk Beach
QLD
NSW

Sundown Resources Reserve
Ballandean
Bald Rock National Park
Bald Rock 1277 m
Cataract National Park
Boonoo Boonoo NP
Bonalbo
Grevillia
Roseberry
Toonumbar NP
Kyogle
Dyraaba Central
Goolmangar
Dunoon
Clunes
Lismore
Alstonville
Wyrallah
Ballina
Lennox Head

Sundown National Park
Lake Glenlyon
Wallangarra
Basket Swamp NP
Drake
BRUXNER
128
Tabulam
Mallanganee
Mongogarie
Mummulgum
HWY
Casino
79
Tatham
Coraki
38
Wardell
Broadwater
Broadwater National Park
Evans Head
Snapper Point

134
B60
Tenterfield
Mole River
Bolivia
Capoompeta NP
Big Mt Spirabo 1492 m
Washpool National Park
Sugarloaf Point 700 m
Rappville
Mount Neville Nature Reserve
Mt Neville 556 m
Baryulgil
Camira Creek
Whiporie
Bungawalbin Nat Park
Bundjalung SCA
Woodburn
PACIFIC
96
Bundjalung National Park
29°

Torrington State Conservation Area
Westminster Mtn 820 m
Torrington
Emmaville
91
Deepwater
Butterleaf NP
Dundee
Banyabba Nature Reserve
Coaldale
Chatsworth
Harwood
Iluka
Yamba
Maclean
The Broadwater

Wellingrove
Gibraltar Range NP
HWY
155
B76
Jackadgery
Fortis Creek National Park
Copmanhurst
Brushgrove
Lawrence
Wooloweyah Estuary

Matheson
Glen Innes
Red Range
GWYDIR
Mann River NR
B76
Barool NP
Nymboida National Park
Newton Boyd
The Brothers 1256 m
Ramornie NP
Grafton
Carrs Creek Junction
Ulmarra
Tucabia
Brooms Head
Yuraygir National Park
Sandon Bluffs
HIGHWAY
66
SOUTH PACIFIC OCEAN

Glencoe
Ben Bomond
Wandsworth
101
Llangothlin
Llangothlin Lake
Guy Fawkes River SCA
Dalmorton
Guy Fawkes River National Park
Chaelundi National Park
Red Herring Hill 930 m
Coutts Crossing
Pillar Valley
Minnie Water
Bare Point
Wooli
Yuraygir SCA
85
Sherwood NR
Red Rock
Corindi Beach
Mullaway
Woolgoolga
Emerald Beach
30°

Guyra
Black Mountain
Mt Gardiner 1150 m
Clouds Creek
Nymboi-Binderay National Park
117
Dundurrabin
Tringham
Hernani
Glenreagh
Nana Glen
Coramba
GREAT DIVIDING RANGE

Armidale
79
Cathedral Rock National Park
Wollomombi
Ebor
Way
Dorrigo
Cascade NP
Bostobrick
88
Dorrigo National Park
Valery
Bindarri Nat Park
22
Sawtell
COFFS HARBOUR
Bongil Bongil National Park

Jeogla
Waterfall
Point Lookout 1562 m
Bellingen River NP
Baalijin NR
Gumbaynggirr NP
Thora
Bellingen
Mylestom
Urunga
NEW ENGLAND

Uralla
70
Hillgrove
New England National Park
Cunnawarra NP
Lower Creek
Bowraville
Macksville
Scotts Head
Missabotti
Valla Beach
Nambucca Heads

Kentucky
Enmore
Comara
Burrapine
Donnellyville

PARK AND RESERVE ABBREVIATIONS
CP   Conservation Park
CA   Conservation Area
Cons Conservation
FFR   Flora & Fauna Reserve
NP   National Park
NCR   Nature Conservation Area
Res   Reserve
Reg   Regional
RP   Regional Park
WPA   Wilderness Protected Area

NORTH
10km 0 10 20 30 40km

© Copyright Westprint Maps Pty Ltd 2022

50' **144°** 10' 20' ◤56◥ 20' 30' 40' 50' **145°** 10' 20' ◤57◥ 30' 40' 50' **146°** 10' 20'

Soonah Crossing Karwalke Wiralla Jandell Alroy Glendilla Kubill Linden
Norley 37 19 23 5 Tilbooroo Hazelfield Nardoo Nardoo Farm stay
8 21 The 23 Bundoona Baroona Horton Vale Nulbear 31
Lake Hutchinson Opal 42 Penaroo Farnham Plains Moonjaree Phillott Mayvale HWY
Lake Toomaroo Yowah Opal Field 42 Kahmoo BALONNE Way
28° Lake Bindegolly National Park Bingara Carpet Springs 51 66 Cunnamulla 49 Adventure Charlotte Plains
Thargomindah Lake House Developmental Mud Springs Eulo 15 5 18 25 33
7 48 Bulloo 129 Springvale Mt Bingara 281 m Eulo 45 30 Hillview Weelamurra
21 Ackland Adventure 42 22 Wandilla Metavale 28 Borambil Widgeegoara
Urimbin Bore 15 Tarko 32 Werai Gumahah 122 68 Gate
20 Yakara Wombula Werewilka Mooning Watercourse 30 Westlea 28 Thurulgoonia Noorama
Wathopa Yenloora Wittenburra 118 Werai Pitherty Tinnenburra 17 Thurulgoonia 32
Mt Torrance 225 m Turn Turn 44 Werai Park Kungie Lake Kungie Lake Approximate site of Tinnenburra Woolshed
Zenoni Boodgheere 28 Cerni Paroo Waterhole Caiwarro Never Fail Binya National Park 26 20 10
170 Kilcowera Lake Wyara Boorara Hungerford Blue Lakes Binya National Park Gilnockie Barringun Tuon Morton Plains
Mt Roy 231 m Lake Numalla The Granites River Rockwell Lake Bulla Border Survey Post Turra Rostella 41 Gerara
Karto Currawinya Currawinya National Park 15 Paroo Lake Thorlindah Lake Wombah **QUEENSLAND** 3 Barringun 18 Ledknapper Nature Reserve
29° Moombidary Waverley Gate 55 Hungerford **NEW SOUTH WALES** 30 Avoca Thumylae 29
Hillside Weebah Rathgar Brindingabba Wancobra Burrawantie 13 Wirrawarra HIGHWAY 18 Enngonia 21 38
Waverley Downs Warroo South Bindra Nahweenah Gummeroo Waterhole 32 Comeroo 35 21 Lochnagar Nulty Springs
Gumbo Whim Plain Thoura Cuttaburra Basin 19 Mungunyah Crossing Springvale Lila Lednapper Crossing
Euroli Willara Crossing Glenhaven Killoween Mullarara Waterhole Yantabulla Mascot 43 Ella Vale 133 Springs Inverness
Barrajong 100 Moreland Downs Moolyearrah Maureen Joy 159 22 Lake Denman North Kirribree Bellenbah Lower Lila Bullaroon Moongulla
Nardoo Tredega 42 Dungarvon Bells Ck Bloodwood 34 Kerribree Creek Green Creek 36 Garlands
Lenroy 68 River 24 Lake Coonany Nellyvale 31 Fords Bridge 19 Glengeera
Wanaaring 41 Braemer Minetta 28 Kerribree Creek Floodout South Kerribree Merita 9 Lauradale 57 Belvedere Warraweena
3 10 21 Yulcarley Lake Burkanoko 45 Maghera 66 Artesia The Lagoon
30° Nocoleche Wongareena 16 Wangamana 12 Lake Nichebulka Tringadee Romani Gumbalie Walkdens 27 The Island
Myrnong Nocoleche Nature Reserve Hopelands Numbardie 190 69 Janina Goonery Yandaroo 62 Fort Bourke 16 North Bourke
Garden Vale Cuttaburra Channels Conlea Darling Farms **Bourke** Mount Oxley
Nantilla Emaroo Salt Lake Glenora Lake Mere Nulty Janbeth Myandetta Prattenville
Noonamah Mount Mulyah Utah Lake Glen Villa Trafalgar Woodstock
View Point Outstation Pelora Lake Toorale Toorale National Park Dicks Dam Ross Billabong Gundabooka SCA Murramburra Dam Kinchela
Lakes Pebbles Dam Talwolla DARLING Ben Lomond Mullagalah
Laurelvale Lake Arthur New Chum Louth Belah Gundabooka National Park Mt Gunderbooka 495 m
Napunyah Station stay Trilby Dunlop Winbar Wee Toura Curraweena Kenilworth
NORTH Carney Idalia Wongowal Deerina Wilgaroona Coronga Peak
10km 0 10 20 30 40km

© Copyright 2014 Westprint Maps Pty Ltd

50' **144°** 10' ◤21◥ 20' 30' 40' 50' **145°** 10' 20' ◤18◥ 30' 40' 50' **146°** 10' 20'

Bowra Sanctuary
This 14,000 ha property is one of Australia's most rewarding bird watching destinations with over 200 species. Now managed by the Australian Wildlife Conservancy.

Binya National Park of 13,700 ha was declared in 2009 and is the first national park to provide protection for a significant area of Warrego River floodplain.

Cobbrum · Carellen · Woodvale · Rutherglen · Belgaum · Powrunna · Cashmere West · Wongola · Lake Kajarabie

Thrushton National Park · Neabul Downs · Beralga

Marango · Binda · Arakoola · Belle Plains · Rosehill

Bendena · Nebinedulla · Cardiff · Mourilyan · Belingra · BALONNE · 112 · HIGHWAY

Blairmore · 179 · Rollo · Yunnerman · Bollon · Mona · St George · Thuraggi

Narkoola National Park · Heather · Wirraninna · Minimi · Doondi · Kurray · Yilgangandi · Chelmer

Bonna Vonna · Narkoola · Moorindoorah · Argyle · Bogong · Honeymah · Mooramanna · Myall Plains · Nindigully

Bendee Downs · Oban · Denholm · Openbah · Whyenbah · Shirley · CARNARVON

South Glen · Murra Downs · Runnymede · Dewurra · 164 · Bullamon Plains · 117

Gamarren · Murra Murra · Fernlee · Kanowna · Andys Crossing · Bullindgie · Hamilton · Dirranbandi · Noondoo · Thallon

Darrawong · South Plains · Armagh · Book Book · Narline · Cubbie · Bonathorne · Johnstone · Gleneve

Rosscoe Downs · Munda Munda · South Muthong · Moorenbah · Nindi-Thana · Bullawarrie

Middleton · Drigalow Downs · Wyagdon · Nulky · Ooraine

ankalilla · Yaralla · Whyenbirra · Mugangulla · CASTLEREAGH · Cavillon · Koomalah · Narine

Bundaleer · Tambingey · Woolerbilla · Euraba · Balgi · Kenmore

Kumbogan · Kulki · Dongon Plains · BALONNE · Wynella · Calooma

Darrawong · Mulga Downs · Combo · Davirton · RIVER · Habnarey · Glenara · Moyen

Mintaka · Myola · Moorefield · Culgoa · Ballandool · Hebel · Lake Bokhara · Myall Grove · Jomara · Cambo

Weona · Culgoa Floodplain National Park · Brenda Gate · Mungalby · New Angledool · Karoola · Whyalla · Gundabloui

Talbalba · Culgoa National Park · Brenda · Mogila · Oowing · Nullawa · Tuttawa · Oakleigh

Dunsandle · Widgee Downs · Burban Grange · Byerawering · Goodooga · Red Plain · Angledool Lake · Narrandool · Birrah · Eurangie · Moongulla · Bukulla

Glenmore · Glenora · Wynbar · Muckerawa · Imbergee · Bangate · Gurson · Rugby · Mogil Mogil

Whyman · Norooma · Caringle · Langboyd · Leander · Mitchell Plains · Aitken · Lightning Ridge · Dunumbral

Myuna · Baringa · Cartlands · Taralba · Bomalli · Coocoran Lake · Weetalibah · Midgery · Collarenebri · Trelawney · Pokataroo

Bora · Inverella · Willoh · 107 · Karinga · Morella · 138 · Heathfield · Franxton · Belarra · Merrywinebone

Innisfail · Talawanta · Bundabulla · Killarney · Mureabun · Strathmore · Cumborah · Nardoo · Dundalla · Mercadool · Beethoven

Mundiwa · Eurah · Glenallyn · Narran Plains · Wee Warra · East Mullane · Bairnkine · Gingie · Glen Eden · Rowena

Wongal · Rosehill · Meadow Plains · Narran Lake Nature Reserve · Roscommon · Wilkie · Eumanbah · Spillbury · Sefton Park · Cryon · Whitewoods

Collerina · Glandore · Penarie · Narran Lake · Remington · Tungra · Gorian · Bugilbone · Omeo

Coolabri · Lilyfield · Coola · Kia-Ora · Walgett · Rayleigh

Beemery · Quantambone · Yappalee · Lexington · 126 · Glenrow · River View · Bugilbone

Yambacoona · Gwandalan · Borooma · Cara Mia · Fairfield · Euroka · Eurabah · Yarraldool

Cedars · Waratah · Bogewong · Netherby · Kincora

Neranghi · Eumarra · Brewon · Borgara · Ashantee · Combogolong · Brantwood · Merridale

Charlton · Yarrawin · Westhoek · Come By Chance · Pilliga

Sainsbury Park · Gongolgon · Billybingbone · Ballarie Vale · Carinda · Nedgera · Pilliga Nat Park

Bobelah · Cowga · Goonaroi · Salisbury · Trafalga · Wingadee · Pilliga West SCA

Wave Hill · Fairlight · Ben Avon · Miltara · Conneelibah · 117 · Wingadee

Wyuna Downs · Nidgery · Branglebar · Wamboin · Macquarie Marshes Nature Reserve · Bora · The Myalls · Gunyillah · Yugilbar

Nemeena · Mulgawarrina · Kimbriki · Edale · Gilgooma

Brewarrina · 98 · Barwon · Bogan

Walgett · GWYDIR · HIGHWAY · 73

Mirra Mitta Bore

Kalla Hill

Mt Hogarth

MUNGERANIE

Salt Lake

Lake Perigundi

Lake Andree

Lake Miraditchie

Andree Waterhole

Lake Bulpanie

Lake Marak- onnamaoka

Gidgealpa

21

B&W Camp 66

B&W Camp 67 (Tilcha Waterhole) & Wills Memorial

22

5

19

Mapaoonie WH

56

No camping at Burke and Wills Bridge. Please use the managed campsite at The Dig Tree.

Sandy Ck

72

Poolbarra Swamp

Yalcuma Waterhole

Merrimelia Gas Field

19

Gidgealpa Waterhole

125

Wadrawadrinna Mile WH

14

Track

15

Innamincka

Hot Rocks Power Station

20

Bore

10

Winthekarrinna Waterhole

35

18

9

Fifteen

32

Wattathoolendinnie Waterhole

Della Waterhole

48

45

30

Track

Numerous oil wells, private roads and tracks in this area

Epsilon Gas Wells

Waukatanna Waterhole

Cooper Creek

Numerous lakes and huge areas of interdune corridors are inundated when Cooper Creek floods.

Gidgealpa Gas Field

GIDGEALPA

VHU8

Dullingari Gas and Oil Field

Innamincka Bore No 3

14

40

Cooper

MULKA

Lake Appadare

Lake Warrakalanna

See inset map for more detail around Moomba (no services available)

MOOMBA

Moomba Oil and Gas Field

6

10

7

34

Moomba Viewpoint

204

16

Della Gas Field

Strzelecki Oil and Gas Field

23

9

11

Bore

Track

19

Epsilon

Lake Teplidlinna

Spencer Oil Field

Big Lake Gas and Oil Field

Big Lake Moomba

66

Farm stay

Lake Hope or Pando

Lake Walpayapeninna

STRZELECKI

Farina Gas Field

Daralingie Gas Field

Strzelecki

Track

43

Lake Moomba

Charles Sturt 1844-46

Strzelecki Oil and Gas Field

Innamincka No 2 Bore

Toolachee Gas Field

9

Gidgee & Munro Oil Wells

DESERT

Strzelecki Track

The Strzelecki Track originally followed the creek. A new alignment was built to provide improved access to Moomba after gas was discovered in 1960.

D96

Lake Murteree

MERTY MERTY

Munkarie No 6 Gas Well

Bore Track closed at reserve boundary

Barren Lake

60

15

Strzelecki Regional Reserve

(No public access)

This station track may ONLY be used when the main track is flooded.

10

43

Old

Merty Merty

Mandibarcbooloo Waterhole

Innamincka No 1 Bore

Pigeon Lake

Lake Killamperpunna

33

STRZELECKI TRACK

For further information between Innamincka and Marree, see the BIRDSVILLE and STRZELECKI TRACKS map from Westprint.

Strzelecki

43

Popes Bore

Caroowinnie Waterhole

54

BOLLARDS LAGOON

Lake Kopperekoppinna

Bucaltaninna

Lake Gregory

Yaningurie Waterhole

Strzelecki Crossing

36

Twilight Bore

Bollards Lagoon

Cameron Corner

15

Corner Store

21

Fortville Gate

29°

DULKANINNA

Manuwalkaninna Creek

Gurra Gurra Waterhole

Cheri Cherri Waterhole

Gas

27

Strzelecki Track

Pioneered by John Costello in 1867 when he overlanded 200 horses from his property in South Western Queensland to Kapunda, north of Adelaide. This journey of 900 kilometres through mostly unknown land, was the first time the Strzelecki Creek was used as a stock route.

LINDON

Fort Grey

Lake Frome

Toontcatchyn Creek

Lindon

Lake Stewart

MURNPEOWIE

Lake Blanche

D96

25

Charles Sturt 1844-46

Strzelecki Regional Reserve

Lake Pinaroo

Waka

Emu Creek

Duck Ponds

Creek

26

Montecollina Bore

Lake Arthur

Toontcatchyn

Creek

Blanchewater

Strzelecki

Track

39

Moppa-Collina Channel

P

Hewart Downs

Murnpeowie

Strzelecki

30

St Mary Pool

Hopeless

Mount Hopeless

Ck

QUINYAMBIE

Creek

274

23

Deans Bore

Mt Hopeless 125 m

VLE8

Lake Callabonna

Reginald

Yandama

George

MacDonnell

Petermorra

Yerila

56

Lake Callabonna Fossil Reserve

Creek

Winnathee

18

MOUNT LYNDHURST

24

Dog Fence

Mt Distance 335 m

Underground

Woolatchi

Green

Gulfy

Creek

12

Hawker Gate (No access through border)

Tindelpina

Pelican

Mt Freeling 384 m

25

MOOLAWATANA

15

Mt Fitton 350 m

Moolawatana

24

Hamilton

Lake Yannerpi

28

Cooney

Taylor

26

Mount Freeling

Mt Fitton Talc Mine

Mount Fitton Ruin

Parabaranna Hill 348 m

Yandama

AME07

Lake Kamerooka

Yandaminta

Tent Hill 245 m

P

Mt Harris 743 m

Mt Neil 549 m

40

STRZELECKI

Smithville House

D96

Yerelina

NORTH

Creek

Lake Callabonna

Boolkaree

Wilkowie Well

28

FLINDERS RANGES

Arkaroola Wildlife Sanctuary

Paralana Hot Springs

Mile Ck

Poontana

DESERT

18

14

Frome River

Mt Curtis 519 m

VLA8

Wheal Turner Mine

Beverley Mine

37

Tea Tree Ck

North Mulga

Lake Cootabarlow

Moorabie

Lake Mock

Wallace

Umberatana

33

Mt Painter

ARK08

28

The Needles 609 m

Arkaroola Village

Lake Pundalpa

Border Downs

Yankaninna

Wooltana Cave

WOOLTANA

Lake Coontayunta

MTR01

18

24

Owieandana

Vulkathunha - Gammon Ranges National Park

Wooltana

19

Munyakina

Starvation Dam

Starvation Lake

Mount Serle

22

Mt McKinlay 1050 m

Balcanoona

National Park Office

LAKE

Poverty Lake

Sanpah

Angepena

DIN02

Italowie Gorge

16

Balcanoona

WER06

FROME

Dog Fence (follows border)

78

Iga-Warta

26

Hawker Hill 756 m

23

Wertaloona

FROME DOWNS

Pine View

ANGEPENA

Moro Gorge

Lake Frome National Park

Lake Elder

Yellow Waterhole

Mt Hack 1087 m

NANTAWARRINA ABORIGINAL LAND

Grave Ck

Big John Ck

Lake Maljanapa

NORTH

10km 0 10 20 30 40km

© Copyright Westprint Maps Pty Ltd 2022

SOUTH AUSTRALIA

QUEENSLAND

NEW SOUTH WALES

WA NT QLD SA NSW VIC TAS

Burke and Wills
Involved in the first expedition to cross Australia from south to north. Their unfortunate death near Innamincka is one of Australia's best known exploring tragedies. More information is found on the INNAMINCKA and COONGIE LAKES map from Westprint.

Adventure Way
The `Adventure Way' stretches east - west across Queensland from Toowoomba to Innamincka in South Australia.

Large areas subject to flooding; track becomes impassable.

Deep creek crossing

Private road (no access)

No public access, no fuel at Jackson

WARNING:
Remote track, rarely used

WARNING:
Tracks in this area are not for public use

STURT NATIONAL PARK
For further information on this area, refer to the STURT NATIONAL PARK map from Westprint.

Bulloo River Overflow
Huge quantities of water flow down the Bulloo River during floods. This water fills numerous small lakes, swamps and waterholes in an area known as the Bulloo River Overflow. This is a terminal flood plain that collects all the excess water from the Bulloo River system.

Large areas subject to flooding

Sturt National Park

QUEENSLAND

NEW SOUTH WALES

GREY RANGE

BULLOO RIVER OVERFLOW
(Large areas subject to flooding)

BULLOO RIVER OVERFLOW

Dog Fence (follows border)

Place names:
Nockatunga, Noccundra Hotel, Norley, Thargomindah, Orientos, Bransby, Santos, Naryilco, Tickalara, Old Tickalara, Mt Morris, Mt Bygrave, Mt Shillinglaw, Mt Lucas 267 m, Orient, Nooyeah Downs, Thyangra, Picarilli, Yakara, Zenoni, Bulloo Downs, Moombidary, Mirintu, Waverley Downs, Hillside, Thurloo Downs, Delalah House, Owen Downs, Barrajong, Wonga, Colane, Yamba, Urisino, Moalie Park, Urella Downs, Reola, Allundy, Myrnong, Salisbury Downs, Bootra, Petita, Willaroy, Wattle Vale, Garden Vale, The Range, Nantilla, Noonamah, Quarry View, Monolon, Myro, Wonga Lilli, Questa Park, Glendara, Mulga Valley, Purnanga, Tonga, Laurelvale, Youldo, Pulchra, Box Vale, Cawnolmurtee, Yantabangee, Klondyke, Caradoc, Oak Vale, Goodwood, Glen Hope, Peery, Lonsdale, Wonnaminta, Morden, Katalpa, Allandy, Yancannia, Yalda Downs, Callindary, Cobham, Pulgamurtie, Dalmuir, Pimpara Lake, Boulia, Mount Arrowsmith, Pincally, Lake Wallace, One Tree, Mount Shannon, Mount Browne, Milparinka, Mount Poole, Theldarpa, Yandama, Whyjonta, Brindiwilpa, Clifton Downs, Narriearra, Connulpie, Teurika, Narcowla, Onepah, Wompah House, Olive Downs, Mount King, Gumvale, Tibooburra, Mount Stuart, Mount Wood, Mount Sturt, Pine Ridge, Yelka, Packsaddle, Nundora, The Veldt, Kayrunnera, Westwood Downs

Mt Sturt 287 m
Mt Wood Gorge
Mt King Bore

Carryapundy Swamp
Jerrira Swamp
Bulloo Lake

B&W Camp 43 to B&W Camp 61 (various)

WINTINNA

CAD02

Wintinna

Mt Willoughby 310 m

ARCKARINGA

Gidyea Creek

VLB8   D95   ALLANDALE

Mt Perrypolkot 199 m

Cadney Homestead

Cadney Park

Mount Willoughby

Copper Hills

San Marino Hut

Mt Arckaringa 243 m

Arckaringa Station stay

Painted Desert

Neales River

Mount Dutton

Mt Dutton 174 m

Mt Harvey

Tarracalena Dome

Algebuckina Hill

Algebuckina (ruin)

Algebuckina Waterhole

John McDouall Stuart
Stuart made several journeys in this approximate location between 1858 and 1862 which resulted in a practical route north - south across Australia.

The Elder Scientific Exploration Expedition
Led by David Lindsay, the expedition left Wartina (on the Oodnadatta Track) for a known point in the Everard Ranges (north-west of Marla). The exploration then extended west through the Great Victoria Desert toward what is now Kalgoorlie and then on to settled areas near Geraldton.

EVELYN DOWNS

Mt Evelyn

Mirackina Creek

MTB04

Mt Kingston 187 m

Peake Creek (ruin)

Peake Hill

Peake Historic Site

Mt Denison 239 m

England Hill 314 m

Evelyn Downs

Mathesons Bore Rest Area

Algebuckina Historic Site
Gibber covered red and purple hills

Algebuckina Waterhole

Oodnadatta Track

Neales Creek

Rail bridge

Pump station (ruins)

Stone cairn (ruins)

Old Overland Telegraph Line (1870s route)

Giles Expedition Memorial

Warrina (ruin)

Elder Expedition Memorial

Peake

MOUNT WILLOUGHBY

190

Mount Barry

MOUNT BARRY

Lake Conway

Lake Warrangarrana

199

NIL06

Mt Margaret 411 m

Nilpinna

Evelyn Downs Rest Area

Pootnoura

Pootnoura Rest Area (emergency telephone)

Mt Eube 240 m

Derangunabula Hill 220 m

Cadaree Hill 151 m

Duff Creek (ruin)

Duff Creek

Boorthanna Siding (ruin)

Mt Anna 266 m

Dog Fence

Bulgara Hill 148 m

Box Creek (ruin)

Anna Creek (ruin)

Anna Creek

Kanku-Breakaways Conservation Park

The Breakaways

Oolgelima Creek

Lake Cadibarrawirracanna

Mootooroorana Swamp

Mount Clarence

Stuart Range

Mabel Creek

Manguri

VLC4

Beadell Highway

Anne

Dog Fence

ANNA CREEK

No permit is required to travel this track.

Coober Pedy
Stuart Memorial

COB02

Hutchinson Memorial

WIL03

WOOMERA PROHIBITED AREA

WIL02

MABEL CREEK

Mabel Creek

Pioneers Swamp

Cairn Hill Mine Ore Loading Facility

Cairn Hill Mine Haul Road

MOUNT CLARENCE

Mt Brady 229 m

Engenina Ck

Cairn Hill Mine (No public access)

Warriner

Wattiwarriganna

Codna

Robin Rise 185 m

Lake Phillipson

A87

Mt Penrhyn 216 m

Balta Creek

Warrinner

NORTH

INGOMAR

Wirrida

Brumby Creek

McDOUALL PEAK

Prominent Hill Mine

Prominent Hill

Halifax Hill 204 m

Mt Hawker 189 m

Lake Wirrida

Ingomar

Ingomar Rest Area (emergency telephone)

(No public access)

Mt Soward 225 m

McDouall Peak

Gina

Hanson Rise 222 m

Mirikata

Hogarth Hill 201 m

MILLERS CREEK

Billa Kalina

McDouall Peak 214 m

The Twins

Millers Creek

VLD8

VLD2

Commonwealth Hill

COMMONWEALTH HILL

BULGUNNIA

Haggard Hill 213 m

Mount Eba

MOUNT EBA

256

VLC5

Mulgathing

Carne Outstation

Carne

Bulgunnia

VLD9

RFDS Emergency Airstrip

Mount Eba

Bamboo Swamp

Reedy Lagoon

MULGATHING

WOOMERA PROHIBITED AREA

Bon Bon Rest Area (emergency telephone)

Bon Bon

Vivian Wells

PARAKYLIA

Trans Australian Railway Access Road
For more information between Kingoonya and Kalgoorlie, refer to the Trans Australian Railway map-on-demand from Westprint Maps

Mentor Outstation

WILGENA

No. 7 Camp

NORTH WELL

STUART

BON BON

Mount Vivian

Lake Parakylia

Lyons

Malbooma

Malbooma Outstation

Tarcoola

WLG06

Wilgena Hill 258 m

Wilgena

Peela Swamp

Lake Labyrinth

Mt Eba 228 m

VLA4

Rocky Hill

HIGHWAY

MOUNT VIVIAN

Lake Reynolds

10km 0 10 20 30 40km

© Copyright Westprint Maps Pty Ltd 2022

Central Australian Railway

Stuart Highway A87

Oodnadatta Track / OLD GHAN RAILWAY D95

NT QLD WA SA NSW VIC TAS

20' 30' 40' 50' **137º** 10' 20' 30' 40' **58** 50' **138º** 10' 20' 30' 40' 50'

Mt Robinson 183 m

Koorakina Creek

THE PEAKE

Anchor Creek

Boy Ck

Lake Pompappilinna

Warburton River

Lake Miamiana

KALAMURINA

Kalamurina

Kalamurina ▲ Cowarie

9

Mirra Mitta Bore

TIRARI DESERT

Mt Hogarth

Birdsville

33

49

Mungerannie Gap

•Uwinya Hill

Kirrawadinna Ck

28º

Dr CT Madigan
After crossing the Simpson Desert Madigan continued south from Birdsville to explore the eastern shore of Lake Eyre and to return his camels to Muloorina.

Twin Lakes

Kalamurra Lake

Lake Koolkootinnie

▪ Mungerannie Hotel

D83 ▪MUN02

40

S t u r t   S t o n y

Lake Kittakittaooloo

D e s e r t

10'

Oroowilanie

TIRARI

Lake Ngapakaldi

Peake Historic Site

Mt Kingston
Peake Creek (ruin)
Ruins
Mine Shaft Grave
Peake Hill

Oodnadatta Track

Old Ghan Line 17

17

Old Overland Telegraph Line (1870s route)

Cairn

The Warburton Groove

Warburton Groove

Kati Thanda – Lake Eyre National Park

Hector Island

Lake Mulapula

Lake Koolkootinnie

DESERT

Mulka •
Mulka Store Ruins

20º

20'

Mulka ▪

23

Natterannie Sandhills

Lake Puntawolona

LAKE EYRE (NORTH) / KATI THANDA

The Warburton

Cooper Creek

Lake Kalaramultu

Tilla Tilla Waterhole

Lake Killalpaninna

Lake Kopperamanna

15

30'

Elliot Price Conservation Park
(No public access)

Erli Island

Outtaprie Waterhole

Carrurama Waterhole

Killalpaninna Mission Ruin

18

21

Lake Killampepunna

33

Telegraph Line

Sunny Creek

Douglas Creek

Halligan Bay

EYR04 Ck

Cooinchina

24

Halligan Bay Point

9

ABC Bay

Brooks Island
Hambidge Point

Artemia Point

Babbage Peninsula

Hunt Peninsula

M a d i g a n

G u l f

ETADUNNA

Obtain permission from Etadunna before visiting Killalpaninna Mission Ruin

Lake Palankarinna

Etadunna ▪

Cannuwaukaninna Bore

William Creek

5 7

Memorial to Caroline Grossmueller

30

Jackboot Bay

Bonython Headland

Campbell Point

Willow Head

Milner Pile

209

40

Gerty Hill 141 m

Belt Bay

Prescott Point

Level Post Bay

Lake Florence

The Birdsville Track
One of the most famous stock routes in the world, its history is a legend in Australian folk-lore. For more information see the Birdsville and Strzelecki Tracks map from Westprint.

29º

Irrapatana (ruin)

30

Lake William

Lake Callara

Goyder Channel

OODNADATTA TRACK
For further information between Marree and Marla, see the OODNADATTA TRACK map from Westprint Maps

Dulkaninna ▪
Coolibah Camp
Conical Hill
Halleem Hill

Birdsville

30

Cairn
DUK06

DULKANINNA

Strangways (ruin)

12

Strangways Historic Site

Beresford (ruin)

24

Beresford Hill 72 m

Warriner Creek

LAKE EYRE (SOUTH) / KATI THANDA

Pelican Point

Lake Frances

Lake Ellen

40

River

Borefield •

Muloorina ▲

Track

23

▲ Clayton

Dog Fence

10'

Clayton Ck

CLAYTON

Kewson Hill 42 m

See inset map 3

Coward Springs

6

Hamilton Hill 40 m

21

Historic site Curdimurka

34

199

Emeroo Point

Borefield •

The Illusion Plains

MULOORINA

VLC7

54

32

Dog Fence

D83

Lake Harry

Lake Harry ▪

Lake Marion

20'

VWC3 Pound

Wabma Kadarbu Mound Springs Cons Park

John McDouall Stuart
Stuart travelled from Adelaide to Chambers Creek (now Stuart Creek). This was the starting point for his later explorations to the north.

Lake Phibbs

Bopeechee (ruin)

D95

16

Hermit Hill 123 m

OLD GHAN

17

Mt Alford 81 m

CALLANNA

Attraction Hill 72 m

Birdsville Mailman
Tom Kruse became a legend during his own lifetime by driving the Marree - Birdsville mail run for almost 20 years. At a time when the isolation of the Birdsville Track was magnified by droughts, dust storms and floods, Tom just battled on because it was his job.

Lake Arthur

Mound Springs

Coward Springs

Coward Spring

6

Wabma Kadarbu Mound Springs Cons Park

The Bubbler

The Blanche Cup

Hamilton Hill 40 m

Margaret Creek

Stuart Creek (Wulley-Yarra)

Alberrie Creek (ruin)

Finniss Springs

19

Wangianna (ruin)

13

Callanna (ruin)

Marree **A**

RAILWAY

MUNDOWDNA

Mundowdna

Lake Pinnarie

40'

Frome River

Screech Ck

Gregory Ck

FINNISS SPRINGS REHABILITATION AREA

Callanna ▪

SANDY Ck

53

78

Witchelina (ruin)

Hayes Ck

Kingsmill River

MOUNT LYNDHURST

50'

Underground Water Pipeline Road

D97

113

VLF6

Stuart Creek Opal Field

Lookout 7

6

Saddle Hill 109 m

5 View Point

30

Mulgaria ▪

Lake Pidleeomina

Mulgaria

Lake Arthur

Request permission from Mulgaria to use track west of the homestead. Ph 08 8675 8313.

A fee is payable to access the scenic drives within Witchelina Reserve.

Mt Nor West

Berlina Dam

55

West Mount Hut

WITCHELINA

Witchelina ▪

24

Witchelina Nature Reserve (Nature Foundation SA)

Minagoona Lake

Wilpoorinna ▪

FARINA

Farina (ruin) ▲

D83

30º

Tent Hill 245 m

Wilkowie Well

Mundy Ck

14

28

Mt Telford 360 m

Telford

MOUNT SERLE

67

BILLA KALINA

KOK04

Red Lake

Parakylia •

Curdlawidny Lagoon

Mattaweara Lagoon

Dog Fence

45

Sink Holes

Mulgaria Ck

Termination Hill 464 m

Lake Watharston

Ochre Cliffs

20

Mt Lyndhurst 287 m

24

14 Ck

Strzelecki

Mount Lyndhurst

Leigh Ck

10'

Avondale ▪

Lyndhurst

38

Borefield

29

Olympic Dam Mine

Andamooka ▪ **A**

White Dam Opal Field

Opal Fields

Bushovie Ck

Myrtle Springs

Leigh Creek Coalfield Lookout

22

Copley

BURR WELL

Mt Serle

Mount Serle

30'

Olympic Dam Village ▪

30

55

Roxby Downs A

Andamooka Ranges

LAKE TORRENS

Depot Ck

Aroona Ck

Aroona Sanctuary
Aroona Dam

MTS02

Leigh Creek **A**

Aroona

Ajax & Copper King Mines

Warraweena 4wd tracks ph (08) 8675 2770

9

Mount Hack 1087 m

Warraweena ▲

Roxby Downs ▪

ROXBY DOWNS

ANDAMOOKA

20

Andamooka ▪

Myall Creek

Lake Torrens National Park

BELTANA

Mt Deception 687 m

Puttapa

65

18 21

Maynards Well

Angepena ▪

13

137º 10' 20' 30' **23** 50' **138º** 10' 20' 30' 40' 50'

NORTH

10km 0   10   20   30   40km

© Copyright Westprint Maps Pty Ltd 2022

NT
QLD
WA
SA
NSW
VIC
TAS

The rare Christmas Tree Mulga

Tjintirkara Rockhole
No camping at rockhole.
A camping area with toilets
and water located is 200 m
west of the turnoff.

Mamungari
Conservation Park

ANNE BEADELL HIGHWAY
For further information between
Coober Pedy and Laverton, refer
to the ANNE BEADELL HIGHWAY
map from Westprint Maps

Beadell
Marker

34   48   Anne   80   Beadell   10   Voakes Hill   106
Tjintirkara   **279**   Corner   Highway
Rockhole   Voakes Hill   Turn off to
347 m   Voakes Hill

Rare Christmas
Tree Mulga   29
Rockhole

No camping permitted
along this section of the
Anne Beadell Highway

Numerous sand dunes.
Tyre pressures may need
to be reduced.   8

Serpentine
Lakes   Eucalyptus gongylocarpa
(Marble gum)   Waldana Well

A transit permit is required to travel
this track. Available from Maralinga
Lands Council in Ceduna.
Ph 08 8625 2946, fax 08 8625 3076.

Serpentine   11
Lakes   17   BMR 3 Road

Churina Native Well
Bringnya Native Well

G R E A T   V I C T O R I A   24

BMR 5 Road   Voake Hill Rd between
BMR 3 and BMR 5 Roads
is closed to traffic.

Nurrari   Koolkoona   Wyola
Lakes   Native Dam   Lake
(two bores)   24

D E S E R T   Halinor Lake

Rare Eucalyptus wyolensis
(Lake Wyola mallee)   Heavy Vehicle
Dispersal Point   20   Tanks   Ingolinna
Rockhole

Forrest   Lake
Lakes   Dey Dey

Lake   Dey   Dey   Road   Oak Valley
55   (No public access)

Tank   Road   51   VLC6   Lake
14   Maurice

Business   Midgening
Native Dam

Aboriginal   56   66

10   Chilbinga
Native Dam

Mamungari
Conservation   **O O L D E A**
Park   **R A N G E**

Lake

115   **MARALINGA TJARUTJA**

Tanks   Warldarie Parlkalidga
19   Rockhole

ABORIGINAL LAND
Choolkooning
Rockhole

Few sheltered camping
areas south of this point   Muckera Rockhole

Dual tracks exist in many
parts of the Nullarbor Plain

A transit permit is required
to travel this track. Available
from Maralinga Lands Council
in Ceduna, ph 08 8625 2946,
fax 08 8625 3076.

76

N U L L A R B O R   P L A I N

Fisher   Trans-Australian   O'Malley
22

Cook   Access   54   Road
Jail cells at Cook, along the Trans Australian Railway   **Nullarbor**
Regional Reserve
Denman   42   Trans

Deakin   Trans-Australian   Railway   46   58   **Trans Australian**
Deakin   Hughes   **Railway Access Road**
Obelisk   53   For more information on this
route, refer to the Trans Australian
Railway map-on-demand from
Westprint Maps

WESTERN AUSTRALIA
SOUTH AUSTRALIA

GREAT VICTORIA

DESERT

ANANGU PITJANTJATJARA

ABORIGINAL LAND

Centreline of fire (Woomera Rocket Range)

Mount Davies Road
This section of the Mount Davies Road was built by Len Beadell's party in 1957. A permit is required prior to travelling this track.

A permit is required to travel this track which is reputed to be in very bad condition

A 'Mustang' aircraft at Emu in 1953

Tallaringa

Conservation Park

Mount

Davies

Road

BMR 3 Road

Anne's Corner

23

28

Lake Meramangye

300 Mile Point on centreline of fire 28° 24' 28" S 132° 27' 38" E

9

Dingo Claypan

51

The area around Emu is excluded from the Woomera Prohibited Area

Emu

18

(NO PUBLIC ACCESS)

MARALINGA TJARUTJA

Atomic Bomb Tests
A large saltbush plain near Emu was chosen as the site for joint British-Australian atomic testing

Ground Zero Obelisks

5

Observation Point

ABORIGINAL LAND

Observatory Hill 271 m

Road

Beadell Marker

250 Mile Point on centreline of fire 28° 50' 20" S 133° 07' 23" E

ANNE BEADELL HIGHWAY
For further information between Coober Pedy and Laverton, refer to the ANNE BEADELL HIGHWAY map from Westprint Maps

323
110

Fence

Beadell

Anne

45

Dog

29°

Emu

A permit is required to travel this track

WOOMERA

PROHIBITED   AREA

Beadell Marker

GREAT VICTORIA

DESERT

25th Avenue

25th Avenue
This is the northern extent of the planned test area for maralinga that was never developed.

Wilkinson Lakes

Wilkinson Lakes

Road

Emu

Northern Barrier Gate

Dog Fence gate

VLD6

West Point Hill 231 m

Mobella

Breakaway   Marcoo   Gona Site
Taranaki Sheds   Five Ways
Beadell Bore   Tietkens Plain

33

FORMER MARALINGA NUCLEAR TEST SITE
This land is part of the Maralinga Tjarutja Lands. Access requires the consent of Maralinga Tjarutja.
TELEPHONE: (08) 8625 2946
The Land contains artefacts of the Nuclear Test Era, including items contaminated at low levels with radioactivity. Any enquiries about such items should be directed to:
Maralinga Tjarutja or the South Australian Environment Protection Agency, Radiation Protection Branch. Telephone: (08) 8463 7826

STOP

Lake Anthony

Challenge Gold Mine

Jumbuck

Half Moon Lake

Tietkins Well

Roadside Village

Dey Dey

125

Road

19

MARALINGA

RESTRICTED   AREA

Dog

Fence

MOBELLA

30°

Maralinga Village
(Restricted access)

Cauley Test Site

Maralinga Gate

10

Entrance to the Maralinga Nuclear Test Site

Lake Bring

Yarle Lakes

14

Choolalie Lake

OOLDEA   RANGE

Parinya Rockhole

Ooldea Hill 278 m

Ooldea Well

Daisy Bates Memorial

Ooldea

MULGATHING

follows

track

Mt Christie 233 m

15

27

33

Railway

Watson

Railway Memorial

Ooldea

Road

32

Immarna

13

Bates

36

Barton

57

Mungala

Mount Christie

32

Wynbring

Dog   Fence   follows   track

42

31

Railway Sidings
Many of the old, original railway sidings have now been removed. Few traces remain at these sites.

Yellabinna
Regional Reserve

Lyo

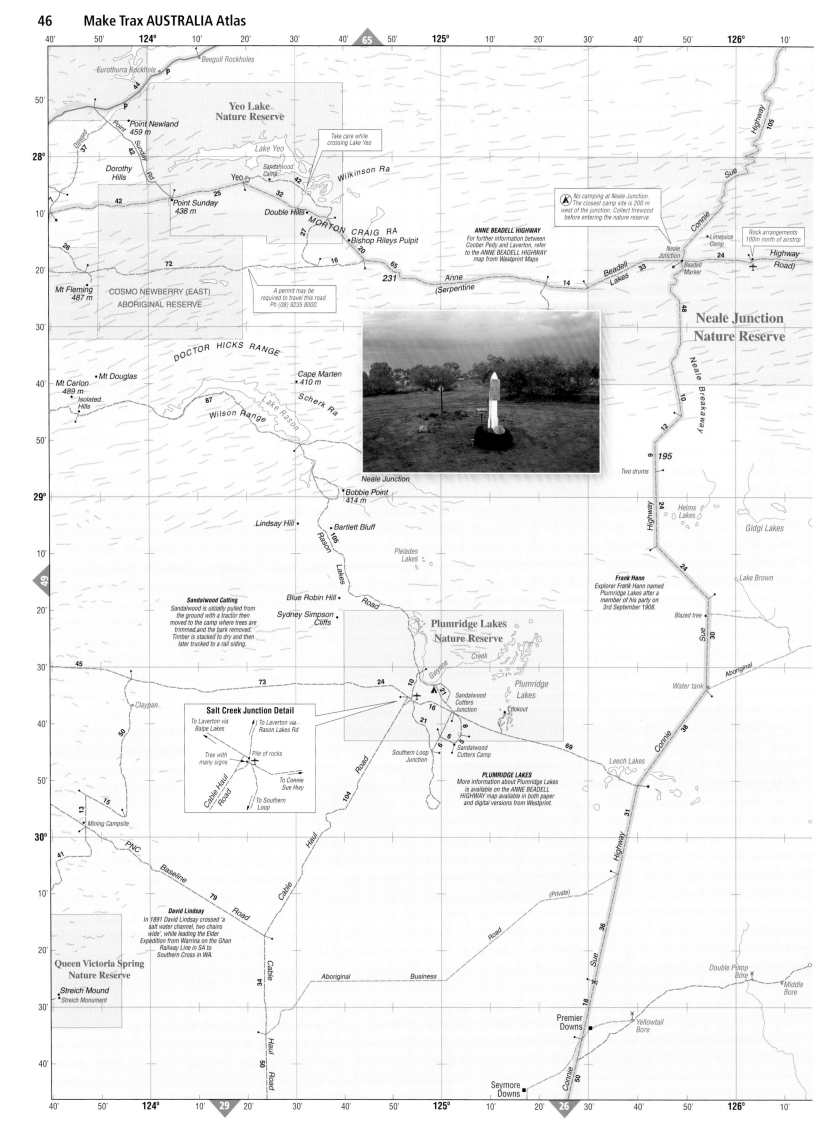

Neale Junction

NGAANYATJARRA

CENTRAL ABORIGINAL

RESERVE

28°

44

*Good travelling
from Neale Junction
to cross roads*

20 dunes to cross.
20 minutes each way.

*Aircraft
crash site*

44

NMF 258

9

10

Toilet, water
& shelter

58

*Tuning Fork
Rockhole*

Ilkurlka Roadhouse
Fuel and some
supplies available at
Ilkurlka Roadhouse

180

47

Anne

*Small salt
lake*

12

Toilet &
water

Some very sharp corners
and 40 km of sand dunes
with winding track, slow
travelling in this area.

Beadell

168

Highway

99

No permit required to travel the Anne
Beadell Highway within Spinifex
Ahoriginal Land Reserve.
www.spinifex.org
Permits required for all other roads.

*Wanna
Lakes*

A permit is required for
travel along this track

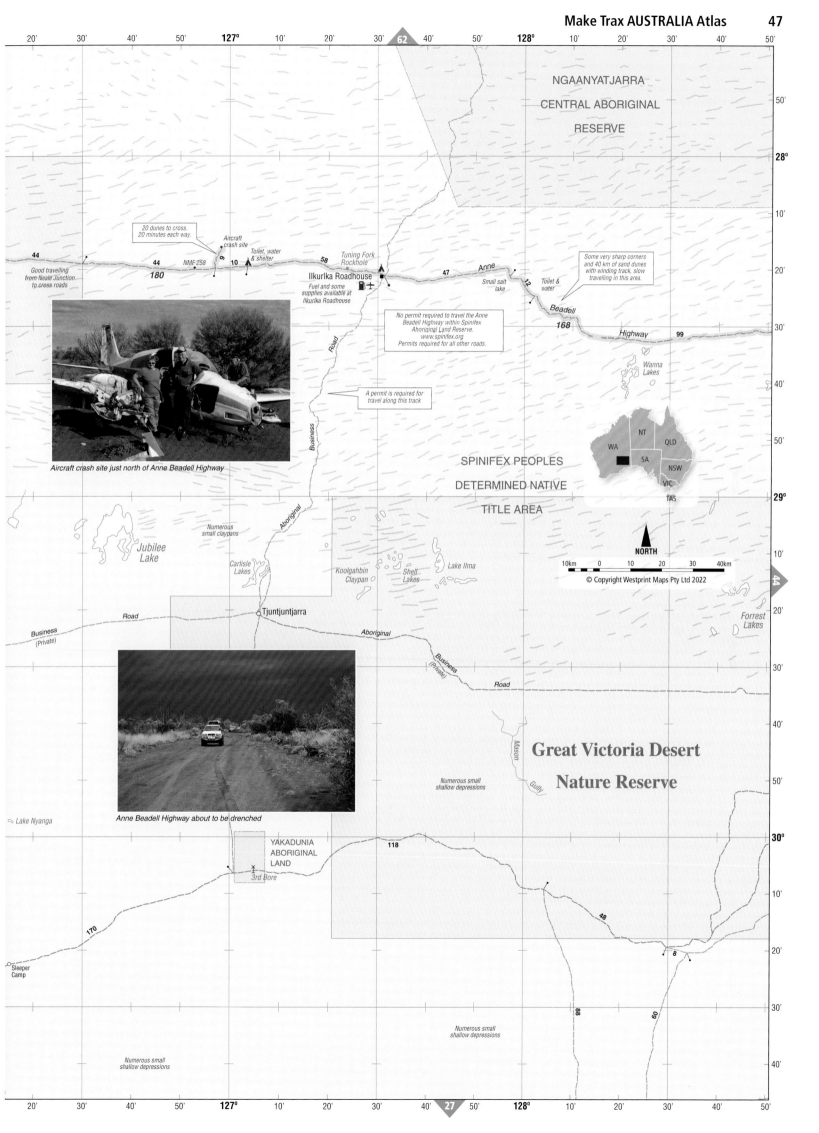

Aircraft crash site just north of Anne Beadell Highway

Road

Business

Aboriginal

SPINIFEX PEOPLES

DETERMINED NATIVE

TITLE AREA

29°

NT
QLD
WA
SA
NSW
VIC
TAS

NORTH

10km   0   10   20   30   40km

© Copyright Westprint Maps Pty Ltd 2022

*Jubilee
Lake*

*Numerous
small claypans*

*Carlisle
Lakes*

*Koolgahbin
Claypan*

*Shell
Lakes*

Lake Ilma

*Forrest
Lakes*

Road

Business
(Private)

Tjuntjuntjarra

Aboriginal

Business
(Private)

Road

Great Victoria Desert

Nature Reserve

Mason

Gully

*Numerous small
shallow depressions*

Anne Beadell Highway about to be drenched

~ *Lake Nyanga*

YAKADUNIA
ABORIGINAL
LAND

3rd Bore

30°

118

48

8

170

88

60

° Sleeper
Camp

*Numerous small
shallow depressions*

*Numerous small
shallow depressions*

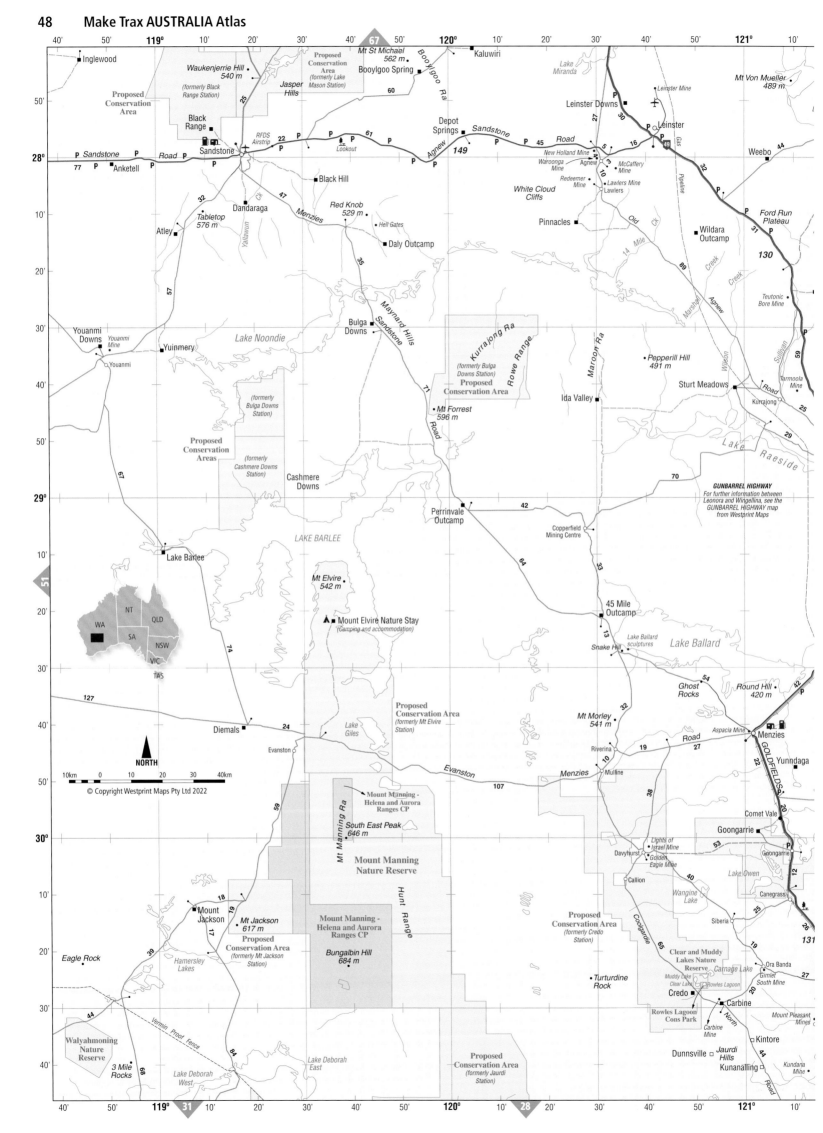

Inglewood

Proposed Conservation Area (formerly Black Range Station)

Waukenjerrie Hill 540 m

Jasper Hills

Proposed Conservation Area

Black Range

Sandstone

RFDS Airstrip

Anketell

Sandstone   Road

Dandaraga

Atley

Tabletop 576 m

Black Hill

Menzies

Red Knob 529 m

Hell Gates

Daly Outcamp

Youanmi Downs

Youanmi Mine

Yuinmery

Youanmi

Lake Noondie

Bulga Downs

Sandstone

Maynard Hills

Proposed Conservation Areas

(formerly Bulga Downs Station)

(formerly Cashmere Downs Station)

Cashmere Downs

Kurrajong Ra

Rowe Range

Proposed Conservation Area (formerly Bulga Downs Station)

Mt Forrest 596 m

Road

Mt St Michael 562 m

Booylgoo Ra

Kaluwiri

Lake Miranda

Mt Von Mueller 489 m

Leinster Mine

Leinster Downs

Leinster

Depot Springs

Sandstone

Agnew

Road

New Holland Mine

Waroonga Mine

Agnew

Redeemer Mine

McCaffery Mine

Lawlers Mine

Lawlers

White Cloud Cliffs

Pinnacles

Gas Pipeline

Weebo

Ford Run Plateau

Wildara Outcamp

14 Mile Ck

Marshall Creek

Agnew Creek

Teutonic Bore Mine

Pepperill Hill 491 m

Ida Valley

Maroon Ra

Wilson Ck

Sullivan Ck

Sturt Meadows

Kurrajong

Tarmoola Mine

Lake Raeside

GUNBARREL HIGHWAY For further information between Leonora and Wingellina, see the GUNBARREL HIGHWAY map from Westprint Maps

Perrinvale Outcamp

Copperfield Mining Centre

WA

NT

QLD

SA

NSW

VIC

TAS

LAKE BARLEE

Lake Barlee

Mt Elvire 542 m

Mount Elvire Nature Stay (Camping and accommodation)

45 Mile Outcamp

Snake Hill

Lake Ballard sculptures

Lake Ballard

Ghost Rocks

Round Hill 420 m

Proposed Conservation Area (formerly Mt Elvire Station)

Mt Morley 541 m

Diemals

Evanston

Lake Giles

NORTH

10km 0   10   20   30   40km

© Copyright Westprint Maps Pty Ltd 2022

Aspacia Mine

Menzies

Yunndaga

GOLDFIELDS

Comet Vale

Goongarrie

Goongarrie

Lake Owen

Riverina

Mulline

Menzies Road

Evanston

Mount Manning - Helena and Aurora Ranges CP

Mt Manning Ra

South East Peak 646 m

Mount Manning Nature Reserve

Hunt Range

Mount Manning - Helena and Aurora Ranges CP

Bungalbin Hill 684 m

Mt Jackson 617 m

Mount Jackson

Proposed Conservation Area (formerly Mt Jackson Station)

Hamersley Lakes

Eagle Rock

Vermin Proof Fence

Walyahmoning Nature Reserve

3 Mile Rocks

Lake Deborah West

Lake Deborah East

Lights of Israel Mine

Davyhurst

Golden Eagle Mine

Callion

Proposed Conservation Area (formerly Credo Station)

Wangine Lake

Coolgardie

Turturdine Rock

Muddy Lake

Clear Lake

Clear and Muddy Lakes Nature Reserve

Carnage Lake

Rowles Lagoon

Credo

Rowles Lagoon Cons Park

Carbine

Carbine Mine

Dunnsville

Jaurdi Hills

Proposed Conservation Area (formerly Jaurdi Station)

Kunanalling

Siberia

Canegrass

Ora Banda

Gimlet South Mine

Kintore

Kundana Mine

Mount Pleasant Mines

20' 30' 40' 50' **122°** 10' 20' 30' 40' **64** 50' **123°** 10' 20' 30' 40'

Banjawarn

Bandya

Mt Cumming
558 m

Lake
Darlot

Vickers *Creek*

NECKERSGAT RA

Borodale

Bandya

A permit may be
required to travel this road.
Ph (08) 9235 8000.

Disappointment
Hill

Truscott
Hills

35

*Darlot
Mine*

Melrose

Lake Irwin

Old Erlistoun
Mine

Mistake

Ck

Central P **316** Road 64 34

Cosmo
Newbery

50'

28°

119

Little Mill Well

75

Mt Boreas
534 m

105

Reichelt
Find Mine

Mt Clarke
565 m

Mt Shenton
520 m

COSMO NEWBERRY (WEST)
ABORIGINAL RESERVE

Disused 37

31

48

Chandlers
Breakaway

Mill Road

Old King of
Creation Mine

Mt Varden
535 m

Great

55

Mt Shenton Yamarna Rd

Yamarna
Point Salvation
508 m

7

10'

Ten Mile
Outcamp

Mt Redcliffe
565 m

Mt Zephyr
522 m

Erlistoun

Monitor
Flats

Swincer

Road

Old Corktree
Well Mine

ADAM RANGE

77

Giles
Breakaway

A permit may be
required to travel this road.
Ph (08) 9235 8000.

84

Road

35

26

Mt Fleming
487 m

20'

Creek

Nambi

49

Dillon

Ck

Ck

Road

37

Laverton Downs

Cliffs

Yamarna

144

COSMO NEWBERRY (SOUTH)
ABORIGINAL RESERVE

The Terraces

West Terrace
Hill 535 m

East Terrace
562 m

71

Korong

Old Mount
Windara Mine

Beasley

P 19 13

Hann's
Camp

White

60

White Cliffs

30'

GOLDFIELDS

Mertondale

Monument Hill
545 m

Road

23

Laverton

Craigiemore

ANNE BEADELL HIGHWAY
For further information between
Laverton and Coober Pedy, refer
to the ANNE BEADELL HIGHWAY
map from Westprint Maps

Hazlett Cliffs

75

This track can be
impassable after
wet weather

Mt Carlon
489 m

Isolated
Hills

40'

Leonora

8

P Leonora

Murrin Murrin
Nickel Cobalt
Project

P Mt McKenzie
480 m

Mt Weld
524 m

Point Bott
472 m

Road

51

A

Leonora

19

Cement

120

Mount Margaret
Mine

Mount Margaret

Mount Marven
Mine

Old
Burtsville
Mine

Burtsville

60

Lakes

Mt Luck
476 m

50'

Sons of
Gwalia
Mine

P Laverton

59

Kowtah

Ck

Granny Smith
Mine

Wallaby
Mine

Plumridge

45

8

Mallee Hen Rocks
474 m

Malcolm

Minara

Laverton

Old

Irwin Hills

29°

P

49 Melita

43

LAKE
CAREY

Mt East
548 m

Mt Dennis
521 m

26

Mineral Patch Hill
Coglia Outcamp

62

Glenorn

Yundamindera

48

Jasper Hill
Mine

Hope Campbell
Lake

10'

104

Tampa

36

Creek

Yundamindra

18

Lake Raeside

40

Linden

45

Hope Campbell
Hill

BALPE LAKES

90

20'

46

Kookynie

Bullock Hole Creek

22

Mount
Remarkable

Davis Creek

9

Stella
Range

Lightfoot
Lake

Morapoi

45

Nine Mile Ck

Prospector
Pool

30

Box Creek

45

Surprise
Granite

Lake
Minigwal

45

P

10

Niagara Dam
Nature Reserve

Yerilla

12

48

49

30'

P

Donkey

37

Rocks

Seven Mile Pool

Boyce

Elora

Mendleyarri

29

44

EDJUDINA RA

PNC

47

40'

14

Lake
Marmion

Blue Duck Ck

40

Barba
Hills

19

Yarri

Lake Raeside

73

Baseline

22

Menangina

Edjudina

23

53

13

Donkey
Rocks

Boomerang Lake

11

19

Road

32

Pinjin

26

Mining Campsite

60

20

4

Road

Kirgella
Rocks

Lords
Bore

Mulga Rockhole

41

30'

30°

Deadman
Soak

25 Mile Rocks
22 Mile Rocks

LAKE REBECCA

Pinjin

7

31

Nippon

57

Highway

Lake
Goongarrie

51

Goongarrie
National Park

Ponton

10'

Old Pinjin

48

LAKE REBECCA

Queen Victoria Spring
Nature Reserve

Creek

41

HWY

31

Bardoc

Hunt Pinnacles

20'

P

49

Gindalbie

Yindi

Round Hill
390 m

Queen Victoria Spring

A

Streich Mound

9

13

Broad Arrow

A

Bullock Holes
Timber Reserve

8 Streich
Monument

Paddington
Mine

P 10

King of
the West Lake

Kanowna

Arrow Lake

28

Lake
Penny

32

Kurnalpi

32

Mt Eric

CUNDEELEE
ABORIGINAL LAND

30'

Black Flag

13

26

Mt Parkin

Mt Quinn

Black Flag
Lake

Kanowna
Belle Mine

Kanowna

31

Bulong Nickel
Project

Jurangie
Hill

36

Lake
Perkolilli

**KALGOORLIE
BOULDER**

A

Bush Two-up School

Super Pit Mine

29

Power
station

28

Bulong

27

Bulong Nickel
Mines

65

Lake
Yindarlgooda

Mt Charnleigh
389 m

Lake
Roe

Kalin Granite Rock
364 m

Cundeelee
Aboriginal Community

40'

20' 30' 40' 50' **122°** 10' 20' 30' 40' **29** 50' **123°** 10' 20' 30' 40'

40'   50'   **114°**   10'   20'   30'   40'   **69**   50'   **115°**   10'   20'   30'   40'   50'   **116°**   10'

Chinamans Rock
12
Kalbarri
Red Bluff, Mushroom Rock
Rainbow Valley
25
Shell House
Island Rock, Natural Bridge
Bluff Point
Ajana Kalbarri
Wittecarra Gully
Kalbarri National Park
Galena Bridge
31
Rocky Pool
Yandi
41
Four Mile Pool
15
Ten Mile Pool
Riverside   Station stay
Galena Nature Reserve
Woolgorong
Lake Nerramyne
Lake Nerramyne Mine
Pinegrove
Bullardoo
30
George
Wagoe Beach
12
Summer Hill
Ajana
13
Mallee Nature Res
Mallee
12
Dartmoor
Station stay
Nandina
Proposed Conservation Area (formerly Woolgorong Station)
Yuin
13

50'

Wileri
Binnu
50
Road
Binnu
32
14
13
Wandana Nature Reserve
Tallering Peak Mine
Mullewa
Road
36

28°
Utcha Well Nature Res
Shoal Point
Hutt Lagoon
Grey
25
Drive
Hutt River Province
Chilimony Nature Res
1
33
33
Urawa Nature Reserve
Hughes Aders
P
15

10'
Port Gregory
Broken Anchor Bay
Big Pool
Proposed Nature Res
Gregory
Rd
41
Ogilvie
32
5
Yuna
McGauran NR
East Yuna NR
36
Bindoo Hill NR
21
Perkins Well
Falls
22
28
Pindar
118
Wandanooka
Tallering
53

HOUTMAN
20'
East Wallabi Island
Wallabi Group
Eastern Island
Long Island
Dick Island
9
Northampton
Bowes
Bowes
32
Greenough River
Magnet
Teninedwa
17
18
Wilroy Nature Reserve
Barrabarra Nature Reserve
38

30°
West Wallabi Island
Middle Channel
Easter Group
Little North Island
Rat Island
Morley I.
Wooded I.
ABROLHOS CHANNEL
Three Mile Beach
Horrocks
21
Isseka
25
24
105
Nabawa
Howatharra
8
Oakajee NR
Nanson
24
Coronation Beach
Proposed NR
14
Drummond Cove
Waggrakine
10
31
95
Wicherina
Mount
123
26
10
Magnet
Butterabby Graves
Wongoondi Grain Storage
Wilroy
22
24
Tardun
Zeewijk Channel
Pelsaert Group
Gun Islands
Middle Islands
Half Moon Reef
Mangrove Group
Pelsaert Lagoon
Pelsaert Island
Wreck Point
Champion Bay
13
Point Moore
11
Geraldton
Geraldton
Tarcoola Beach
Moonyoonooka
Narngulu
The Forty Four Mile Nature Res
Indarra Spring Nature Res
Beetalyinna NR
30
8
16
P
Canna
24

40° / 50'
Cape Burney
1
21
Georgina
32
17
P
Gutha
56

Greenough
1
Walkaway
Burma Road Nature Reserve
Coalseam Cons Park
Pintharuka

29°
65
44
Irwin River
32
15
13

10'
INDIAN OCEAN
Midlands
Mingenew Nature Reserve
46
116
Mingenew
61
Morawa
Koolanooka Dam NR
Koolanooka

20'
Dongara
Port Denison
8
Yardanogo Nature Reserve
20
Rd
Yandanooka
Billeranga Hills
Bowgada
Bowgada NR
42
Beekeepers Nature Reserve
Ten Mile Beach
White Point
24
Mt Adams
Wilson Nature Res
17
P
Arrino
17
24

30'
Cliff Head
BRAND
Arrowsmith
1
Wotto Nature Res
Dookanooka Nature Res
Yarra Yarra Lakes
Three Springs
32

40'
Illawong
27
56
HIGHWAY
Depot Hill NR
White Gums NR
65
Yarra Yarra Lake Cons Park
Carnamah
50
Beekeepers Nature Reserve
20
Lake Logue NR
Eneabba
Eneabba North Mine
RGC North Mine
Tathra National Park
67
Winchester
Capamauro Nature Res
27

50'
Coolimba
29
Leeman
9
RGC South Mine
South Eneabba Nature Reserve
Coorow
Marchagee NR
16
116

30°
13
Point Louise
Green Head
41
29
Lesueur Nat Park
22
Alexander Morrison National Park
81
Pinjarrega Nature Res
Marchagee
30

10'
Jurien Bay Marine Park
Radbury
Lesueur Nat Park
153
Coomallo Nature Reserve
Boothendarra Nature Reserve
Watheroo National Park
Gunyidi
Gunyidi Nature Reserve

20'
Boullanger, Whitlock, Favourite, Tern & Osprey Islands Nature Reserve
North Head
Drovers Cave NP
38
Jurien Bay
23
Dinner Hill 345 m
Namban NR
Longreach
Watheroo

Escape Island NR
Jurien Mine
Hill
Badgingarra
Twyata NR
Nature Reserve
Manaling NR
40
Coomberdale

Southern Beekeepers Nature Reserve
Ronsard Bay
Nambung Bay
37
51
12
Badgingarra National Park
Mungedar
Chelsea
59
81
Moora

NORTH
10km 0 10 20 30 40km
Cervantes
Thirsty Point
Nambung National Park
The Pinnacles
Wongonderrah Nature Res
Cooljarloo Mine
Minyulo Nature Reserve
Billinue
Dandaragan
63
Jam Hill Nature Reserve

© Copyright Westprint Maps Pty Ltd 2022
Jurien Bay Marine Park
Grey
Wanagarren Nature Reserve

40'   50'   **114°**   10'   20'   30'   **115°**   10'   20'   30'   **30**   **116°**   10'

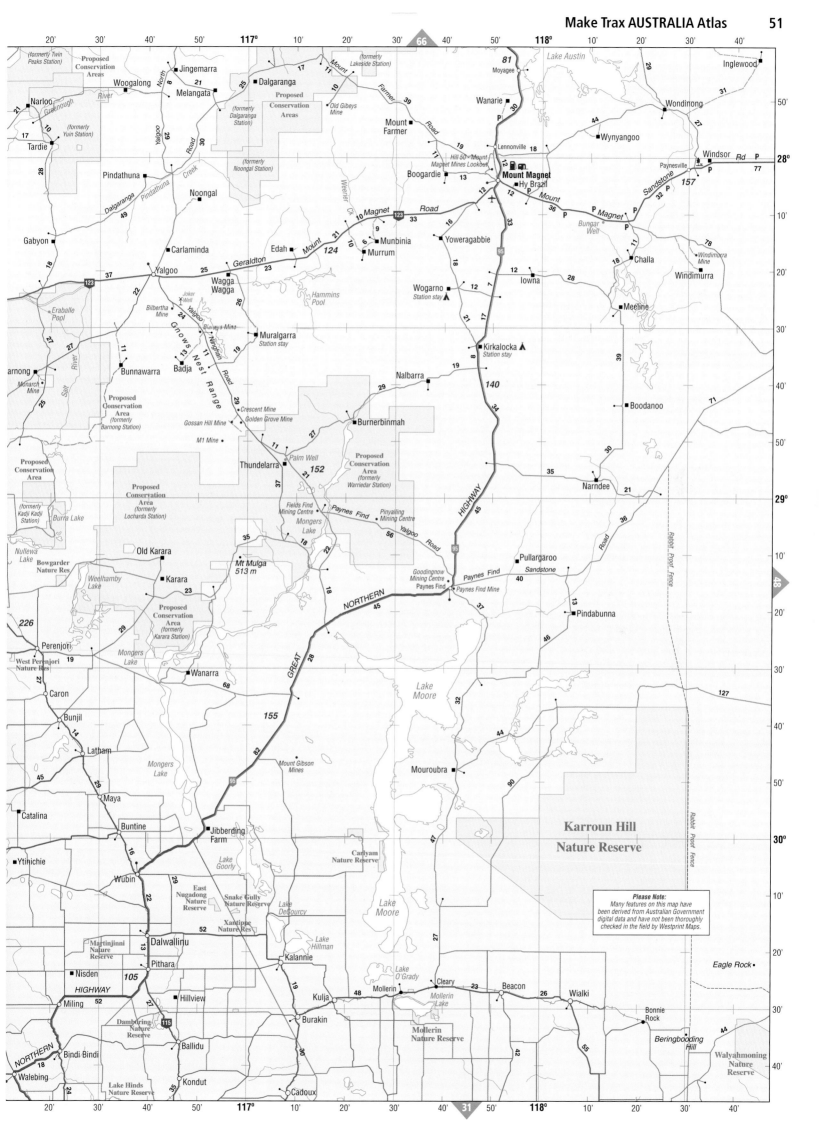

Natural Bridge Springbrook National Park, Queensland

4WD crossing a river in the Kimberley

Manning Falls, Kimberley

Brachina Gorge, Flinders Ranges National Park, South Australia

Numbung National Park, Western Australia

Broome, Western Australia

Outback Church

Savannah Way

Bungle Bungles, Purnululu

Map Grid — Coordinates (top)

50' 152° 10' 20' **71** 30' 40' 50' 153° 10' 20' 30' 40' 50' 154° 10'

NORTH

10km 0 10 20 30 40km

© Copyright Westprint Maps Pty Ltd 2022

Littabella NP
Lake Monduran
Yandaran
Meadowvale
Burnett Heads
Bundaberg Harbour
Bargara
Monduran
Bingera
Bundaberg
Bullyard
Kolan South
Elliott Heads
Gin Gin
Wallaville
Bingera National Park
Cordalba NP
Cordalba
Childers
Woodgate
Burrum Coast National Park

Hervey Bay

Great Sandy Marine Park
Rooney Point
Marloo Bay
Orchid Beach
Platypus Bay
Waddy Point
Fraser Island

BRUCE
HWY
112
Burrum Pt
Burrum Heads
Toogoom
Howard
Torbanlea
Hervey Bay
Urangan
Happy Valley

Good Night Scrub NP
Woowoonga National Park
Wongi National Park

Great Sandy National Park
Mile Beach

Biggenden
Brooweena

River

Maryborough
Maaroom
Boonooroo
Tuan

Coalstoun Lakes
Sunny Glen
Tiaro
Poona National Park

Seventy Five Mile Beach
Hook Point

Mount Walsh National Park
Ban Ban National Park
Glenbar National Park
75
Bauple

150

Grongah National Park
Theebine
Miya
Gunalda

Mary River

Tin Can Bay
Toolara Forest
Rainbow Beach
Wide Bay
Double Island Point

S O U T H   P A C I F I C

O C E A N

Mudlo National Park
Gympie NP
Tansey
49
Kilkivan
63
Cloyna
BAY HWY
Oakview National Park
WIDE
Goomeri
Nangur NP

Murgon
Cherbourg
Wondai
Tingoora
Wooroolin
Memerambi
Lake Barambah
Cherbourg CP

Barambah Ck

Wrattens National Park
Wrattens Resources Reserve
Amamoor
Kandanga
Gallangowan

Gympie
Goomboorian National Park
Woondum NP
81
Kin Kin
Cooran
Pomona

Great Sandy National Park
Lake Cootharaba
Lake Cooroibah
Tewantin National Park
Boreen

Kingaroy
82
Nanango
Jimna
Imbil
Lake Borumba

North Arm
Mapleton NP
Yandina
Noosa
Noosa National Park
Cooroy
Eumundi
Lake Weyba

Coolum Beach
Marcoola
Mudjimba

Tarong NP
Yarraman
D'AGUILAR
A17
Linville
Moore
Benarkin
45
Blackbutt
Cooyar
Wutul
121
Haden

Kenilworth
Mapleton
Maleny NP
Woombye
Kondalilla NP
Palmwoods
Conondale
Conondale National Park
Maleny
Landsborough
Beltthorpe National Park

Nambour
Maroochydore
Buderim
Sunshine Coast
Mooloolah River National Park

Caloundra

Kilcoy
Woodford
120
Hazeldean Deer Reserve NP
Toogoolawah
Nukinenda
Somerset Dam
Lake Somerset
Beerwah
Glass House Mountains
Beerburrum

98
Bribie Island National Park
Bribie Island

Mount Binga National Park
Goombungee
Crows Nest
Crows Nest NP
Esk
Wamuran
Dayboro
Narangba

Caboolture
Burpengary
Donnybrook
Meldale
Bellara
Woorim
Bongaree
Beachmere
Deception Bay
Redcliffe

Bulwer
Cape Moreton
Moreton Island
Moreton Island National Park
Tangalooma

Meringandan
Murphys Creek
Kingsthorpe
Highfields
Toowoomba
Helidon
Hampton
Haden

D'Aguilar National Park
Lake Wivenhoe
Lake Samsonvale
Petrie
Strathpine
Mount Nebo
Samford
Brisbane Airport

Kooringal
Moreton Bay
Amity
Point Lookout

Lockyer National Park
136
Lowood
Fernvale
Mount Crosby
BRISBANE
South Brisbane
Mt Gravatt

Dunwich
Capalaba
Cleveland
North Stradbroke Island

Wyreema
Cambooya
Gatton
Forest Hill
Grantham
Plainland
125
Minden
Marburg
Laidley
Rosewood
Walloon
Ipswich
Swanbank
Logan
Redland Bay
Macleay Island
Russell Island
Naree Budjong Djara NP

Mcgrath Crossing
Grandchester
Purga
Peak Crossing
Harrisville
Logan Village
Plinkett CP
Pimpama
Beenleigh
Southern Moreton Bay Islands NP
South Stradbroke Island CP

Please Note:
Many features on this map have been derived from Australian Government digital data and have not been thoroughly checked in the field by Westprint Maps.

PARK AND RESERVE ABBREVIATIONS

CP	Conservation Park
CA	Conservation Area
Cons	Conservation
FFR	Flora & Fauna Reserve
NP	National Park
NCR	Nature Conservation Area
Res	Reserve
Reg	Regional
RP	Regional Park
WPA	Wilderness Protected Area

50' **147°** 10' 73 20' 30' 40' 50' **148°** 10' 20' 30' 70 40' 50' **149°** 10' 20'

Salvator Rosa Section
Mount Playfair
Spyglass Peak
Mt Salvator
Mt Flat Top

Ka Ka Mundi Section
Mt Ka Ka Mundi
Carnarvon

Carnarvon National Park
Round Mtn
Kenniffs Lookout
Consuelo Peak
Rewan
Ingelara
Carnarvon Gorge Section
Early Storms
Bandana
Mt Moffatt

Nuga Nuga National Park
Warrinilla
Wyseby
Lake Nuga Nuga

Fairfield
Purbrook
Glenidal
Iron Pot

Palmgrove National Park
Bedourie
Mapala

16 Mile Spring

Torres Park
Babbiloora
Mount Tabor

The Chimneys
Bullen Bullen
Cathedral Rock

Mount Hetty
Glenolive

Moolayember Gorge Section

171
DEVELOPMENTAL

Wallaroo

Cannondale Mtn
The Battery
Expedition National Park
Surprise Mtn
Mt Weldon

Forfar
Charlies Creek
Darkwater

East Sunrise
Sunrise

Yoothappinna

Boxvale

Pyramid Hill

Sandstone

Chesterton
Bogarella
Lorne
Derbyshire Downs

Crystalbrook

Merivale

Westgrove

Mau Lau

Currajong

Lucknow
Willara
Waverley
Bellona
Connemara
Wetlands

Hoganthulla

Redford

Oak Vale

Silverleaf
Munnaweena

Womblebank

Rockvale
Kildare

Garlands

Ridgeland

Home Paddock

Warndoo

Waterview

Fairview

Expedition Resources Reserve

Bonnie Doon
Myrtle Vale

Baroondah

Hutton

Quida Downs
Glenallen

Bungaringa
Boxland

Tooloombilla

Forest Vale

Blue Hills
Bendoba

Mount Hutton
Injune
Glengarry

Kevington
Pony Hills

Scott Creek

Dungowan

Angellala Downs

26°

Yo Yo Park

LANDSBOROUGH

90

Bellrose

Moyallen

Mount Maria

Chesterton Range National Park

Mount Elliot

Currawarra

Verniew

Kilmorey

Claravale

Mountain View

Katanga

Woodlawn

Gunnewin

Hendon Park

Cornwall

Walhallow

Bungil Creek

89

Clissold Downs

Eurombah Creek

169

Durham Downs

HWY

Cashalton
Pickabox
Alice Downs
Morven

Armadilla

Ivanhoe Downs
Dulbydilla

HWY

88

Mungallala

Mount Lonsdale
Curraweena

Wattamolla

Mitchell

The Peaks

Maranoa River

Eastern Creek
Heather Downs

Waroonga

Echo

Landreath

Thornhill

Dargal

Miawood

A7

Roma

WARREGO

Wallumbilla

A2

Tregole National Park

Rocky
Maryvale

Tregoning

Lilly Pool

Amby Downs
Amby

Eurella

Bindango

87

Roma Downs

Kincora

Mulgavale
Womalbrook

Muckadilla

Massey Downs

Richmond Downs

Durella
Kyarra
Albury

Eversfield
Bonus Downs

Cotswold

Summerhope

Wyoming
Blairmack

Bulala
Ardno

Wununa

Wallabella

Lowood

Ularunda

Durella Bore

Springfield

Rockybank

Hollyrood
Inniscraig

78

Tinowon

Urana

Leinster

Cedarvale

Megine

Garraburra

Combarngo
Balonne

Sherwood

Glenorie

Preston

Cytherea

Teeswater
Balford

Beldene

Yannagan
Eulorel

Spring Grove
Newington

Rockdale
Rockton

27°

Aqua Downs

Gunnawarra
Lolworth
Tullachard

Byzantium

Katarvon

Albany Downs
Tamanick

Naldera

Royston

South Coogoon

Newstead

Surat

Marlee Downs
Boatman

Tongy
Ashling

Glenalvon
Coolibah

Woodlands
Wahcumba

Cogoon R

Ballaroo

Weribone

Brynog

Warroon

Parknook

Dingwall
Wongamere

Grassmere

NORTH

Abbieglassie

Ravenscourt
Arlington

Cunnyana West

Araluen

Hillsborough

North Quibet
Tarmoola
Quibet

Tartulla Ck

Balnakeil
Morocco

116

Weeallah

Billinbah
Glen Fosslyn
Cooma

Dundee

10km 0 10 20 30 40km

© Copyright Westprint Maps Pty Ltd 2022

Homeboin

Southampton
Glenmuir
Landridge

Maronga
Waterloo

Powrunna

Woodburn

Donga

CARNARVON

Glenearn

Glenmore

Neabul
Rutherglen
Belgaum
Neabul Downs
Belle Plains
Beralga

Cashmere West

Lake Kajarabie

A55

Boxleigh

Thrushton National Park

Marango
Arakoola

Woodvale

50' **147°** 10' 39 20' 30' 40' **148°** 10' 20' 30' 40' 50' **149°** 10' 20'

30' 40' 50' 150° 10' 20' 30' 40' 71 50' 151° 10' 20' 30' 40' 50'

Junedale
Nipan
59
Lonesome Creek
Coominglah
A3
Caniaview Po
Lake Monduran
A1
Thomby
Glandore
Rawbelle
Wingfield
Monto
Monduran
Forest Hills
Stonecroft
Boonarga
Theodore
Mulgildie
25°
Coorada
Glenbar
Camboon
Barram
Tuturi
Bania National Park
Ghinghinda
Isla Plains
Kildare
Dareen
Mount Perry Resources Reserve
Reedy Creek
Isla Gorge National Park
Glencoe
Tireen
Rosslyn
Mount Perry
10'
Jamberoo
Karinya
Dawson Park
Precipice National Park
Cracow
Telemark
Euroka
111
Good Night Scrub NP
94
Cloncose
Eidsvold
A3
Nour Nour National Park
20'
Pine Hills
Hedley Hill
Spring Creek No 2
Fairyland
Rockybar
Wathonga
Widbury
Coonambula
Cronulla
Burnett River
Bluchers Gully
Boxgrove
A5
Spring Vale
Quaggy
Redbank
Binjour
Byrnestown
30'
Broadmere
Nunbank
The Bend
Nantglyn
Coalstoun Lakes
Kerwongah Park
Rocky Springs
Mundubbera
Wilga Park
Taroom
Lilyvale
Dawson Vale
Gayndah
40'
Taroom
Two Up
Dykehead Crossing
Boyne River
Hornet Bank
Cockatoo
Sujeewong
Hawkwood
Cooranga
Aranbanga
A3
150
Sutherland Park
Eurombah
Clonduff
Leichhardt
Benvenue
50'
Richon
Currawong
Auburn
Beeron National Park
Wigton
Beninbi National Park
Thordon Park
Bungaban
Auburn
Bimbadine
Culgowie
Monogorilby
Manar
26°
Broadmere
Wondaree
Coondarra
Allies Creek
Lake Boondooma
Abbeywood
Cloyna
Wandoah
Aqua Downs
Proston
Hivesville
10'
125
Hippong
Lismore
Brigooda
Murgon
49
Lucky Downs
Kroombit
Jimnora
Boondooma
Cherbourg
53
Stanley Park
Wondai
20'
Highway
Glenrowan
Durong
Woordolin
Tingoora
Pelham
Wongongera
Memerambi
Bendemere
Noonga
Barakula
Riverview
30'
Warramoo
Woodstock
Kingaroy
Walton Park
Fairyland
Stoneleigh
HWY
Dulacca West
Boortkoi
Canaga
Woodburn
Karrween
49
Kumbia
40'
Yuleba
141
Jackson
Dulacca
Drillham
Miles
A2
Chinchilla
Bunya Mountains National Park
Tarong NP
Wyandra
Killawarra
Jandowae
Bell
50'
Springlea
Berwyndale
Warrego
126
Warra
Jimbour
Macalister
A2
Kaimkillenbun
Cooyar
Banjo Gully
Kentara
Gunbarwood
Bunya
Wutul
27°
Rostock
Callitris
Moraby
Boorameal
Condamine
Kogan
Mirrabooka
49
Quinalow
Maclagan
Peranga
121
Salisbury Creek
Wurama
Brooklyn
Beelbee
Kulpi
Warkon
Govana
Dalby
Haden
10'
Erambie
Glenmorgan
Dunkerry
Leichhardt
Bilbah
Bowenville
Acland
Goombungee
Blenheim
Cainable
Meandarra
The Gums
Tara
Karee
84
Jondaryan
Meringandan
20'
124
Currajong
Wahroonga
Tipton
Formartin
Oakey
Kingsthorpe
Sandalwood
110
Cecil Plains
Aubigny
30'
Doonba
Coomrith
Logeah
Boongala
Kiama
A5
Moonie
Waar Waar
Mount Tyson
Benroy
Pampas
A2
Toowoomba
Wongle
Sedgeley
St Hilliers
New Dunmore
Brookstead
82
Wyreema
40'
Teelba
Glengarry
Enarra
Moonie
49
Southwood National Park
Pittsworth
Southbrook
Cambooya
Felton East

30' 40' 50' 150° 10' 20' 30' 36 40' 50' 151° 10' 20' 30' 40' 50'

Top coordinates: 50' **142°** 10' 75 20' 30' 40' 50' **143°** 10' 20' 72 30' 40' 50' **144°** 10'

Needle Creek   Opal Hill   Bellevue   Ungo

Braidwood   *169*   Mt Aaron   Mt Brookes 379 m   Konupa

Lina Hill   Jundah   Mt Perrier 338 m   Kiama Park   Yaraka

Lina Glen   Prairie   Glenvalley

CHANNEL COUNTRY   Glenlock   Mt Marlow   Merry Peaks 368 m

Longford   Wandsworth   16   Merrigal

Turret Hill   Cardinals Cap

Moyen   Welford National Park   Jedburgh   Retreat

44   Haughton Vale   Welford   Bush Christening

Galway Downs   Romula   Retreat   Mt Welford 255 m

Diamantina - Cooper Watershed
A ridge divides the Diamantina River and Cooper Creek catchments. Both drain into Lake Eyre.

Three Sisters 300 m   Cooper Creek Junction   Yellow Mtn 259 m   The Whale 322 m

JC Hotel ruins and cemetery   Coniston   Advance   Budgerygar

Carranya   Ourravoo   Oakham   **Hell Hole Gorge National Park** (No public access)

Diamantina   Developmental *108*   Windorah   Hammond Downs

Mt Butler 297 m   Canterbury   Thunda

DIAMANTINA LAKES
For further information north of this area, refer to the DIAMANTINA LAKES map from Westprint Maps

Mt Wilkie   Moothandella   Alfred Bluff   Trinidad   Gooyer

Adavale Stock Route
An important stock route developed between Windorah and Charleville during the 1880s. Extension of the railway from Charleville to Quilpie in 1917 caused a dramatic decline in its use and now only a 130 kilometre section remains. Permission from station owners is required for access to the stock route.

South Galway   Tenham   Clifton North Bore   Lynwood

Channel Country
Heavy rain in the catchment of the Diamantina, Georgina, Thompson and other rivers cause flooding over thousands of square kilometres of channel country creating one of the largest naturally irrigated areas in the world.

Tanbar Waterhole   Tanbar   Bulgroo   Araluen

Opal
The largest open-cut opal mine in the Southern Hemisphere is located on Canaway Downs

Springfield   Baxter   Canaway Downs

Keeroongooloo   Lula Outstation

Wombunderry Waterhole   Eulbertie Waterhole   Currawonga Waterhole

Breakfast Ck   The Duracks settled Thylungra in 1868   Thylungra   Ray   Alaric   Goombie

Mt Rouse   Terachie   Bull Creek Opal Field

Dingo Barrier Fence
This fence extends from the Great Australian Bight near Ceduna in SA to the Great Dividing Range west of Brisbane, a distance of 4850 km. It is the longest man-made barrier in the world, more than three times the length of the Great Wall of China. Known as the Dingo Barrier Fence, the Dog Fence or the Vermin Proof Fence, it generally defines cattle country in the north from sheep country in the south.

Bull Creek
Some mines are abandoned and permission may be given for camping and fossicking. Contact Quilpie Visitor Centre for information on 07 4656 2166.

Raymore   Cornwall   Nickavilla   Tintinchilla   Como

Malagarga   Kyabra   Earlstoun   Bull Creek Mine

Table Top Peaks   Byrock   *239*   Pinkilla

Caution: Minor Tracks
Numerous minor tracks not shown on this map may lead to oil and gas fields. These are private tracks and public access is restricted.

Mount Howitt   Cooma   Murreewathalow   Old Kyra   Naretha   Quilpie

Cooper Creek
Numerous channels and waterholes form Cooper Creek; large areas are subject to flooding

Plevna Downs   Mt Bellalie 212 m   Black Stump Oil Field   Kenmore Oil Field   Whynot

Mt McCallum   Eromanga   Bargo Bargo Mountains   Boolbanna

The Blue Hills 170 m   Developmental *112*   Mount Margaret   Congie   Moble

SOUTHWEST QUEENSLAND
For further information east of this area, refer to the SOUTHWEST QUEENSLAND map from Westprint Maps

Durham Downs   Bellalie   Nerrigundah   South Comongin   Piastre

Channel Country
Naturally irrigated by periodic flooding from Cooper Creek, flood plains grow huge quantities of clovers and grasses. Grazing cattle grow fast with the basic elements of feed, water and warm climate. The channel country is known as some of the best natural fattening country in the world. If good rains or floods do not re-occur within a couple of years, these grasses can disappear to leave a desolate wasteland.

Mt Tabbathcubbah   *160*   Bowali   Tobermory   Tinderry

Channel Country
This whole region is covered with numerous channels and waterholes. Large areas are subject to flooding.

(No services) Ballera Gas Plant   Karmona   Old Bundeena   Kihee   Ardoch   Kiandra

Jackson Oil Field
Jackson is Australia's largest on-shore oil field. Oil is pumped 800 kilometres by pipeline to Moonie and then on to Brisbane.

(No services) Naccowlah Oil Plant   Goonbabinna Waterhole   Road subject to flooding

Naccowlah Waterhole   (No services) Jackson Oil Plant   Stock route - difficult when wet

Cooper Creek
Numerous channels and waterholes form Cooper Creek; large areas are subject to flooding

Large areas subject to flooding; track becomes impassable   Nockatunga   Developmental *124*   Karwalke   Soonah Crossing   Wiralla

Noccundra Hotel   Nockatunga Waterhole   Norley   Quilpie Thargomindah

Bottom coordinates: 50' **142°** 10' 20' 30' 40' 41 50' **143°** 10' 20' 30' 40' 50' **144°** 10'

Idalia National Park

Mariala National Park

Bosses Gorge
Access is permitted to this impressive and unusual gorge on private property, but all rubbish must be removed. Do not drive near the edge of the gorge because it has been undercut by water action and could be dangerous.

Record Shearing
In 1892, 720,000 sheep were shorn on Milo Station, a world record for one property.

Limited access to Mariala National Park.

Bilby (Macrotis lagotis)
The Bilby is one of Queensland's most endangered species and is currently being bred in captivity at Charleville. Ph 07 4654 3057.

Cosmos Centre (Charleville)
By day fascinating interactive displays increase our understanding of earth. At night powerful Meade telescopes give visual access to deep space. Ph 07 4654 3057.

Wyandra
Established as a railway settlement when the line from Cunnamulla to Charleville was built. Information is available from the hotel.

Duck Creek Opal Field
Opal mining began in the early 1890s. The population grew to 300, but dropped to 70 by 1900. some mining continues on this historic field, visitors welcome. Bushwalk, camp and fossick for free. Few facilities, no power or shops.

Please Note:
Many features on this map have been derived from Australian Government digital data and have not been thoroughly checked in the field by Westprint Maps.

Stock route and fishing access

Plane crash memorial

Duck Creek Opal Mines
Sheep Station Creek Opal Mines
Koroit Opal Field

NORTH
10km 0 10 20 30 40km
© Copyright Westprint Maps Pty Ltd 2022

WA NT SA QLD NSW VIC TAS

Place names and features:

Mt Ellen 427 m, Mount Harden, Idalia, Highlands, Colabara, Warringah, Homebush, Terrick Terrick Stud, Allambie, Effra, Macfarlane Downs, Innis Downs, Bexhill, Gartmore, Tambo, Mount Pleasant, Carlow, Ravensbourne, Coolatai, Sumnervale, Prospect, Isoroy, Koondoo, Dumfries, Jynoomah, Minnie Downs, Lansdowne, Manning, Caldervale, Gowan, Brides Creek, Glanmire, Stirling Downs, Yandarlo, Alva, Allawah, Woolga, Westbourne, Westquarter, Listowel Downs, Milray, Myall Creek, Tarrina, Chatham, Akarayu, Amaroo, Lumeah, Toliness, Lower Landsdowne, Listowel Valley, Cave Hill, Caranna, Oxford Downs, Bayswater, Glanworth, Bayrick, Aubigny, Wellclose, Bull, Byrganna, Cunalama, Lucknow, Arlington, Willara, Waverley, Wakes Lagoon, Baykool, Oakwood, Claren Park, Poseidon, Connemara, Milo, Gundary, Bronte, Koorangie, Wadeholme, Buckeys Creek, Gladys Downs, Rosewood, Burenda, Sherwood Park, Mount Morris, Biddenham, Augathella, Wansey Downs, Reynella, Gundare, Dungowan, Adavale, Wade Hill, Ambathala, Kurrajong, Oakleigh, Koreelah, Oak Park, Barduthulla, Ard-Na-Ree, Bundoo, Yo Yo Park, Etona, Milroy, Bulls Gully, Emudilla, Gumbardo, Varna, Ravenscourt, Langlo Crossing, Rocksville, Calewrie, Woolabra, Helvetia Park, Dunvegan, Bellrose, Granville, Mona Vale, Grenfield, Norah Park, Cairns, Gowrie, North Yarrawonga, Yarrawonga, Cashalton, Dungiven, Patrick Park, Burrandilla, Bonella, Maxvale, Collaroy, Thurlby, Wyoming, Alice Downs, Lochabie, Boothulla, Nimboy, Glenallen, Auburn, Charleville, Cosmos Centre, Lesdale, Moble Springs, Tiranna, Old Gowrie, Comongin, Colac Farm stay, Pingine, Merrigang, Rocky, Maryvale, Coolbinga, Winbin, Loddon, Coothalla, Wanko, Westgate, Woodside, Authoringa, Cheepie, Yalamurra, Cooladdi, Diamantina, Mayfield, Wallal, Colombo, Riversleigh, Shelbourne, Lowood, Lanherne, Chums Plain, Weaner Creek, Merigol, Wooyenong, Mangalore, Aldinga, Dempsey, Yarronvale, Bierbank, Napolean, Cowley, Fairlie, Armoobilla, Coolabah, Allambie, Riverview, Yanna, Kenmore, Fortland, Sherwood, Pinkenetta, Murweh, Wheatleigh, Ludston, Beechal, Coparella, Quilpeta, Mount Alfred, Doobibla, Quilberry, Rosevale, Quilberry, Wyandra, Alpha, Boatman, Toompine Hotel, Wareo, Buthana, Big Creek, Eulolo, Aldville Farm stay, Come by Chance, Humeburn, Mt Goolgoolwaddy 300 m, Warrego Park, Northam, Wongalee, Mervyndale, Prairie, Paracoona, Dundoo, Boobera, Yerrel Creek, Cocklarina, Retreat, Claverton, Nombardie, Mirrabooka, Woodlands, Belmore, Elmina, Dingwall, Alroy, Jandell, Mt Herbert 241 m, Hazelfield, Glendilla, Wallen, Ardrossan, Offham, Charlotte Vale, Coongoola, Kubill, Nardoo, Nardoo Farm stay, Nulbear, Cobbrum, Corfu, Carellen, Ferndale, Woodvale, Elverston

Roads and highways: Landsborough Hwy, Mitchell Hwy, Warrego Highway, Mitchell Highway, Charleville Road, Adavale Road, Quilpie Road, Old Charleville Road, Developmental Road, Diamantina Developmental Road, Cunnamulla

Poeppel Corner

NORTH
0   5km

Bypass track

QAA   Line

Poeppel Corner to Birdsville 170 km

Alternative route if Lake Poeppel is impassable, tracks may be indistinct

Lake Poeppel

18

Poeppel Corner

French   Line

To Simpson Desert

Disused shot-line

K1 Line

Poeppel Corner to Birdsville Track 191 km

▲ Madigan Camp 10

Madigan Camp 16

Madigan Camp 17

Dr CT Madigan
Madigan led a scientific expedition across the Simpson Desert in 1939. His party of nine with 19 camels took about three weeks to cross from Andado Station to Birdsville.

40

Small Claypan
GPS 25° 01' 49"
137° 53' 55"

38

16   Shotline

Sand dunes on this shotline are stable, but travel is slow.

Beachcomber No 1 Oil Well

Hay River Track

58   River Track

Hay River Track on CD
For more information on travel between Poeppel Corner and the Plenty Highway, refer to the Hay River map and guide on CD Rom from Westprint Maps.

Kilpatha Native Well

Poeppel No 1 Oil Well

Simpson Desert
This is the largest parallel sand dune desert in the world. It is a beautiful place but can also be dangerous. Always exercise care and common sense.

Perlanna Native Well

3

Mirranpönga Pongunna Lake

Detour north of salt lakes when they are impassable due to flooding

Lake Poeppel

18

Thomas Track (no entry)

Poeppel Corner

NORTHERN TERRITORY
QUEENSLAND

S I M P S O N   D E S E R T

Munga-Thirri National Park

Queensland's largest national park. Formerly known as Simpson Desert National Park.

Permission may be required to cross the Simpson Desert National Park and Adria Downs Station.

GLENGYLE   Creek   Tomydonka Waterhole

Titchery   Eyre   Waterhole

ADRIA DOWNS

Mudloo Well

Madigan Camp 18

Cowarie Waterhole

Cattle Industry
Many huge cattle properties are found in Western Queensland. Only 14 properties make up the Diamantina Shire which is twice the size of Denmark. Some properties are accredited with 'organic beef' certification.

Madigan Camp 19

Muncoonie Waterhole

Titheropatchie Lakes

Kuddaree WH

■ Muncoonie

Muncoonie Lake East

Muncoonie Lake West

ADRIA DOWNS

Burke & Wills
Follow the explorers with a Burke & Wills map package from Westprint Maps.

Annandale □

Madigan Camp 20

Madigan Camp 21

No public access to Annandale or Muncoonie without prior permission.

BIRDSVILLE TO BOULIA
For further information between Birdsville and Boulia, see the PLENTY HIGHWAY map from Westprint Maps

Dickerrie WH

Vermin   Old

Madigan Camp 22

Eyre

Proof

Goonamillera Waterhole

Goonamillera Crossing

Fence

Mickrapyra Waterhole

NOTE: Use of the Goonamillera Track is only permitted during flooding of the QAA Line.

NOTE: Vehicles heading west should reduce tyre pressures at this point. UHF channel 10 is recommended.

Madigan Camp 23

SIMPSON DESERT
For further information on crossing the Simpson Desert, refer to the SIMPSON DESERT TRIP PLANNING map from Westprint.

Tilkerran Sandhill

S I M P S O N   D E S E R T

Big

Bear

28

31

QAA   71   Line   170

15   23   40

See Inset Map 3

Lake Thomas

Lake Nappanerica

See Inset Map 2

The   Poeppel   Line

NORTHERN TERRITORY
SOUTH AUSTRALIA

French   Line

Erabena Oil Well

8

Erabena Junction

53   264

Lindsay Junction

35

Lake Tamblyn

Approdinna Attora Knolls

Jacks Junction (no entry)

Knolls Track is sometimes covered with drifting sand

40

Erabena

31

Colson Junction

23

Oolarinna Oil Well

Linnies Corner

WAA   55

Walporican Native Well

WAA Junction

Line   30

Knolls Track

34

Georges Corner

Rig

WAA   Track

12

Beelaka Native Well

WAA Corner

7

Poolawanna Oil Well (Abandoned)

86

K1   Line

DESERT PARKS PASS
A pass is required to travel east of Dalhousie Springs or through Simpson Desert Regional Reserve. Passes are available from National Parks and Wildlife Service offices and agencies.

Terrachi Waterhole

Wompananie Waterhole

Dickeree Waterhole

The West Lake   □ Alton Downs

8 Mile Waterhole

Karrathunka Waterhole. September 14, 1970.
Kidnap victim, Monica Schiller, is rescued by police on the Inside Track. Terrence Haley, Raymond Gunning and Andrew Brooks had escaped from an Adelaide prison taking Schiller hostage. They were re-captured by Detective Sergeant Giles at Karrathunka Waterhole.

Karrathunka Waterhole

S I M P S O N   D E S E R T

ALTON DOWNS

Mulligan River

Kooringala Waterhole

Narrabutiannie Waterhole

44

Macumba Oil Well

34

Killumi Oil Well

Murraburt Native Well

Rig   47   Road

Walkandi Junction

17

Lone Gum Tree

Poolowanna Lake

Burraburrinna Native Well

35

Walkandi Oil Well and Airstrip (abandoned)

Rig

102

Road

The K1 Line follows dune corridors for most of its length.

THE RIG ROAD
was constructed with a clay surface to enable drilling rigs to be moved by road trains. Most other tracks in the Simpson Desert are sandy.

THE RIG ROAD
was constructed with a clay surface to enable drilling rigs to be moved by road trains.

Beelpa Native Well

Lake Peera Peera Poolanna

Live sand dunes in this area often make travelling difficult. Road graded June 2014.

Kuncherinna Oil Well and Airstrip (abandoned)

Warburton Track - K1 Line
Once the main access for road trains travelling to Poeppel Corner, it is now a Public Access Route (PAR) through Clifton Hills Station.

K1 Line

Warburton

60

Tepaminkanie Waterhole

Inside   Track

The Inside Track is NOT maintained and becomes impassable when wet.

56   271

Track

Pelican Waterhole

14

Goyder   Lagoon

Munga-Thirri – Simpson Desert National Park

Lake Griselda

S I M P S O N   D E S E R T

Lake Umaroona

Apawylaranie Lake

Koomarinna Lake

Goyder Lagoon Waterhole

Numerous station tracks on gibber plain

CLIFTON HILLS

Tracks in this area are often closed due to flooding.

Edge of floodplain

Track

19   18

Clifton Hills ■   14

Outside

8   10

7 Mile Ck

Sturt Stony Desert

Lake Eyre Yacht Club
Club members claim this circuit of about 600 kilometres along the Kallakoopah Creek and Warburton River provides the best yachting experience within a desert landscape that can be found anywhere in the world.

NORTH

10km   0   10   20   30   40km

© Copyright Westprint Maps Pty Ltd 2022

White sand dunes and coolibah trees in this area. Easy travelling, road graded June 2014.

Yards

Yelpawaralinna Waterhole

26

186

Tippipilla

S I M P S O N   D E S E R T

Lake Willawilaninna

Kallakoopah

Wurdoopoothanie Waterhole

Mt Gason Wattle Project

• Milkapurda Hill

Lake Willawilaninna

Lake Pirriepatchillie

Kuncherinna Waterhole

Pathraootara Lake

Mt Gason Bore

Mt Gason

Lake Milkapurda

Kanakaranthina

Approximate position of stock route prior to the sinking of bores

COW04

46

Lake Koodnanie

COWARIE

Lake Pialpotingoona

Lake Pantoowarrina

Lake Warrandirinna

Marroo Hill

• Powana Hill 103 m

TIRARI DESERT

Lake Peera Mudla Yeppa

Lake Pompapillinna

Lake Howitt

Mirra Mitta Bore

• Kalla Hill

KALAMURINA

Warburton   River

Lake Noolyeana

Lake Millyeewilpa

■ Cowarie

Kalamurina ■   9   49

Lake Warrewarrana

MACUMBA   RIVER

NT   QLD
WA   SA   NSW
VIC
TAS

Glengyle
Monument to W.J.S. Hutchison
Lake Machattie
Lake Mipia
Lake Koolivoo
Bunk Waterhole
Cuttaburra Crossing
Permanent waterhole, toilet, table & bird hides
B&W Camp 80
Umpadloo Creek
Whitianta
Gerara Waterhole
Cemetery
Sallen Creek
Monkira
CLUNY
MONKIRA
Carbine Creek
81
Farrars Creek
The Nob
Palparara
Cungabulla Waterhole
Conanbulla Waterhole

Travelling Stock
Stock for market often travelled east from Davenport Downs via Palparara and Windorah to the rail-head at Quilpie.

30
186
Road
Bilpa Morea Claypan
Largest claypan in the world

Channel Country
Heavy rain in the catchment of the Diamantina, Georgina, Thompson and other rivers cause flooding over thousands of square kilometres of channel country creating one of the largest naturally irrigated areas in the world.

MOORABERREE
Round Mtn
144
Narradunna Hill
Currawilla
3
31
19
Farrars Creek Channels
Bore
26

Cacoory
Bore
Toilet, dump point
B&W Camp 79
Three Sisters 300 m
Flat Top 158 m
Gas Station
Lookout
Toilet, dump point

69
65
Mooraberree
Meipunga Lake
Kingadurka Waterhole
Montapira Waterhole
Pitchuricoppa Waterhole
Doorie Waterhole
15 Mile Ck
62
Morney Plains
15
29
Hamilton Bluff
Mt Butler 297 m

Developmental
Old Roseberth
ROSEBERTH
DURRIE
Wilpungra Waterhole
Cooningheera Waterhole
Windaroo Waterhole
Mt Collins 225 m
Farrars
Morney
Road
Byway
52

SOUTHWEST QUEENSLAND
For further information east of this area, refer to the SOUTH-WEST QUEENSLAND map from Westprint Maps.

Leave all gates as found when travelling this track

Eyre
Developmental
83
DIAMANTINA
B&W Camp 78
Alligator Sandhill
40
Durrie
Cyrill's Sandhill
Durrie Jump-up
John McKinlay 1861-62
14
Toilet, table
Mount Leonard
Betoota Jump-up
Betoota Hotel
Farley Jump-up
Deon's Lookout & Picnic Area
Developmental
43
10
Country Channel
Billabooroo Ck
Tarchara Ck

Waddi Trees
Mt Lewis 96 m
Roseberth
117
B&W Camp 77
30
Emergency airstrip
Cuppa Creek Rest Area has a toilet, table & dump point
Birdsville
103
28
Wyerie Ck
Planet Downs
9
13
17
Galah
Lake Cuddapan
Mosquito Ck
Tanbar Waterhole

12
29
Birdsville
BIRDSVILLE TRACK
For further information between Birdsville and Marree, refer to the BIRDSVILLE and STRZELECKI TRACKS map from Westprint.
B&W Camp 76 (Diamantina River)
Queensland

Burke & Wills Maps
Maps showing the Burke & Wills exploration from Melbourne to the Gulf are available from Westprint.

Shallow Lake
26
Moonda Lake
MT LEONARD
Mt Oakes

Queensland State Border
The boundary of Queensland originally extended to the north coast along the 141st meridian. It was moved 3° to the west in 1862 so as to incorporate the Savannah grasslands called the Plains of Promise and a safe anchorage off Sweers Island, both adjacent to Burketown.

The Poeppel Line
SOUTH AUSTRALIA
28
24
Pandie Pandie
B&W Camp 75
123
May Hill

The Poeppel Line
The surveyed border line from Haddon Corner to Poeppel Corner is now known as the Poeppel Line following official registration of the name in 2003. The name recognises the work of Surveyor Augustus Poeppel who led the survey party working on the Queensland/South Australian border from 1878 to 1881.

Mt Frew 117 m
Cadelga
Nappamilkie Ck
The Sisters
Piniewirrie Hill 248 m
VLB6
Hadden Corner
13
9
Yards and dam
14
Eulbertie Waterhole
Lake Barrolka
Gilpeppee
Currawonga Waterhole

Diamantina
Outside
PAN07
93
Track
Lake Uloowaranie
B&W Camp 74
PANDIE PANDIE
Lake Etamunbanie
Lake Moorayepe
CORDILLO DOWNS
50
160
Kertiemucka Hill
Haddon
Mt Howie 248 m
Bore and tank
Terrietcha Yards
17
127
Nulla Outstation
Tank
12
QUEENSLAND
SOUTH AUSTRALIA
Lake Yamma Yamma
130

Alton Downs
Andrewilla Waterhole
B&W Camp 73 (Goyder Lagoon)
Koonchera Waterhole
No entry without prior permission
Page Family Grave (Private property)
Geake Hill
D83
Koonchera Dune
My Mountain 228 m
Providence
Creek
INNAMINCKA
For further information south of this area, refer to the INNAMINCKA and COONGIE LAKES map from Westprint Maps.
VHD7
Deep creek crossing
20
10
Wicho Creek
Cook Oil Field
Cooks Well
Macgregor Range

57
Track
2
7
14
B&W Camp 72 (Strzelecki Desert)
Old fence
Walkers
Lake Willara
Lake Cooreeninnie
Lake Kertieyanta
Bull Hole
26 Ck
11
Cordillo Downs
No camping between these two gates
27
Old yards
9
12
8
6
Arrabury
10
Yards
9
Old yards
16
Macgregor
Barrolka Gas Field
130
Kokopera

Sturt Stony Desert
Somewhere near this point in August, 1845 explorer Charles Sturt stood on a high sand dune and looked upon a 'gloomy stone-clad plain' unlike any 'similar geographical feature (he had seen) in any other part of the world'. Sturt named it Stony Desert.

Diamantina - Cooper Watershed
A ridge divides the Diamantina River and Cooper Creek catchments. Both drain into Lake Eyre.

Caution: Minor Tracks
Numerous minor tracks not shown on this map may lead to oil and gas fields. These are private tracks and public access is restricted. Some such tracks are shown thus;

Walkers Crossing Track is a Public Access Route, or 'PAR'
Lake Golgoopiarie
8
30
Yards
Lake Strangways
Lake Karangie
Lake Toontoowaranie
Lake Apanburra
Lake Goyder
Lake Chewruganie
Lake Koonoomoorinna
Lake Sir Richard
Mitkacaldratillie Lakes
Leap Year Bore
No 3 Grid
Leap Year Dam
18
55
102
Lake Pure

Coongie
Lake Apachirie
Coongie Lake
22
Malkumba-Coongie Lakes National Park
INNAMINCKA
For further information on this area, refer to the INNAMINCKA and COONGIE LAKES map from Westprint Maps.
Candradecka Ck
Candradecka Dam
13
12
138
Patchawara Ck
Policeman Dam
Patchawara Bore
SAINT ANN RANGE
Pudlapatchie
Sealing the Adventure Way to the SA border should be completed some time in 2012.

89
26
Crossing
B&W Camp 71 (Kernacoopinna WH)
Lake Macnamara
Kudriemitchie Outstation
B&W Camp 70
Lake Amagooranie
12
Wattacupine Yards
Coongie
First oil exploration well in Cooper Basin 28 Apr 1959
Bartons Well
BKB06
Beantree
Sturt Stony
19
189
78
Way
Adventure
(No services)
Ballera Gas Plant
35
13
7
35

Innamincka Regional Reserve
B&W Camp 69 (Moran Waterhole)
Walkers Crossing
14
Boggy Lake
16
104
John McKinlay 1861-62
27
B&W Camp 68
22
Sandy Ck
31
Desert
Nappa Merrie
B&W Camp 63 (Maapoo Crossing)
Maapoo Waterhole
B&W Camp 64
56
Burke and Wills Bridge
B&W Camp 62 (Wilson River)
Cooper Creek
Numerous channels and waterholes form Cooper Creek, large areas are subject to flooding.

Lake McKinlay
Lake Kanchie-mulanie
Lake Yarowinie
Ooga-Boogina Waterhole
Lake Andree
19
Fly Lake
Tirrawarra Oil and Gas Field
Scrubby Camp WH
Scrubby Camp
21
Track
See inset map
B&W Camp 67 (Tilcha Waterhole) & Wills Memorial
B&W Camp 66
Cullyamurra WH
13
10
Burke and Wills Dig Tree (Camp 65)
Innamincka No 1 Bore
Oontoo
17
10
Nappacoongie WH
No camping at Burke and Wills Bridge. Please use the managed campsite at The Dig Tree.
B&W Camp 61 (Nockanoora Waterhole)
B&W Camp 60 (Tookabarnoo)
Tookabarnoo Waterhole

Lake Perigundi
Lake Bulpanie
Andracunie Swamp
Taierrinie Creek
Coori Coori Tillie Lakes Moolionburrinna
Lake Kanchiemulanie
Lake Miraditchie
Andree Waterhole
Lake Marackorinnanboka
Gidgealpa
Merrimelia Gas Field
22
14
Innamincka

ANGAS DOWNS

Rd

16

79

Desert Oak Hill

The Twins

P

Palmer Valley

3

33

Lurilja

PALMER VALLEY

18

Salt Creek Rest Area

76

Percy Hill

Charlotte Range

44

43

Castle Rock

Pinnacle Hills 435 m

Angas Hill 611 m

25°

P

Chambers Pillar

Chambers Pillar Historical Reserve

Alice Well

CURTIN SPRINGS

MOUNT EBENEZER

IDRACOWRA

22

Idracowra

10

Angas Downs

18

LASSETER

34

Imanpa Aboriginal Community

Ippia Hill 638 m

11

41

21

Mt Casuarina 449 m

8

RED

10

Mount Ebenezer Roadhouse

HORSESHOE BEND

25

244

CENTRE

Erldunda

Impadna

Curtin Springs

6

HWY

WAY

56

4

Tower

17

Horseshoe Bend

Mt Squire 410 m

10

Lookout

17

Mygoora Lake

Karinna

Ck

STUART

BLACK HILL RANGE

70

Mt Conner 859 m

60

P

ERLDUNDA

Eileen Hill 484 m

IDRACOWRA

LILLA CREEK

Creek

CURTIN SPRINGS

LYNDAVALE

87

95

Katamurta

Lilla Creek

58

Mt Gordon North 463 m

34

Lyndavale

Spring

Umbeara

Creek

Ck

MULGA PARK

HWY

UMBEARA

22

Mt Hopetoun 508 m

170

Kulgera

P

60

VICTORY DOWNS

Kulgera

13

Kulgera

31

7

Goyder

Old

Highway

77

Mt Cavenagh 669 m

Outounya

20

31

7

Mt Cecil 547 m

32

64

Gunbarrel

Johnstone Geodetic Stn

MOUNT CAVENAGH

NORTHERN TERRITORY

Victory Downs

Mount Cavenagh

24

SOUTH AUSTRALIA

26°

Border Rest Area

AYERS RANGE SOUTH

Sentinel Hill 905 m

Birthday

Alcurra

38

Creek

Hamilton

Stevenson

Mt Cuthbert 1030 m

Marryat

10'

63

McNamara Hill 1069 m

Numerous roads and tracks exist in this area. Permits are required for access to all of them.

Tietkens

MUSGRAVE RANGES

Creek

A87

Tieyon

35

Mt Woodroffe 1435 m (Highest peak in SA)

Pukatja (Ernabella)

Yunyarini (Kenmore Park)

Pine Ridge 617 m

P

Marryat Rest Area (emergency telephone)

Ernest Giles

Giles travelled from Peake Telegraph Station in an attempt to reach the west coast of Australia. He was repelled by the Gibson Desert named after Alfred Gibson who lost his life during the exploration.

Curralilla

Umuwa

Eateringinna

Marryat

Watinuna Community (Officer Creek)

The Elder Scientific Exploration Expedition

Led by David Lindsay, the expedition left Warrina (on the Oodnadatta Track) for a known point in the Everard Ranges (north-west of Marla). The exploration then extended west through the Great Victoria Desert toward what is now Kalgoorlie and then on to settled areas near Geraldton.

Echo Hill 599 m

De Rose Hill

Alberga

DE ROSE HILL

158

Officer

Currie

Creek

Fregon (Kaltjiti)

Creek

Marble Hill 510 m

76

Agnes Creek Rest Area

Agnes Ck

Creek

Mulga Bore

68

Tarcoonyinna

Ck

Chandler Rest Area

Lambina

51

Walalkara

Paw Paw

Kulitjara

Victory Well

Mimili Community (Everard Park)

27°

Chandler

13

Granite Downs

58

LAN07 Seven Waterholes

Eteamerta Hill 723 m

THE EVERARD RANGES

Mt Etitinna 733 m

Indulkana Community

Private

LAMBINA

Lambina Opal Diggings

Teeta Bore

Mt Carmeena 747 m

Ammaroodinna

Chambers Bluff 592 m

Mt John 562 m

Central Australian Railway

40

Road

Nicholson Hill 404 m

Mt Illilinna 604 m

Travel permits for the road to Mintabie are available at Marla.

A

Locked gate

MAR04

Coongra

Coongra Creek

54

Track

Mintabie

Marla

D95

Oodnadatta

44

WEL06

Welbourn Hill

Trainor Hill 417 m

35

Marla Bore

STUART

WELBOURN HILL

Wallatinna

Ammaroodinna Hill 355 m

GREAT VICTORIA

ANANGU PITJANTJATJARA

60

A87

HIGHWAY

OODNADATTA TRACK

For further information between Marla and Marree, refer to the OODNADATTA TRACK map from Westprint Maps

Wintinna Rest Area

WINTINNA

15

DESERT

ABORIGINAL LAND

CAD02

Wintinna Ck

23

20' 30' 40' 50' **135°** 10' 20' 30' 40' **77** 50' **136°** 10' 20' 30' 40' 50'

NORTH

10km 0 10 20 30 40km

© Copyright Westprint Maps Pty Ltd 2022

HORSESHOE BEND

ANDADO

Fletcher Hill 232 m

Highway Bore

Madigan Camp 2 · The
Poodinitterra Hill · Twins
Crocker Hill 229 m

Bundooma (ruin)

228

34

Old Andado Track

Middle gate

Marshall Bluff 224 m

Geosurveys Hill 156 m

Engordina (ruin)
44
Point Eremophila 451 m

Yellow King Ochre Mine

Yellow King Ochre Mine
Mined extensively during WWII when
yellow paint was required for camouflaging.
No public access.

Madigan Camp 1

Madigan Camp 1A

25°

NEW CROWN

Mount Squire (ruin)
27

North Bore

38

East Bore

9

Hubbard Hill 225 m

**Mac Clark Acacia
Puece Reserve**

NT
WA
QLD
SA
NSW
VIC
TAS

Colson Pinnacle 452 m
Mt Rumbalara 449 m
39 Rumbalara (ruin)

ALICE SPRINGS TO OODNADATTA
For further information between
these two towns, see the ALICE
SPRINGS to OODNADATTA map
from Westprint Maps

ANDADO

ANDADO

River

Colson

Crown Point

Finke (Apatula)

18
70 Andado

Old Andado

Yalura Hill 218 m
Moolta Hills

118

Colson Track
A permit from the Central Land
Council is required prior to travel
the Colson Track.

205

Lambthe Centre
13 20
15

30 Grave
New Crown

15

Mt Day 249 m
Peebles Bore

PMER ULPERRE
INGWEMIRNE ARLETHERRE
ABORIGINAL LAND TRUST

Colson Oil Well

Mt Beddome 425 m

Mt McGowan 367 m

Duffield (ruin)

31

Mt Peebles 258 m

Waggon Claypan Dam
29

Mayfield Swamp

Ted Colson
Colson was the first European to cross
the Simpson Desert when in 1936 he travelled
from his home at Bloods Creek to Birdsville and
return. Colson used camels and was accompanied
by an Aboriginal person named Peter.

BEDDOME RA

NEW CROWN

Charlotte Waters

FINKE RIVER

Mayfield Bore
10

Mt Daer 163 m

Mt Etingambra 171 m

Duffield Creek

Charlotte Bore
Coglin Ck

41 Whitewood Bore

17

McDills Bore

NORTHERN TERRITORY

Coglin Creek

14

SOUTH AUSTRALIA

Lindsay Creek
Wall Creek

25

CROWN POINT

10

Mount Dare

Mt Apperda 245 m

NOTE; Vehicles heading east
should reduce tyre pressures
at this point. UHF channel 10
is recommended.

Colson Junction
Line

Eyutalyera Creek

Abminga (ruin)

Abminga

Mt Weeahlakiminne 285 m

Witjira National Park

Oasis Bore

29

38
Ted Colson 1936

French

Wonga Junction

13
23
Oolarinna Oil Well

Linnies Corner

58

17

20

24

Mt Hammersley 225 m

Alka Seltza Bore

17
Purni Bore

Glen Joyce Oil Well

34

Eringa

37

Bloods Ck

16

Bloods Creek
Federal

Red Mulga Creek crossing

VLD7

55

Alka Seltza airstrip

Freeth Junction

Mokari Oil Well
and Airstrip
(abandoned)

Rig Road

Georges Corner

34

John McDouall Stuart
Stuart made several journeys in this
approximate location between 1858
and 1862 which resulted in a practical
route north - south across Australia.

Ross Creek

76

Ilbunga (ruin)

34

Mt Crispe 278 m
VLB7

Dalhousie Springs

Lookout

Ambullinna Waterhole

Oolerinna Waterhole

Etelkertinna Native Well

DESERT PARKS PASS
A pass is required to travel east of Dalhousie
Springs or through Simpson Desert Regional Reserve.
Passes are available from National Parks and
Wildlife Service offices and agencies.

Macumba Oil Well

Killumi Oil Well

HAMILTON

EMERY RA

Three O'clock Creek

9

3

No access past lookout

Mt Emery 280 m

Dalhousie

Mt Attacherrikanna 238 m

SIMPSON DESERT
For further information on crossing the
Simpson Desert, refer to the SIMPSON
DESERT TRIP PLANNING
map from Westprint.

THE RIG ROAD
was constructed with a clay surface
to enable drilling rigs to be moved
by road trains. Most other tracks in
the Simpson Desert are sandy.

BAGOT RANGE

VLC8
Bluff Point 342 m

286

Stevenson Creek

Pedirka (ruin)

43

Pedirka Track is
generally rough

Algoochinna Ck

17

24

Hamilton

Ernest Giles
Giles travelled extensively across
Australia during his five major explorations.
He passed this way in 1873-74.

Hamilton Creek

VLB3

Mt Rebecca 288 m

MABEL RANGE

Arrabunda Ck

Mt Yangalee 237 m

Malakilla Ck

SIMPSON DESERT

An old station track
between Macumba and
Freeth Junction is NOT
for public use.

John Forrest
Forrest's exploration party left Geraldton on
the west coast on April 21, 1874 and reached the
Overland Telegraph Line on September 27, 1874.
Forrest then followed the line south to the Peake Repeater
Station where he advised the WA Government of
the success of his exploration.

Mount Sarah (ruin)
Mount Sarah
Mt Sarah 259 m

MOUNT SARAH

Fogartys Claypan

Mt Alexander 478 m

Gercheena Ck

MACUMBA

27°

Dalhousie Springs
to Purni Bore
71 km

Spring

Creek

Dalhousie Springs

Gluepot Bog

Witcherrie Mound

To lookout
(no through road)

Todmorden

Alberga Ck

33

MJN01

Mt Herbert North 326 m

208

Oodnadatta

TODMORDEN

Alberga (ruin)

VLE6
Mt John 267 m

MACUMBA

Macumba

Ranger

Dalhousie Springs
to Mount Dare
71 km
34

Bog detour

3

Tenacity Bog

9

Witjira National Park

ALICE SPRINGS TO OODNADATTA
For further information between
these two towns, see the ALICE
SPRINGS - OODNADATTA map
from Westprint Maps

Oodnadatta Track

66

60

Neales River

Branch of

Western Bluff 207 m
Mt O'Halloran 174 m

Angle Pole

17

Mt Guy 255 m

Dalhousie Pile

Dalhousie

0 5km

NORTH

Dalhousie Springs

Flemings Ck
North Branch of
Camel Ck

South Branch

5
Oodnadatta
A

Cecilia Ck

Mt Areebunna 241 m

Hann Hill 234 m

VLG2

Mt Edarteenya 238 m

Woodmurra Creek

MACUMBA RIVER

Mt Willoughby 310 m

Mt Albany 224 m

46

14

Allandale

VLB8
D95

ARCKARINGA

Hann Ck

37

Mount Dutton (ruin)
Mt Dutton

ALLANDALE

Mt Perrypollkot 199 m

Tarracalena Dome

Mt Robinson 183 m

Boy Ck

20' 30' 40' 50' **135°** 10' 20' 30' **42** 40' 50' **136°** 10' 20' 30' 40' 50'

40' 50' **127°** 81 10' 20' 30' 40' 50' **128°** 10' 20' 78 30' 40' 50' **129°** 10'

Lake Farnham

Mt Johnno
751 m

RAWLINSON RANGE

Beadell Tree

Private

Road

SCHWERIN MURAL CRESCENT

Kulail
23

P 27
Tower

27

50'

16 13 15 5

Blazed tree

Old Blazed tree

Gunbarrel

46

Sladen

Water

Gill Pinnacle
869 m

Beadell tree

Docker River
(Kaltukatjara)

41

Blazed tree

31 **344**

Highway

Lapaku

Mt Russell
785 m

49 92

Umputjutu

Alfred Gibson
Gibson died somewhere in
this area while exploring with
Ernest Giles in 1874.

20

25°

Million Dollar
Corner

9 16

Van Der Linden
Lakes

Warakurna

Giles Meteorological Station

Dean Ra

Petermann Ranges

Wankari Walka

Mippiltjarra
Rockhole

This bore water not
suitable for drinking
(Aug 2000)

Beadell Marker

Warakurna Roadhouse

13

26

Tower

Giles Creek

Kunapula

Kurkatingara

The abandoned section is so named
because in 1977, a new road was built
between Warburton and Giles (part of
the Great Central Road). This section
of the Gunbarrel Highway was
no longer used.

Road

36

P

GUNBARREL HIGHWAY
For further information between
the WA Border and Wiluna, see the
GUNBARREL HIGHWAY map
from Westprint Maps

Beadell Marker

(Old Giles Gunbarrel

WESTERN AUSTRALIA / NORTHERN TERRITORY

Mulyati

UHF 3

Wanarn
Community

20

NGAANYATJARRA

Beadell Marker

15

9

Bore

Central

20

Tjukurlapini
Rockholes

33

CENTRAL ABORIGINAL

20'

17

16 Tjulun Rockholes

RESERVE

162

The original Gunbarrel Highway extends
through the Pitjantjatjara Aboriginal Lands
in South Australia to Victory Downs Station
near the Stuart Highway. Permits are
required to travel this route.

Alkata

229

Great

Walu Community

28

Permits are required
for travel along all
roads in this area

Park

30'

Len Beadell
The Gunbarrel Road Construction
Party, led by Len Beadell, built
6,000 kilometres of roads in the
Western Deserts.

Yarla Kutjurra
Rest Area

42

27

74

600 Mile Point
on centreline of fire
25° 45' 23" S
128° 35' 45" E

Marker thought
to have been burnt

Highway

Ukatjupa

Jackie
Junction

Dry Hill

Tower

82

Jameson
(Mantamaru)

70

36

22

Mt Gosse
881 m

Road

Kurkutjara

Beadell Tree

50'

Kurrkarturtu
Outstation

37 P

Amy Giles
Hill

Tower

7

26

Surveyor
Generals
Corner

Mummine Well

UHF 6

Blackstone
(Papulankutja)

15

Arnold
Creek

33

6 5
4

Nyikukura

26°

33

Waratjara

Blackstone Ra

Wingellina
(Irrunytju)

22

Kalka

129

Red Rock

Lightning
Rock

Mt Hinckley
1017 m

Mt Elvire
602 m

Bilbring
Waterhole

CAVENAGH RA

TOMKINSON RA

Pipalyatjara

Thomas
Hill

Mt Eveline
631 m

Mt Cooper
Fort Mueller

Mt West
862 m

550 Mile Point
on centreline of fire
26° 12' 20" S
129° 13' 40" E

10'

Mt Herbert

Mt Squires
704 m

BARROW RANGE

Bell Rock Range

Mount

Kunatjara

Borrows Hill
694 m

Kunmanara
Bore

64

20'

NGAANYATJARRA
WARBURTON
ABORIGINAL RESERVE

Lilian Ck

NGAANYATJARRA

A permit is required for
travel along this track

Makurapiti

30'

CENTRAL ABORIGINAL

Road

RESERVE

Lake Kadgo

Tjinturritjan Community

Business

Nyintjilan Community

Mt Agnes
676 m

Blyth
Hills

50'

27°

56

Sydney Yeo Ra

19

Kuruala Community

Sydney Yeo
Chasm

Mt Irving

Milne
Rock

Point Bowzer
Bower

Aboriginal

Ernest Favenc Breakaways

GREAT VICTORIA

10'

DESERT

WA NT QLD
SA
NSW
VIC
TAS

*Waigen
Lakes*

A permit is required for
travel along this track

NGAANYATJARRA

40'

NORTH

CENTRAL ABORIGINAL

10km 0 10 20 30 40km

© Copyright Westprint Maps Pty Ltd 2022

RESERVE

40' 50' **127°** 10' 20' 30' 40' 47 50' **128°** 10' 20' 30' 40' 50' **129°** 10'

20' 30' 40' 50' **130°** 10' 20' 30' **79** 40' 50' **131°** 10' 20' 30' 40' 50'

LAKE AMADEUS

PETERMANN ABORIGINAL

LAND TRUST

Winnall Ridge
605 m

50'

Tower
Karukaki

• Mt Currie
664 m

KATITI ABORIGINAL
LAND TRUST

CURTIN
SPRINGS

25°

Tjunti
Community

25

Puta Puta
Community

*Lasseter's
Cave
(No camping)*

Mt Fagan
905 m

36

Mt Miller

Conellan
Airport

Yulara ⓐ

28

LASSETER

56

4

Curtin
Springs

10'

PETERMANN RANGES

229

81

Road

Tjukururu

Kata Tjuta
(The Olgas)

6

HWY

11

Pilatal

• Mt McCulloch
832 m

*Lasseter's
Grave*

• Mt Olga
1066 m

Uluru (Ayers Rock)
863 m

20'

ALICE SPRINGS TO ULURU
For further information on the area
between Alice Springs and Warakurna
including details of Lasseter's Lost Reef
and the MacDonnell Ranges, see the ALICE
SPRINGS TO ULURU map from
Westprint Maps.

Pilakatal

Katamala Cone
828 m

40

Uluru - Kata Tjuta
National Park

Stevensons Pk
1032 m

Ernest Giles
Giles made several exploratory
journeys throughout the area
covered by this map. A
selection are shown.

**ULURU, KATA TJUTA AND
WATARRKA NATIONAL PARKS**
For further information on these areas,
see the ULURU, KATA TJUTA and
WATARRKA map from Westprint Maps

30'

Mt Jenkins
• 844 m

Foster Cliff
1025 m

GUNBARREL HIGHWAY
For further information between
Wingellina and Leonora, see the
GUNBARREL HIGHWAY map
from Westprint Maps

Butler Dome
1107 m

40'

PETERMANN ABORIGINAL

Gordon Hill
• 938 m

LAND TRUST

Mt Robert
796 m

MULGA
PARK
(Emergency
only)

68

50'

Irkini

Mt Cockburn
• 1134 m

Britten
Creek

Mulga Park

Mt Mann
• 1167 m

Jones

Walytjatjata

NORTHERN TERRITORY

26°

MANN

Inarki

Mt Edwin
1193 m

Mt Charles
1269 m

Mt Whinham
1232 m

SOUTH AUSTRALIA

*Numerous roads and tracks exist
in this area. Permits are required
for access to all of them.*

20

Old
Puta Puta

41

Gunbarrel

Aparatjara

RANGES

Angatja

Hwy

58

Kanpi

*Beadell
Marker*

Umpukulu

78

Aparina

Mt Woodward
• 1221 m

65

Creek

MUSGRAVE

RA

McNamara Hill
1069 m

10'

• Mt Davies
1053 m

Mt Morris
1286 m

4

Amata
(Musgrave Park)

Mt Davenport
• 1140 m

*A permit is required to travel
all tracks in the Anangu Pitjantjatjara
Aboriginal Lands area.*

Tankaanu

38

Kintore

Wilitjara

Harry Creek

Wintawata

*Beadell
Marker*

Manyirkanga

Mt Woodroffe
1435 m
(Highest peak
in SA)

20'

Willi Willi

Ulkiya

Wallany

Yurangka

Davies

Kunytjanu

Bryson Hill

Kunamata

Mt Kintore
• 1067 m

Mt Harriet
• 933 m

ANANGU PITJANTJATJARA

Currie

30'

Mount Davies Road
This section of the Mount
Davies Road was built by
Len Beadell's party in 1956.
A permit is required prior to
travelling this track.

Road

*500 Mile Point
on centreline of fire
26° 39' 07" S
129° 51' 51" E*

56

• Pinundinna Hill
759 m

ABORIGINAL LAND

Creek

40'

70

• Mt Tietkens
776 m

Avenue

*A permit is required to travel
all tracks in the Anangu Pitjantjatjara
Aboriginal Lands area.*

50'

*A permit is required
to travel this track
which is reputed to be
in very bad condition.*

63

Maryinna Hill
• 623 m

Dry Hill
639 m

27°

Permano Hill
730 m

Wartaru

Mt Lindsay
• 813 m

Oompeinna Hill
• 627 m

Makiri

Walalkara

Birksgate Ra

Gilby Hill
605 m

Wintiginna Hill
579 m

10'

Mt Sir Thomas
803 m

Pilkinga

Mt Illillinna
604 m

59

57

*Futarinna
Native Well*

Pilgna

20'

ANANGU PITJANTJATJARA

Mount

ABORIGINAL LAND

30

*Purndu
Saltpan*

Cheesman Peak
654 m

Davies

*400 Mile Point
on centreline of fire
27° 32' 09" S
131° 09' 07" E*

30'

Unmoorinna Hill
639 m

Lake Wright

Iltur

Road

40'

20' 30' 40' **130°** 10' 20' 30' **44** 40' 50' **131°** 10' 20' 30' 40' 50'

Well 11
(Goodwin Soak)
15
McConkey Hill 553 m
21
Well 10

Well 9 Well
Oldham Range

Brassey Range

25°

57
Digby Hill
564 m

A $20 fee is charged by Glen-Ayle for the use of this private station track. Ph 08 9981 2990.

No 9 Well

Mt Sir Gerard

Lake Hoar *Lake Jones*

Lake Keerie

MUNGILLI ABORIGINAL RESERVE

Calvert Expedition
Larry Wells led expeditions starting from the gold rush settlement of Lake Way, now Wiluna.

Salvation Well

Glen-Ayle

Mangkili Claypan Nature Reserve

No permit required to travel this section of the Gunbarrel.

Mangkili Junction

41

Mt Evelyn 631 m

Sydney Heads Pass
This pass appears similar to Sydney Heads

Nunegoo Pool

91

Kaljahr Pinnacle

Len Beadell
The Gunbarrel Road Construction Party, led by Len Beadell, built 6,000 kilometres of roads in the Western Deserts.

Mt Nossiter

47
238

Mt William Lambert 514 m

23

Christmas Bore

Proposed Conservation Area
(formerly Earaheedy Station)

Keatland Hills

105 Highway

Mt Archie

Lake Buchanan

Genbirr Creek

FAME RANGE

39

Calvert Expedition
Larry Wells returned from Midway Well to Harry Johnston Water where he re-provisioned. He then returned to Midway Well and continued north.

Mt Moore
Forrest Cairn

30

Carnegie

John Forrest
Explored to the Overland Telegraph Line near the present-day town of Oodnadatta.

Forrest's campsite

Mingal Pool

40

Nooloo Breakaway

Harry Johnston Water

Mt Hooley

BOODIE BOODIE RANGE

Linke Lakes

The Eagle Highway was built in 1980 for oil exploration access. The southern section was re-named David Carnegie Road in 1996.

58

Carnegie

Mt Hoskin 538 m

Mt Throssell 552 m

Square Hill 539 m

26°

Charles Wells Creek

LAKE CARNEGIE

Lake Bedford

PRINCESS

Wongawol **RANGES**

Wongawol Creek

WELLINGTON RANGE

21

Mt Alexandra 496 m

137

Point Robert 516 m

67

Little Banjo Bore

32

Ck Ck

Miligarrie Creek

WELSTEAD RA

Beatrice May Bluff 491 m

50

Windidda

Tooloo Bluff 538 m

A fee of $20 applies for the use of this station track

Banjo Well

Miningarra Creek

Fourteen Mile

Banjo Creek

Prenti Downs

Windidda Ck

Mt Dora 540 m

Mt Smith 465 m

Yelma

74

VON TREUER TABLELAND

Bonython

33

Ck

Lake Wells

Welstead Hill 516 m

Parsons Bluff
Lyell Brown Bluff 524 m

Kyffin Thomas Hill Potter Bluff 485 m

Larry Wells Ra

Blaxland Range

EARNEST GILES RANGE

27°

130

72

FARQUHARSON TABLELAND

Lake Wells

NORTH

10km 0 10 20 30 40km

© Copyright Westprint Maps Pty Ltd 2022

GRANT DUFF RANGE

12 *Lake Wells*

De La Poer Range

Mt Arthur 563 m

Road

90

De La Poer Nature Reserve

12

23

David Carnegie 1896

Lake Throssell

Mt Maiden 590 m

This track is in poor condition

Creek

Milurie Outcamp

107

NECKERSGAT RA

Lake Duketon

Sandstone Ra

71

Mt Granites 505 m

COSMO NEWBERRY (NORTH) ABORIGINAL RESERVE

Vickers Creek

Bandya

Mt Cumming 558 m

Eurothurra Rockhole

Beegull Rockholes

Lake Darlot

44

20' 30' 40' 50' **125°** 10' 20' 30' 40' 81 50' **126°** 10' 20' 30' 40'

50'

Eagle

Highway 145

Gary Highway 58

YOUNG RA

• Mt Colin
530 m

**Gibson Desert
Nature Reserve**

Lake Newell

56

Tikatika
Rockholes

25°

Charlies Knob
547 m

14

Browne Ra

• Tsakalos Hills
540 m

ALFRED AND MARIE RANGE

12

Million Dollar
Corner

Mippiltjarra Junction

9

Beadell Tree

32

Everard
Junction

9

Mt Gordon
537 m

Mt
Everard
539 m

Gunbarrel

Mippiltjarra
Rockhole

Geraldton Bore
(hand pump)

G I B S O N   D E S E R T

Highway

87

10'

Mungkili
Outstation

54

48

Oil company
survey marker

Hunt

Lake
Gruszka

20'

• Mangkili Claypan

• Mt Johnson

15

Oil

Lake
Sprenger

Len Beadell
The Gunbarrel Road Construction
Party, led by Len Beadell, built
6,000 kilometres of roads in the
Western Deserts.

Gunbarrel

30'

Mike Kendall's
burnt-out Nissan

Taratara Rockhole
Mt Boadoll
526 m

Highway

Bore

18

Camp
Beadell

13

Notabilis Hill
463 m

249

41

Beadell
Tree

Mt Samuel
514 m

36

Todd

Mt Charles

Old

46

Jackie
Junction

• Dry Hill

40'

Herbert

29

Oil

Road

Seismic Line

GUNBARREL HIGHWAY
For further information between
Wiluna and the WA Border, refer to
the GUNBARREL HIGHWAY map
from Westprint Maps

Bore

Thryptomene Hill
438 m

Bore

Lake
Breaden

Ranges

Mangi
Rockholes

Heather

37

Hwy

Beadell Tree

Kurrkarturtu
Outstation

Mt Harvest
553 m

37

This track is in
poor condition
(Aug 2000)

50'

BM GY-9

20

(See inset
below)
Alexander
Spring

Sutherland
Range

Solar-powered
bore

59

**NGAANYATJARRA TJIRRKARLI
ABORIGINAL RESERVE**

Boyd
Lagoon

Blyth

Tjirrkarli

• Blyth Pool

13

15

Heather

47

Highway

36

UHF 2

Warburton

Tower

Mummine Well

33

26°

David

133

Carnegie

Wash

Alexander Spring Detail

Two steel
posts indicate
turn-off

• Alexander Spring

• Mt Allott 458 m
Forrest Cairn

Mt Worsnop •

A deviation north from
Alexander Spring by-passes
washouts on the
Hunt Oil Road.

• Mt Allott 458 m

Mt Worsnop

Hunt Oil Camp
(disused)

40

Murray

11

Caves

Caves

55

Ck

34

17

4

65

**NGAANYATJARRA
ABORIGINAL
RESERVE**

8

Steptoe's
Corner

P

20

41

Bore

**NGAANYATJARRA
WARBURTON
ABORIGINAL RESERVE**

62

10'

Lake Gillen

• Hand pump

Hunt

35

Disused

55

20'

Road

Empress Spring

21

Oil

Kanpa

26

Central

Road

Warburton Shire sign

Baker
Lake

Watt

**NGAANYATJARRA
YAPUPARRA
ABORIGINAL
RESERVE**

Manton
Knob

Beadell Ridge

7

Sue

Mackenzie Gorge

Highway

43

30'

40'

59

Road

Breaden Bluff
465 m

Disused

27

24

244

Point Craig
Harkness Gorge

16

Creek

A permit is required to travel
this section of the Connie Sue
Highway. Ph (08) 8950 1711

50'

Terhan
Rockholes

55

P

P

40

Great

43

Parallel

Muggan
Rockhole

High point -
excellent views

Road

No 2

Bore

22

Breakaways

Waterfall
Gorge

5

permit

required

56

27°

15

26

Tjukayirla Roadhouse

'The Zoo' is a rock
arrangement about
1 km southwest of
Tjukayirla Roadhouse

Connie

Sue

30

Hanns Tabletop Hill
492 m

Woods Pass

Ryans Bluff 491 m

10'

Desert Discovery
Camp 2000

9

Sykes Bluff
490 m

Solar-powered
bore

20'

68

The road complex linking Laverton
to Alice Springs (NT) and Winton (Qld)
has been named the 'Outback Highway'.
The plan is for a sealed road to connect
Central Australia with both the east
and west coasts.

G R E A T   V I C T O R I A

Frank Hann
Hann explored this area
extensively, naming most of the
features including Point Lillian and
Sydney Yeo Chasm.

30'

• Gnamal Rockholes

D E S E R T

40

305

• Point Sandercock
443 m

4

Point Lilian
430 m

40'

**Yeo Lake
Nature Reserve**

20' 30' 40' 50' **125°** 10' 20' 30' 40' 46 50' **126°** 10' 20' 30' 40'

Waldburg
Proposed Conservation Area (formerly Waldburg Station)
Woodlands
Mulgul
Collier Range National Park
Mingah Springs
Proposed Conservation Area (formerly Dalgety Downs Station)
Landor Racecourse
GASCOYNE RIVER
Mount Clere
Milgun
Three Rivers
Landor
Mt Labouchere 715 m
Mt Pleasant
Macadam Plains
Bubbagundy Well
Earabiddy
Fortnum Village and Mine
GASCOYNE RIVER
Tibingoona Pool
Beasley Pool
Horseshoe Lights Mine
Mt Erong 435 m
Erong Springs
Mount Seabrook Mine
Trillbar
Yarlarweelor
Horseshoe North and South Mines
Horseshoe and Cassidy Mines
Horseshoe
Bryah
Proposed Conservation Areas
Mt Seabrook 547 m
Mount Padbury
Yulga Jinna
Peak Hill Mine
(formerly Doolgunna Station)
Yundra
Mt Gould 681 m
Historic Mount Gould Lockup
Mount Gould
Harmony Mine
Mount Gould Mine
Moorarie
Oilba Pool
Mount Fraser
261
GREAT
Proposed Conservation Area (formerly Mooloogool Station)
Beringarra
Murchison River
Cashman Mine
Mooloogool
Jack Hills
Mount Hale
Karalundi
24hr stop, toilets
Glengarry Ranges
Nookawarra
Whela
Yallagibbie Ck
Koonmarra
Hope River
Belele
Berrin Pool
Munarra
Killara
Mileura
Yalgar River
Tieraco Ck
GOLDFIELDS
Twelve Mile Creek
Yoothapina
Sherwood
Murchison Downs
Mudgianna
Bilaby Pool
Meekatharra
Old Haveluck Mine
Boolardy
Kalli
Gibralter Mine
Paddys Flat Mine
Bluebird Mine
Roderick Woolshed
Madoonga
Beebyn
WILGIE MIA ABORIGINAL LAND
Wilgie-Mia 653 m
The Gap
Norie
120
Annean
Nannine Mine
Gabanintha
Hill View
Noondie
Glen
Cue
Afghan Rock
Stakewell
Lake Annean
Gabanintha Mine
Kurara Mine
Boomerang Mine
Sandstone Road
Coodardy
Mindoola Bore
Old Poona Mines
Tuckanarra
Rand Mine
Reedy
Triton Mine
Numerous small mines
Yarrabubba
Barlangi Rock
Big Bell Mine
Old Big Bell Hotel
Cuddingwarra Mine
Nallan
Wanmulla
Meka Station
Austin Downs
Walga Rock 478 m
(formerly Lakeside Station)
Cue
Old Golden Crown Mine
Day Dawn
Tuckabianna Mine
Cogla Downs
Vermin proof fence
Mount Wittenoom
Proposed Conservation Areas
Lakeside (formerly Lakeside Station)
Proposed Conservation Areas
Proposed Conservation Areas
Lake Austin
Old Comet and Pinnacles Mines
Inglewood
Proposed Conservation Area (formerly Black Range Station)
Jingemarra
Dalgaranga
(formerly Dalgaranga Station)
Austin Historic Site
Melangata
81
Moyagee
Lake Austin

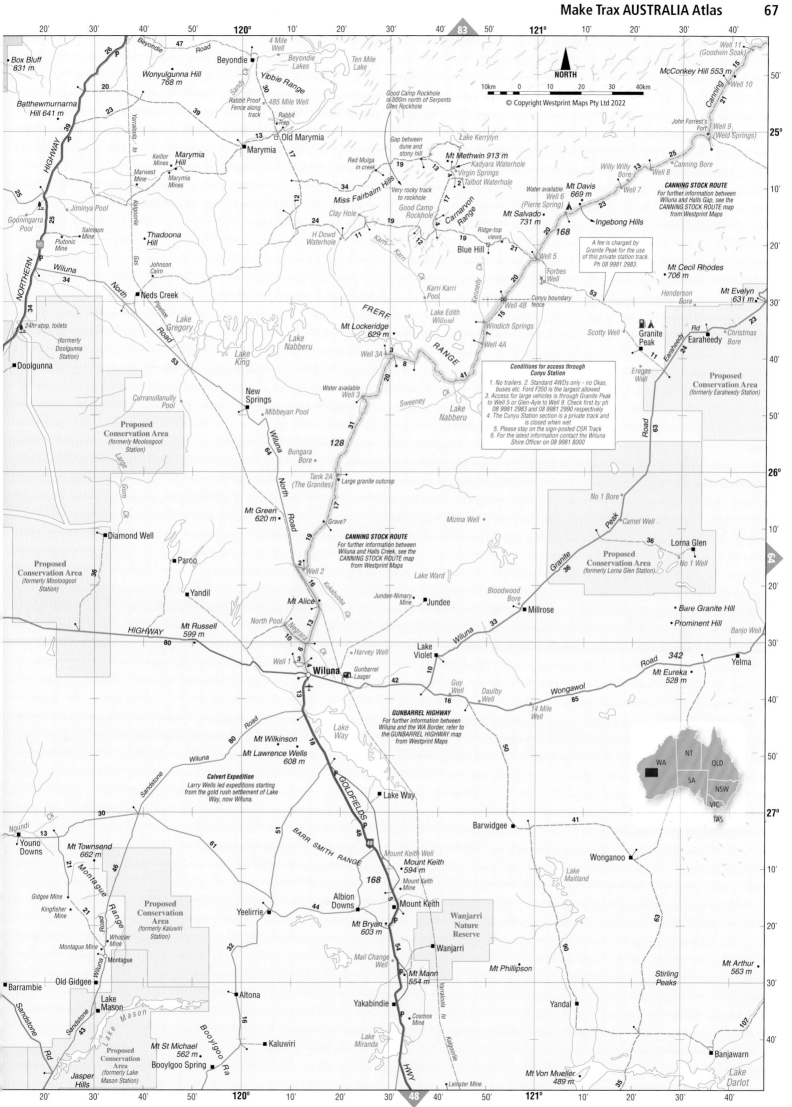

NORTH

10km 0   10   20   30   40km

© Copyright Westprint Maps Pty Ltd 2022

CANNING STOCK ROUTE
For further information between
Wiluna and Halls Gap, see the
CANNING STOCK ROUTE map
from Westprint Maps

A fee is charged by
Granite Peak for the use
of this private station track.
Ph 08 9981 2983.

**Conditions for access through
Cunyu Station**
1. No trailers. 2. Standard 4WDs only - no Okas,
buses etc. Ford F350 is the largest allowed
3. Access for large vehicles is through Granite Peak
to Well 5 or Glen-Ayle to Well 9. Check first by ph
08 9981 2983 and 08 9981 2990 respectively
4. The Cunyu Station section is a private track and
is closed when wet
5. Please stay on the sign-posted CSR Track
6. For the latest information contact the Wiluna
Shire Officer on 08 9981 8000

CANNING STOCK ROUTE
For further information between
Wiluna and Halls Creek, see the
CANNING STOCK ROUTE map
from Westprint Maps

GUNBARREL HIGHWAY
For further information between
Wiluna and the WA Border, refer to
the GUNBARREL HIGHWAY map
from Westprint Maps

Calvert Expedition
Larry Wells led expeditions starting
from the gold rush settlement of Lake
Way, now Wiluna.

Box Bluff 831 m
Batthewmurnarna Hill 641 m
Gooningarra Pool
Doolgunna
Proposed Conservation Area (formerly Mooloogool Station)
Diamond Well
Proposed Conservation Area (formerly Mooloogool Station)
Paroo
Yandil
Mt Russell 599 m
Youno Downs
Ngundi
Mt Townsend 662 m
Gidgee Mine
Kingfisher Mine
Montague Mine
Whistler Mine
Montague
Old Gidgee
Barrambie
Lake Mason
Proposed Conservation Area (formerly Lake Mason Station)
Mt St Michael 562 m
Booylgoo Spring
Kaluwiri
Jasper Hills
Beyondie
Wonyulgunna Hill 768 m
Beyondie
Marymia Hill
Keillor Mines
Marwest Mine
Marymia Mines
Thadoona Hill
Johnson Cairn
Salmaon Mine
Plutonic Mine
Jiminya Pool
Wiluna
Neds Creek
Lake Gregory
Lake King
Lake Nabberu
New Springs
Mibbeyan Pool
Curranullanully Pool
Mt Green 620 m
Grave?
Bungara Bore
Tank 2A (The Granites)
Large granite outcrop
Mt Alice
North Pool
Negrara Ck
Well 1
Wiluna
Gunbarrel Laager
Harvey Well
Kukabubba Ck
Jundee-Nimary Mine
Jundee
Lake Way
Mt Wilkinson
Mt Lawrence Wells 608 m
Yeelirrie
Albion Downs
Mount Keith Well
Mount Keith 594 m
Mount Keith Mine
Mt Bryan 603 m
Mount Keith
Wanjarri
Wanjarri Nature Reserve
Mail Change Well
Mt Mann 554 m
Yakabindie
Cosmos Mine
Lake Miranda
Altona
Leinster Mine
Beyondie Lakes
Ten Mile Lake
4 Mile Well
Yibbie Range
Rabbit Proof Fence along track
485 Mile Well
Rabbit Trap
Old Marymia
Marymia
Red Mulga in creek
Miss Fairbairn Hills
Very rocky track to rockhole
Clay Hole
Good Camp Rockhole
H Dowd Waterhole
Good Camp Rockhole is 500m north of Serpents Glen Rockhole
Gap between dune and stony hill
Mt Methwin 913 m
Kadyara Waterhole
Virgin Springs
Talbot Waterhole
Lake Kerrylyn
Carnarvon Range
Karri Karri Ck
Blue Hill
Mt Salvado 731 m
Ridge-top views
Karri Karri Pool
Water available Well 6 (Pierre Spring)
Mt Davis 669 m
Ingebong Hills
Well 5
Forbes Well
Well 4B
Cunyu boundary fence
Windich Springs
Well 4A
Water available Well 3
Mt Lockeridge 629 m
Lake Edith Withnel
Well 3A
FRERE RANGE
Sweeney Ck
Lake Nabberu
Mizina Well
Lake Ward
Bloodwood Bore
Millrose
Lake Violet
Guy Well
Daulby Well
14 Mile Well
Wongawol
McConkey Hill 553 m
Well 11 (Goodwin Soak)
Well 10
Canning
John Forrest's Fort
Well 9 (Weld Springs)
Canning Bore
Willy Willy Bore
Well 8
Well 7
Mt Evelyn 631 m
Henderson Bore
Scotty Well
Granite Peak
Eregas Well
Earaheedy
Christmas Bore
Earaheedy Rd
Proposed Conservation Area (formerly Earaheedy Station)
No 1 Bore
Granite Peak
Camel Well
Lorna Glen
No 1 Well
Proposed Conservation Area (formerly Lorna Glen Station)
Bare Granite Hill
Prominent Hill
Banjo Well
Mt Eureka 528 m
Yelma
Barwidgee
Wonganoo
Lake Maitland
Mt Arthur 563 m
Mt Phillipson
Stirling Peaks
Yandal
Mt Von Mueller 489 m
Banjawarn
Lake Darlot

WA NT QLD SA NSW VIC TAS

Dirk Hartog Island
Now a national park, this island was the
first site on the west coast visited by European
explorers when Dutchman Dirk Hartog
landed in 1616.

4WD access to Dirk Hartog Island is
via a barge from Steep Point. Only eight vehicles
are permitted on the island at one time, between
March and October each year.
See www.sharkbay.org for further information.

Steep Point
Most westerly point
of the Australian mainland

**Bernier and Dorre
Islands
Nature Reserve**

Cape Ronsard
Wedge Point
*Bernier
Island*
Boulder Point
Red Cliff Point
Cape Couture
Cape Boullanger
Low Point
Quoin Bluff North
*Dorre
Island*
Castle Point
White Beach
Cliff Point
Cape St Cricq

*Blowfish
Banks*
Miaboolya Beach
Ingada Village
Point Whitmore
Carnarvon
Mangrove Point
Gascoyne Flats
Greenough Point
Uendoo Creek
Grey Point
Bush Bay
New Beach

Brick
House
Carnarvon
GASCOYNE
*Rocky
Pool*

Callagiddy

40 Mile Tank

Toilets

*SHARK BAY
(World Heritage Area)*

Naturaliste Channel

Cape Inscription
Urchin Point
West Point
'The Block'
Withnell Point

Cape Levillain
Dampiers Landing/
Sammys Well

Cape Peron North
Skipjack Point
Bottle Beach
Gregories
South Gregories

*Shark Bay
Marine Park*

Turtle Bay

Mystery Beach

*Dirk
Hartog
Island*

*DENHAM
SOUND*

Herald Bight

Guichenault Point
Herald Bluff

*Francois Peron
National Park*

*Hopeless
Reach*

Sandy Point
West Coast Well
Louisa Bay
Quoin Head

Cape Lesueur

*Big
Lagoon*

Middle Bluff

*PERON
PENINSULA*

Monkey
Mia

*Sedimentary
Deposits
Reserve*

*Faure
Island*

Pelican I.

**Dirk Hartog Island
National Park**

Herald Bay

Quoin Bluff South

Tetrodon Loop
Notch Point

Cliff Lookout

Cape
Bellefin

Cape
Heirisson

Freycinet Reach

Dubaut
Point

Potit
Point

*Sedimentary
Deposits
Reserve*

Lagoon Point

Denham

Dirk Hartog
Eco Lodge

Useless Prong

Shark Bay
Salt Works

Useless
Loop

Eagle
Bluff

Fowlers
Whalebone

*L'Haridon
Bight*

*HAMELIN
POOL*

Surf Point

South Passage

Steep Point
Lighthouse

Bellefin Prong

Blind Strait

Ranger

Harrisson Prong

Useless Loop
Mine

Goulet
Bluff

Shell
Beach
CP

(formerly
Nanga
Station)

*Hamelin Pool
Marine Nature
Reserve*

**Proposed
Conservation Area**
(formerly Carrarang Station)

Salt
pans

Nanga Bay Resort

*Nanga
Bay*

Thunder Bay Blowholes

Crayfish Bay
Marinus Point
False Entrance
Popper Point
False Entrance
Blowholes

Useless

*Cararang
Peninsula*

*Shark Bay
Marine Park*

*Henri Freycinet
Harbour*

Cararang
Giraud Point

*Proposed
Conservation
Area*

Loop

Zuytdorp Cliffs

Salutation I.

*Baba
Head*

Road

P
Tamala

(formerly
Nanga Station)

*Proposed
Conservation
Area*

I N D I A N   O C E A N

*Proposed
Conservation Area*
(formerly
Tamala Station)

*Zuytdorp
Nature Reserve*

*Zuytdorp
Nature Reserve*

*Proposed
Conservation
Area*
(formerly Murchison
House Station)

*Gantheaume
Bay*

Chinamans Rock

Red Bluff, Mushroom Rock
Rainbow Valley

Shell House

NT
QLD
WA
SA
NSW
VIC
TAS

NORTH

10km   0   10   20   30   40km

© Copyright Westprint Maps Pty Ltd 2022

20'   30'   40'   50'   115°   10'   20'   30'   40'   85   50'   116°   10'   20'   30'   40'

RIVER

36
Doorawarrah

169

Meeragoolia

37

Mullewa

Fishy Pool

P

Mooka

P

Khyber Pass

Road

22

30

Jimba Jimba

Bidgernia

(formerly Jimba Jimba Station)

(formerly Bidgemia Station)

KENNEDY RA

63

48

(formerly Mooka Station)

Proposed Conservation Area

Police Station Woolshed

57

GASCOYNE RIVER

Proposed Conservation Area (formerly Dalgety Downs Station)

50'

Weedarrah

Mombo   Creek

Mooloo Downs

Mooloo

25°

Gascoyne Junction

Cream   Creek

Carnarvon

77

GASCOYNE

Dalgety   28

Brook

Dairy Creek

Mullewa   Road

31

Dalgety Downs

47

Dalgety

10'

Ellavalla

34

Yalbalgo

Proposed Conservation Area (formerly Pimbee Station)

Winderie

18

Towrana

Pimbee   Road   31

36

Geeranoo   Creek

Glenburgh

20

24   23

Erong   Road

Mt Erong 435 m

Erong Springs

14

20'

Edaggee

Marron

12

Road   44

29

Pell   Creek

Daurie   Creek

Congo   Creek

Coor-De-Wandy

22

Yalbra Outcamp

30'

Wahroonga

26

Pimbee

17

36

Carey Downs

Wooramel   River

North   Wooramel   River

Innouendy   14

25

27

Wooramel   River

41

Wooramel   River   47

40'

Meedo

40

Callytharra Springs

River

Woorarmel   Roadhouse   P

P

20   P

Gilroyd

44

Yaringa

7

Gladstone Jetty

Lookout   P

30   P   P

Woodleigh

27   18

Old Woodleigh

10   P

Carbla

17

Byro   21

Woodleigh   26

Byro Plains

53

Byro

Woodleigh   Road

Yalardy Farmstay

20

33

23

Talisker

Ballythunna

Yarra Yarra   Creek

47

26°

Byro

53   Tathire   Ck

15

Mardagee   52

Yarra   Ck

10'

25   NORTH   WEST

Hamelin Pool Telegraph Station Museum

Road   29

Overlander Roadhouse

P

55

Proposed Conservation Area (formerly Muggon Station)

Breberle Lake

44

Moolarah Pool

Manfred

20'

Lake Ceasar

Lake Tilly

42

26

Muggon

Butchers

Mount Narryer

Track

48

Murrum   River

Scrubby Range

30'

COASTAL

25

P

Butchers   7

Coburn   26

Meadow

1

13

Billabong Roadhouse

67

Track

29

Mungawolagudi Claypan

Track

Errabiddy Hills

Murchison

Roderick   River

32   Bilaby Pool

40'

Murchison

Meeberrie

50'

HIGHWAY

35

Toolonga Nature Reserve

Yatlamia Pool

Wail Outcamp

Road

Carnarvon   Mullewa

Wooleen Lake

Wooleen Station stay

Cundarra Pool

27°

Nerren Nerren

Proposed Conservation Area (formerly Nerren Nerren Station)

178

Billilly Claypan

Pia Wadjari

PIA ABORIGINAL LAND

Boolardy

55

RFDS Airstrip

P

New Forest

E T Hooley Well

Twin Peaks

Murgoo

Medado Pool

10'

20'

Bungabandi Creek

Wilgiamia Pool

Coolcalaya

River

Murchison   River

Yallalong

Billabong

Sanford   River

McNab   Creek

Mount Wittenoom

30'

Station stay

Eurardy Station

The Loop

Murchison River Gorge

19

Kalbarri National Park

Galena Bridge

Rocky Pool

Ballinyoo Bridge (built in 1932)

Proposed Conservation Area (formerly Woolgorong Station)

Proposed Conservation Area

Coolarburtoo   Brook

Woogalong Ck

Woogalong

Jingemarra

8

40'

12   Kalbarri

25

Ajana   Kalbarri

Hawks Head Lookout

Ten Mile Pool

31

Yandi   41

Lake Nerramyne   Lake Nerramine Mine

Pinegrove

Woolgorong

(formerly Twin Peaks Station)

Proposed Conservation Areas

20'   30'   40'   50'   115°   50   10'   20'   30'   40'   116°   10'   20'   30'   40'

148° 10' 20' 30' 40' 50' 149° 10' 87 20' 30' 40' 50' 150° 10' 20' 30'

Goonyella/Riverside Coal Mine
Hamilton Park
Tierawoomba
Undercliff
West Hill Island
Poynter Island
Bedwell Group
Northumberland Isles

50'
Wotonga
Annandale
Mt Flora
Carmila
Carmila West
Red Clay Island
Bamborough Island
Duke Islands
Marble Island

22°
Moranbah 70
Daunia
Olive Downs
Cockenzie
Dipperu National Park
Collaroy
Cardowan
Marylands
Elalie
196
Clairview
Broad Sound Islands National Park
Wild Duck Island
Tynemouth Island
Broad Sound
Hexham Island

Grosvenor Downs
Poitrel
Winchester
Deverill
Morpeth
Saltbush Park
Markwell
Broad Sound Islands National Park
Long Island
Quail Island
Stanage Bay
Leicester Island

145
Iffley
Rookwood Outstation
Broad Sound
Mangrove Islands
Shoalwater Bay Conservation Park
Collins Island
Akens Island

20'
Saraji
Saraji Coal Mine
Bombandy
Batheaston
Markwell
Killarney
St Lawrence
Rosewood Island
Charon Point Cons Park
Couti Uti
Sabina Point
Shoalwater Bay

Cumberland Downs
Vermont
111
Carfax
Croydon
Rosedale
Torilla
Fernlea
Waratah

30'
Luxor
Cosmos
Barmount
Burwood
Tanderra
Raspberry Vale

Dysart
Picardy
May Downs
Langley
Ogmore
Glenprairie
SHOALWATER BAY MILITARY AREA

Cotherstone
Norwich Park
Warwick
Angleside
Marlborough
Raspberry Creek

Peak Range National Park
Booroondara
Middlemount
Essex
Junee National Park
Clive
BRUCE
Marlborough
Eden Garry
The Oaks

50'
Coomburragee
Foxleigh
Manly
102
Glenavon
Montait

Lake Bundoora
Woollamba
Junee
HIGHWAY

23°
Talarah
Tieri
Developmental
Apis Creek
Rossmoya

Capella
Oaky Creek Mine
Mount Stuart
Wilpeena Park
119
Werribee
Goodedulla National Park
Fitzroy River
Yaamba

104
HWY
Gregory Mine
Leura
Mount Etna Caves NP
The Caves

73
Kestrel Coal Mine
Fairhill
Jellinbah
Yarrabee
Ridgelands
Alton Downs

Cooroorah
Melaleuca
Barcomba
Rockhampton

Nogoa
Mayfield
Taunton National Park
Gracemere

30'
Emerald
118
Tolmies
Blackwater
CAPRICORN
Foleyvale
Stanwell
Kabra

Weemah
Yamala
Comet
Bluff
Dingo
Wycarbah
Bouldercombe

Fairbairn Dam
Lochmead
Rhudana
Blackdown Tableland
Namoi Hills
Duaringa
Edungalba
Gogango
149
Old Westwood
71
Mount Morgan

Bonnie Doon
Blackwater Coal Mine
Dawson Range
HIGHWAY

Gindie
Annie Vale
Olive Vale
Blackdown Tableland National Park
Coomooboolaroo
Dululu

65
Fernlees
Glenora
Turkey Creek
Comet Downs
East Brook
Wowan
Deetford
Dixalea

24°
Minerva Hills National Park
Arcturus Downs
South Blackwater Coal Mine
Wooronah
A5
Tomlin

Springsure
Moorooloo
Struan
Humboldt
Spring Hill
Woorabinda
Perch Creek
Baralaba
Rannes
75
Goovigen

Historic cutting
Orion Downs
Mira
Brackenley
Taylors Creek
Mimosa Park
78
Jambin

Spring Hill
Carina Downs
Humboldt National Park
Goomally
Blue Hills
Rosedale
Callide

Nalcoombie
Dalmally
71
Conomara
Redcliffe
Pine Hut
Bindaree
Dakenba

Heathwood
Meteor Downs
Mimosa Vale
Avoca
Coolibah
Banana
45
60

Wealwandangie
Avoca
Albinia National Park
Walba
Oombabeer
Beckersley
Torsdale

Goathland
Meteor Park
Rolleston
Bauhinia
Laurel Hills
165
Moura
Cedars
Barfield

Mt Cheops
Springwood
Planet Downs
DAWSON
Maloneys
Kianga

Carnarvon National Park
Consuelo
Fairfield
Junedale
Nipan
59
Lonesome Creek

Mt Lane
Peawaddy
Boonberry
Thomby
Glandore

Round Mtn
Purbrook
Iron Pot

148° 10' 20' 30' 40' 54 50' 149° 10' 20' 30' 40' 50' 150° 10' 20' 30'

SWAIN REEFS area and coastal Queensland map.

40' 50' 151° 10' 20' 30' 40' 50' 152° 10' 20' 30' 40' 50' 153°

Heralds Prong No. 2

Swain Reefs

Gannett Cay

NT
QLD
WA
SA
NSW
VIC
TAS

Great Barrier Reef Marine Park
(Mackay - Capricorn Section)

High Peak Island

NORTH

10km   0   10   20   30   40km

© Copyright Westprint Maps Pty Ltd 2022

**Broad Sound Islands
National Park**

Cheviot Island

Channel

S O U T H   P A C I F I C

O C E A N

Townshend Island

Reef Point

*SHOALWATER BAY
MILITARY AREA*

Pearl Bay

*Warginburra
Peninsula*   Perforated Point

Cape Clinton

Freshwater Bay

Cliff Point

Cape Manifold

Please Note:
*Many features on this map have
been derived from Australian Government
digital data and have not been thoroughly
checked in the field by Westprint Maps.*

Historic cutting located south-east of Springsure (grid ref 24° 13' S, 148° 14'E)

Brampton
Vale   Samuel Hill

Mt Atherton

Byfield

Stockyard Point

Byfield National Park

Maryvale

Water Park Point
Corio Bay

C O R A L   S E A

Bungundarra   Farnborough

North Keppel Island

Barmoya
East

Yeppoon
Rosslyn Bay

**Keppel Bay Islands
National Park**

Mulambin
Kinka

Great Keppel Island

Cawarral

Emu Park

*Capricorn
Coast*

Broomfield Reef

Mount Chalmers

Wilson Island

**Mount Archer
National Park**

Keppel Sands

North West
Island

**Flat Top Range
Resources Reserve**

Hummocky Island

Heron Island

*Capricorn
Group*

Midgee

Cape Keppel

Cape Capricorn

Mast Head
Island

One Tree Island

**Curtis Island
Cons Park**

Port Alma

Curtis Island National Park

Polmaise Reef

Bajool

Monte Christo

Fitzroy Reef

Marmor

Curtis Island

Black Head

Llewellyn Reef

Raglan

**Bouldercombe
Gorge
Resources
Reserve**

Boult Reef

Ambrose

Proposed
LNG Plants

Southend

Hoskyn Islands

Mount Larcom

Facing Island

*Bunker
Group*   Fairfax Islands

Langmorn

Yarwun

Gladstone

Lady Musgrave Island

Tooloola

Boyne Island
Tannum Sands

Upper
Calliope

Wild Cattle Island NP

Richards Point

Eurimbula National Park

Mount Alma

Benaraby

*Hummock
Hill Island*

Bustard Point

Calliope

Middle Island

Turkey

Eurimbula Resources Reserve

Craiglands

**Dan Dan
National Park**

*Lake
Awoonga*

Bustard Bay

Lady Elliot Island

Bocoolima

Mt
Castletower

Seventeen Seventy

**Eurimbula
National Park**

Agnes Water

Diglum

Bororen

**Castle Tower
National Park**

**Deepwater
National Park**

Callide Coal Mine
and Power Station

**Wietalaba
National Park**

Miriam Vale

Amys Peak

Nagoorin

**Broadwater
Conservation Park**

Callide Dam

Ubobo

Taunton

Biloela

**Kroombit Tops
National Park**

Littlemore

Thangool

Kroombit

**Dawes
National
Park**

Lowmead

Blue Hills

Builyan

**Littabella
CP**

Scoria

**Dawes
National
Park**

**Bulburin
National
Park**

Rosedale

*Lake
Cania*

**Warro
National
Park**

**Littabella
NP**

**Cania Gorge
National Park**

Cania Dam

Kalpower

Yandaran

Moore Park Beach

Coominglah

*Lake
Monduran*

Meadowvale

Bundaberg Harbour

Burnett Heads

Caniaview Po

Bargara

*Great Sandy
Marine Park*

Bundaberg

Rooney Point

PARK AND RESERVE ABBREVIATIONS
CP   Conservation Park
CA   Conservation Area
Cons   Conservation
FFR   Flora & Fauna Reserve
NP   National Park
NCR   Nature Conservation Area
Res   Reserve
Reg   Regional
RP   Regional Park
WPA   Wilderness Protected Area

143° 10' 20' 30' 40' 89 50' 144° 10' 20' 30' 40' 50' 145° 10' 86 20'

Wirilla
Belfield
Coralton
Cressy
Glenreigh
Rockwood
Bannockburn
Wyora
Escombe
Malboona
Burnside
Catumnal
Birricannia
Rainsby
Olio
Luckham
Harwood
Thornville
Elis
Enryb Downs
Adirel Downs
Branga Downs
Burslem
Eastfield
Corinda
22°
Hexham
Belmont
Tarragona
Orielton
Maroomba
Hardington
Caledonia
Camara
Daintree
Bonnie Downs
Eskdale
Marengo
Forest Den National Park
Oondooroo
Rangelands
Aldingham
Jessamine Creek
Mahrigong
Levuka
Hillview
Lilarea
Carella
19
Lord
Bangall
Landsborough
Winton
5
Marita
Kensington
Tragowel
Llorac
Barcoorah
15
Western
Oondooroo Ck
Dillcar
Fairymead
Wando
Fisken Creek
Muttaburra
10
8
Bladensburg (Ranger)
Engine Hole
Skull Hole
Top Crossing
30
Drumlion
Chorregon
Culladar
Western Creek
15
Rosebery Downs
Wilton
Kingsborough
Cherhill
Logans Falls
Mount Landsborough
35
Cronulla
Rosehearty
Green Hills
21
Barataria
Melrose
Bude
Llewellyn
Maronthona
Tuaburra
Merino Downs
Stagmount
170
Rimbanda
21
Darr River Downs
18
Darriveen
Westbury
Glenample
Powella
Aramac
Ravenswood
Bladensburg National Park
Scenery ranging from flat topped mesas to tree lined valleys can be enjoyed by visitors to this park.
Denton
Hereward
17
Morella
Breedon
13
Talleyrand
Camoola Park
Camoola Park
Summer Hill
Shandon Vale
23°
Walters Knob 296 m
39
Evesham
Payne
39
Dalmore
Marchmont
Auteuil
Maranda
Euston
45
17
Neenah Park
Bexley
Rodney Downs
Daunton
Balonne
Mildura
Fermoy
36
Darr
38
Fairfield
Coreena
Mt McEvoy 384 m
34
43
Hulton
Moonya
Bessie Castle Georges Seat
35
Maneroo
43
Longway
Oakley
Norbert Park
The Ranch
Alroy
Cramsie
Camden Park
25
39
32
Longreach
Australian Stockman's Hall of Fame
27
Ilfracombe
Barcaldine
Vergemont
Strathmore
Wellshot
Black
Gin Ck
107
El Kantara
Campsie
44
31
Avoca
Tara
Spring Plains
Toobrack
Arrilalah Town Ruin
Arrilalah
Jindalee Transmitter
Fernhurst
Clovelly
46
Willowie
Barcaldine Downs
Tocal
Langdale
150
28
Evanston
Killara Park
Pegasus
Mount Arthur
Clover Hills
Tulga
45
Bandon Grove
Nerrena
Amor Downs
Dandaraga
Urambie
Withywine
52
20
30
Silverwood
Wellshot
Wynstay
107
Tocal Hotel
Bogewong
Westland
Latrobe
24°
Sunnyside
25
Boree Downs
Gaza
Honan Downs Stratavon
Mulgrave
Mellew
Mooney Valley
Hickleton
35
34
Avington
Mayfair
Tarcombe
Ban Ban
26
Wakefield
Portland Downs
Melrose
Mena Park
Noonbah
Lochern
30
42
Greenwoods
13
Isis Downs
Gowan Downs
Avondale
Tarves
Alice Downs
Thurles Park
Bimerah
Meroondah Downs
17
Arrowfield
37
Isisford
Springfield
Clarendon
Mt Warbreccan 265 m
Depot Glen
Flora Glen
10
Ventry
Ruthven
Thornleigh
Norwood
56
Stonehenge
29
Isisford
Russleigh
Bimerah
10
Rutland Park
47
Moorlands
Mt Doubletop
Barnsdale
Black Mtn
Wahroongah
Rivington
Selvister
Mt Affleck 305 m
Glenariff
John Egan Memorial Drive
Cecil Downs
Glen Afton
Mariana
Idalia Stud
Blackall
Carella
18
Swan Vale
66
Bothwell
Bilbah Downs
Benalla
Wooroolah
Athol
Braidwood
169
Needle Creek
Mt Misery 235 m
41
Mount Grey
Lowana
Alamay
Milton Park
22
14
Jundah
Yellow Mtn Opal Hill
Arno
45
Bellevue
Konupa
Ungo
Emmet
Mt Ellen 427 m
Morundah
Terrick Terrick Stud
Flemington
Mt Aaron
Mt Perrier 338 m
Mt Brookes 379 m
Albilbah
Mount Harden
Warringah
Homebush
Allambie
Carlow

143° 10' 20' 56 30' 40' 50' 144° 10' 20' 30' 40' 50' 145° 10' 20'

30' 40' 50' **146°** 10' 20' 30' 40' 50' **147°** 10' 20' 30' 40' 50' **148°**

Bowie
Moonoomoo
Carmichael
Ulcanbah
Doongmabulla
Fleetwood
Tomahawk
Jochmus
Lou Lou Park
Bimbah East
Hazelmere
Lake Dunn
Eastmere
Lockholm
Barbarah
The Lake
Maynard
Lestree Downs
Dunrobin
Clunie Vale
Clare
Hexham
Lennox Outstation
Fortuna
Albro
Degulla
Trelawney
Winhaven
Rangers Valley
Boongoondoo
Lennox
Forrester

Disney
Beenboona
Cassiopeia
Old Twin Hills
Twin Hills
Moray Downs
Avon Downs
Labona
Elgin Downs
Laurel Hills
Middle Creek
Willesby
Waminda
Bygana
Durdham
Frankfield
Epping Forest National Park
Epping Forest
Waltham
Beresford
Laglan
Kalang
Monteagle
Springvale
New Banchory
Narrien
Narrien Range National Park
Telerah
Old Banchory

Goonyella/Riverside Coal Mine
Wotonga
Nungaroo
Talki
Dooruna
Diamond Downs
Moranbah
Grosvenor Downs
Amaroo
Wentworth
Ellenor Downs
Mazeppa National Park
Solferino
Mount Wilkin
Boolaroo Downs
Barcombe
Kilcummin
Logan Downs
Undara Downs
Colin Downs
Cumberland Downs
Niagara
Merriwonga
Mooramin
Miclere
Peak Range National Park
Blair Athol
Birimgan
Clermont
Pioneer
Clydevale
Redrock
Mountain View
Sunny Park
Eton Vale
Retro
Nanya
Talarah
Capella
Valeria

Taree
Murrabit
Stirling
Texas
Blairgowrie
Rosedale
Garfield
Locharnoch
Hillalong
Hanley
Edwinstowe
Richmond Hills

Eulimbie
Kingston
Windaree
Burtle
Hobartville
Tressillian
Monkland
Cavendish
Gadwell
Eureka
Melton
Beaufort

Craven
Peak Vale
Florence Vale
Woodbrook
Rubyvale
Sapphire
Anakie

Bogantungan historic site

Capricorn Highway
Lochinvar
Alice
Lochnagar
Jericho
Beta
Alpha
Wololla
Burgoyne
Summerdell
Armagh
Allanard
Mafeking
Blendon
Rosemount
Delta South
Stratford
Mendip Hills
Rostrevor
Helen Vale
Tumbar

The Grove
Capricorn Highway
Bogantungan

Brookwood
Chesalon
Dahlonega
Portwine
Kulumur
Lochington
Fairbairn Dam
Lake Maraboon
Craigmore

Alpha Creek
Kurrajong
Narounyah
Cloyne
Rivington
Sedgeford
Avoca

Boorara
Yalleroi
Sydenham
Evora
Tilbury
Henley Park
Navena
Champion
Unavale
Vinetree Downs
East Lynne
Harden Park
Allandale
Erne
Thrungli

Durrandella
Avonmore
Glen Avon
Joe Joe
Alpha
Cheshire
Skye
Shady Downs
Green Hills

Rooken Glen
Glenlee
Connemarra
Millthorpe
Snake Range National Park
Vandyke
Dunstable
Echo Hills
Shadeville
Nandowrie
Riverside
Coranderrk
Nalcoombie
Heathwood
Hillview
Wealwandangie
Spring Creek

Minerva Hills National Park

Mantuan Downs
Castlevale
Petrona
Buckland Plains
Kia-Ora
Metro
Tanderra
Goathland
Kareela

Forest Park
Northampton Downs
Colart
Effra
Macfarlane Downs
Ravensbourne
Innis Downs
Bexhill
Tralee
Windeyer
Gartmore
Killarney Park
Kelpum
Highlands
Mount Pleasant
Cungelella
Wharton Creek
Salvator Rosa Section
Ka Ka Mundi Section
Carnarvon National Park
Mt Cheops
Mt Lane
Spyglass Peak
Mt Salvator
Mount Playfair
Mt Ka Ka Mundi
Carnarvon
Round Mtn

30' 40' 50' **146°** 10' 20' 30' 40' 50' **147°** 10' 20' 30' 40' 50' **148°**

NORTHERN TERRITORY
QUEENSLAND

91
88

95

Moontah Ck
Binyeah Outstation
Serpentine Crossing
RIVER
25
17
31
Carandotta
The Steamboat 302 m
MANGANESE RIDGE
Sulleman Ck
Rufus Ck
STANDISH
The Monument
6
39
Big Red Bluff
Phosphate Hill Mine
Signal Hill
B&W Camp 93
Swift Hills
Chatsworth
8

Brooks Lagoon
32
Duck Creek
Middle Ck
17
Waukaka Waterhole
Split Ck
Four Mile Ck
Romans Ck
Quita Ck
St Ck
Buckingham Downs
Digby Peaks
36
Mort River
55
Kolar Ck
Dot Creek

Manners Creek
Tobermorey
11
DONOHUE
Pituri Ck
Linda Downs
15 Mile Ck
17 Mile Ck
41
Smoky Creek
Mindyalla Creek
DE LITTLE RANGE
147
41
B&W Camp 92
Windsor Park
31
Corrie Downs
Two Rivers
Eastern Ck

TOKO RANGE
HIGHWAY
82
Pituri Creek
Kelly Ck
Blue Mtn 211 m
Roxborough Downs
27
Georgina River Crossing
This crossing on the Donohue Highway was very difficult during the wet. A bridge built in the early 1990s improved access along the highway. Pituri Creek and Cottonbush Creek can also be very difficult when wet. www.racq.com.au Ph 1300 130 595
Longsight Peak
Alderley
Bengacca Ck
Gidya Ck
65
Limestone Ck
Peak Ck
33
Burke Ck
B&W Camp 91
Mt Unbunmaroo 387 m
BOULIA TO BIRDSVILLE
For further information between Boulia and Birdsville, see the PLENTY HIGHWAY map from Westprint Maps
63

Donohue Highway
The Donohue Highway is named after G J (Cliff) Donohue MBE in recognition of outstanding service to the community and Shire of Boulia.

256
55
39
Lake Wonditti
Wheelaman Creek
10 Mile Ck
Basin Waterhole
9
Glenormiston
Lake Idamea
Lower Lake
44
DONOHUE
Georgina
Little Ck
Cottonbush Ck
Stockport
Maryvale
83
8
Badalia
Boulia
A
HIGHWAY
Macsland
51
Kennedy Ck

Pituri Creek
Pituri Creek is crossed at one of its narrowest points which may be difficult when wet. It is named after the pituri bush which provides the basis for a mild narcotic used by Aborigines. The maze of channels and lignum bushes spreading out on either side is typical Queensland channel country.

Glenormiston
This large station fronts the Georgina River and the homestead is near a permanent waterhole once regularly used by drovers. The station has huge areas of naturally irrigated channel country along Pituri Creek and the Georgina River.

Herbert Downs
4
27
Dog Fence
Wirrilyerna
Goodwood
40
Montagu Downs
Waddi Trees
B&W Camp 89
Mudgeacca
Paton
Westward Ho
Gas Pipeline
Bore
39
RIVER
Parapituri Waterhole

Cravens Peak Reserve
(Bush Heritage Australia)

Twin Hills 244 m
Mulligan River
Cravens Peak
Lake Namabooka
Mt Whelan
Mt La Touche 234 m
Bucket Ck
Sugarloaf Hill 186 m
Mt Tobin 231 m
Marion Downs
The first station in the sandhill country south of Boulia was named by ER Edkins after his wife, Marion.
Marion Downs
Mailman Sign
Tropic of Capricorn (Lat 23)
62
Road (The Channel Country Byway)
83
Burke Ck
41
B&W Camp 88
Mile Ck
Five Ck
King Ck
Canary
61
Lorna Downs
Creek

Bush Heritage Australia
A national, independent non-profit organisation focused on the long term protection of Australia's unique and abundant bio-diversity. They achieve this by acquiring and managing land, water and wildlife of outstanding conservation value.

Carlo
Wandera Waterhole
Barrington Peak 125 m
MARION DOWNS
Mailman Sign
Eddie Miller was the last of the Boulia-Bedourie mailmen whose job it was, come hell or high water, to get the mail through. This crossing of the Georgina Channels was particularly difficult during the wet.
Hilary Ck
Hilary Floodplain
Developmental
58
Twelve Mile Mtn 161 m
53
Gidyea Ck
Mitchell Grass Plains

Lake Wongitta
Sylvester Ck
The Sisters 213 m
The Knob
Bellevue Ck
Bellevue Floodplain
190
Diamantina Shire Boundary
B&W Camp 85
B&W Camp 86
Bindy Ck
Grasstree Ck
Grassy Waterhole
Coorabulka

Ethabuka Reserve
(Bush Heritage Australia)

Wongitta Waterhole
Pulchera Lake
Ethabuka
30
Grave
Reynold's Grave
In memory of Kathleen Reynolds (Tootles) Accidentally drowned 21st May 1918 Aged 13 years RIP
Humpy Ck
Cooramarina Ck
Breadalbane
Grave
4 Mile Waterhole
Cuckoo Waterhole
B&W Camp 84
GEORGINA
Mulya Ck
Tent Hill
No 4 Bore
COORABULKA

Montara Waterhole
Pulchera Waterhole
Palilou Ck
40
COORABULKA
Diamantina
RIVER
Mitchell Grass Plains
Terriboah Ck
71
No 5 Bore

Tribilkie Waterhole
Sandringham
45
4 Mile Creek Rest Area
Note: Rest area and memorial are on a side track east of the main road
63
83
Eyre
Mt Woneeala 133 m
Cootah Ck

SANDRINGHAM
Tracks in this area are not for tourist use
13
6
7
No 10 Bore
Warra Ck
Curica Ck

(Inset map of Australia showing WA, NT, SA, QLD, NSW, VIC, TAS)

NORTH
10km 0 10 20 30 40km
© Copyright Westprint Maps Pty Ltd 2022

KAMARAN DOWNS
Kamaran Downs
Mumbleberry Lake
Lake Phillipi (Lake Wickamunna)
Bedourie
22
Afghan Grave
Cluny 24
King Ck
Toilet, table & dump point
B&W Camp 82
28
No 3 Bore
Griffiths Tank Corner
22
B&W Camp 83

Public Roads
The Diamantina Shire has almost 1800 km of roads to serve a population of only 350 people.

Mumbleberry Waterhole
Black Hill
King Creek Crossing
Nine Mile Plain
Diamantina
137
Mt Cuttiguree 160 m
The Sugarloaf
69

Permission may be required to cross the Simpson Desert National Park and Adria Downs Station.

Madigan Camp 17
Lake Torquinie
GLENGYLE
Will Hutchison
A plaque erected by the Coober Pedy Historical Society commemorates the life of the founder of this opal mining town. Will drowned nearby in the Georgina River on 9 July 1920.
Glengyle
53
Monument to W.J.S. Hutchison
Lake Machattie
CLUNY
CHANNEL
B&W Camp 81
B&W Camp 80
89
Gerara Waterhole
Devel Ck

Mudloo Well
Titchery Waterhole
Tomydonka Waterhole
Eyre Ck

138° 10' 20' 58 30' 40' 50' 139° 10' 20' 30' 40' 50' 140° 10' 20'

Ranges Valley
Wongan
164
Brooklyn
Belfield
Wirilla
Cannington Mine
Cannington
Dagworth
Werna
Cooinda
Ayrshire Downs
Toolebuc
Cathedral Hill
Amelia Downs
Weston
Strathfillan
Camara
The Brothers
Robins
Lovelle Downs
Leeson
Carella
Woodstock
166
Kennedy
Narangie
Pathungra
Llanrheidol
Archervale
John Hills
Elderslie
Developmental
Road
Lorrett Downs
Lookout
Dunbar Ck
Western
Winton
St Lucia
Middleton
Kalkadoon
Bladensburg
Warenda
Gnalta
Mackunda Downs
Jarvisfield
River
Engine Hole
Skull Hole
This road is often impassable after wet weather
Bladensburg National Park
Top Crossing
Logans Falls
Outback Highway
Named in 1998, this road is planned to be a major link between Kalgoorlie and Winton via Alice Springs.
Tulmur
Carisbrooke Station stay
Lilleyvale Rest Area
Mt Skipper
Lilleyvale
Dermod WH
Whyralla
Carisbrooke Station
Lyndon B Johnson was aboard a US Flying Fortress forced down near here in 1942.
Warnambool Downs
Cawnpore Lookout
Chiltern Hills
Pollygammon
Lucknow
Min Min Hotel
Mt Williams 257 m
Hamilton Hotel
Developmental
Road
198
Cawnpore Lookout
Offers views of unique mesa formations found only in Australia and South America
Mackunda
Cork
Wantalanya
Only the fireplace remains today.
Slashers Creek
Cambeela
Munduran
Narcissus
Mueller's Range
Walters Knob 296 m
Mitchell Grass
Franklin
Old Cork
Historic homestead
Arthurs Mtn
Fermoy
Plains
Verdun Valley
Lark Quarry Cons Park
Dinosaur footprints
Warra Hill 199 m
WARNING
All minor unsealed roads in this area are impassable when wet
Diamantina Stock Route
A stock route follows the Diamantina River south-west to Birdsville where it joins the Birdsville Track and finally the railway at Marree
Mt Holberton 257 m
Warra
McBride
Eildon Park
Not suitable for camping
188
Elizabeth Springs Conservation Park
Mt Macartney 146 m
Canis Tank
Opalton
Opalton
Some commercial mining still exists. A fossicking area is available for visitors.
Elizabeth Springs
Brighton Downs
Kangaroo Mtns
Elvo
SPRINGVALE
Diamantina National Park
Mt Edward Graves 168 m
Mayneside
Mt Vergemont 318 m
Springvale
Goyder Range
Mayne Junction Hotel
Maynes Peak 167 m
Mayneside
Vergemont
DAVENPORT DOWNS
Leave gates as found
Gum Hole
Hunters Gorge
Janets Leap
Private road
Private road
Mt Hunter 121 m
Point Remarkable
Mount Windsor
Gumhole Yards
Diamantina Gates
Diamantina Lakes
Ranger
Diamantina Floods
Floods attract birds and wildlife to waterholes along the Diamantina River. Bush flies and sand flies may also appear at this time.
Goneaway National Park
(No public access)
Mungeroo Knobs 121 m
Ruins
Yards
Lake Constance
Diamantina National Park
MT WINDSOR
Tonkoro
Diamantina National Park
The Bluff
Commissioner Mtn 317 m
Westerton
Moon Rocks
Astrebla Downs National Park
(No public access)
Copra Waterhole
Coota Waterhole
Davenport Downs
Suspension Bridges
Once common along these large rivers, they were made from twisted wire, rope and wooden slats and could carry light foot traffic. One built at Diamantina Lakes in 1898 cost £20 ($50). A very short section remains today but virtually nothing remains of one built at Davenport Downs.
Onoto
Mt Fairview 245 m
Mt Flat Top
Mt Felix 355 m
Thurles Park
Connemara
This crossing impassable when river in flood
KURRAN
Warbreccan
Mt Doubletop
20 Mile Yards
158
Corrikie
Mt Affleck 305 m
Peleenah Waterhole
The Three Brothers Mt
Mt Dot
DAVENPORT DOWNS
Grahgor Downs
Stock Routes
The Diamantina Shire is covered by a vast network of stock routes. The two shown illustrate the importance of major rivers to the droving industry. This situation changed dramatically with the introduction of road trains in the 1960s.
Mt Square Top
HARDINGS RANGES
Bull Waterhole
COUNTRY
Mitchell Grass
Plains
18 Mile Tank
Diamantina Shire Boundary
Lily Lagoon
Flodden Hills
Trewalla
Juno
Mt Barri
The Nob
Lochiel
Travelling Stock
Stock for market often travelled east from Davenport Downs via Palparara and Windorah to the rail-head at Quilpie.
Cemetery
Monkira
WARNING: All minor unsealed roads in this area are impassable after wet weather
Palparara
Lina Hill
Lina Glen
Braidwood

133° 10' 20' 93 30' 40' 50' 134° 10' 20' 30' 40' 50' 90 135° 10' 20'

ANNINGIE

Anningie

Johns Range

43

Camel Soak Bore

Mt Judith
705 m

Central Mt Stuart
846 m

Teamster Memorial

44

89

STIRLING

ALAYAWARRA
ABORIGINAL LAND
TRUST

28

floodout

No 8
Bore

18

Corella Bore

18

Urapuntja

Atheleye

31

Irultja

Derry
Downs

Mt Chisholme
723 m

Central Mt Stuart
Historical Reserve

22°

Western

Anningie Ck

Hanson

15

AHAKEYE ABORIGINAL
LAND TRUST

MOUNT SKINNER

17

14

Arlparra Store

ANGARAPA
ABORIGINAL LAND
TRUST

35

Nturiya
(Ti Tree)

Ti Tree

15

Sandover Highway
The Sandover Highway is a graded, earth
road linking station properties between the Plenty
Highway and Lake Nash on the Queensland border.
It was developed as a 'beef road' along with the
Tanami Road and Plenty Highway. Other roads link
with Camooweal and Mt Isa. The Sandover Highway is
a dry-weather-only road usually suited to conventional
vehicles with good ground clearance.

Sandover

MACDONALD
DOWNS

MacDonald
Downs

Old MacDonald
Downs

42

Mt Ultim
612 m

Saltbush Creek

Mt Solitary
679 m

50

26

Mount Skinner

Mt Skinner
673 m

Utopia Community

Bundey

Tower Rock
554 m

Mac & Rose
Chalmers CR

Pmara Jutunta

Tea Tree Farm

Gorries Bore

Woolla
Downs

180

Ledan Peak
558 m

DELMORE
DOWNS

Delmore Downs

Mount Swan

Boxhole
Meteorite
Crater

22

Dneiper

7

PINE HILL

Pine Hill

43

ATARTINGA

Atartinga

5

Waite River

Angula

Delny

DELNY

Mt Swan

30

DNEIPER

Entire Point
516 m

Woodforde

32

Territory
Grape Farm

SANDOVER

76

ALCOOTA

Mueller

Bundey

River

Mt Mary
909 m

Prowse Gap
Rest Area
(toilets)

Prowse Gap

Anna's Reservoir
Conservation
Reserve

17

125

STUART

AILERON

BUSHY
PARK

PLENTY HIGHWAY
For further information between Alice
Springs and Mount Isa, see the PLENTY
and SANDOVER HIGHWAYS map
from Westprint Maps

Engenala

The Twins
628 m

Alcoota

Table Hill
613 m

Conical Hill
588 m

Plenty

Creek

River

25

12

Aileron Roadhouse

13

Glen Maggie (Historic ruin)

Ryan Well
Historical
Reserve

Hann Range

Mt Ewart
804 m

Native Gap
Conservation
Reserve

52

14

Bushy Park

MT RIDDOCK

Harts Range
Police Station

22

281

Atitjera

25

12

Mount
Eaglebeak

Reaphook
Hills

Amadeus Basin to Darwin Gas Pipeline (underground)

Amadeus Basin to Darwin Railway

P

P

Conners Well

Conners Well

PLENTY

18

HIGHWAY

32

Gemtree

Mud Tank

23

Harts Range
Fossicking Area

Zircon Field
Fossicking Area

6

Mount Riddock

42

Mt Riddoch
1101 m

Mt Brassey
1203 m

Fossicking Area

HARTS

RA

Ambulbinya Peak
859 m

Huckitta

Injulkama

AMBURLA

Mt Chapple
Bore

25

188

Limestone
Bore

27

19

Mt Strangways
1028 m

Mt Pfitzner
1052 m

43

Alatyeye

Station Well
Fossicking Area

56

This track not
recommended
for trailers

AMBALINDUM

Mt Emma
809 m

Mt Karina
768 m

Stanovos

MPERINGE-ARNAPIPE
ABORIGINAL LAND

YAMBAH

P

Warburton Memorial

Yambah

Burt Ck

Pinnacles
Bore

Narbib Range

31

22

Cattlewater

Harts Range
Fossicking Area

Cattlewater Pass

8

Claraville

Mt Ruby
853 m

Mt Ruby

15

TANAMI

Milton
Park

Amburla

HAMILTON
DOWNS

BURT PLAIN

Harry Ck

McGrath Ck

17

22

Black Tank

MPERINGE-ARNAPIPE
ABORIGINAL LAND

THE
GARDEN

The Garden

Winnecke
Gold Mine

26

Hale

8

Ambalindum

12

Star Ck

11

Atnarpa RA

Atnarpa

Glen Annie Gorge
Ruby Gap

Ruby Gap
Nature Park

Charlie Creek

23

ROAD

25

Cadney
Bore

Kunoth
Bore

5

Everard

Sixteen Mile Ck

30

68

BOND
SPRINGS

87

Tropic of Capricorn marker
(Lat 23)

Radio
receiving
station

Trephina Gorge
Nature Park

Trephina
Gorge

John Hayes
Rockhole

Old Arltunga Hotel

Arltunga
Historical Reserve

Fossicking Area

32
(2 hrs)

Aremera

Illogwa

Hamilton
Downs

MACDONNELL

23

Cadney Bore

24

Monument

Mt Everard
949 m

Bond Springs

RANGES

19

Todd

5

Ross

33

Atnarpa Ra

Old Telegraph Station

LOVES CREEK

Mt Giles
1389 m

West MacDonnell
National Park

Hamilton Downs
Youth Camp

Brinkley Bluff
1209 m

Simpsons
Gap

Standley
Chasm

Flynn's
Memorial

ALICE SPRINGS

A

Emily & Jessie Gaps
Nature Park

Corroboree
Rock CR

8

Hwy

N'dhala Gorge
Nature Park

14

FERGUSSON RANGE

Pulya

Cleary

Ochre
Pits

Serpentine Chalet (ruin)

Hugh Gorge

23

Birthday WH

Honeymoon Gap

Ross River
Resort

8

8

Serpentine
Gorge

23

Namatjira

42

2

Iwupataka

40

6

Temple
Bar

Kuyunba
CR

6

Pine Gap
(No access)

Amoonguna

31

27

15

Giles

20

Allua
Well

27

Ringwood

Mt Kathleen
387 m

Limbla

Ellery Creek Big Hole

Drive

Todd

RINGWOOD

ROULPMAULPMA

Drive

5

Owen Springs
Ranger

Owen Springs

48

21

UNDOOLYA

Todd River

51

Casey
Bore

URUNA

Larapinta

18

42

OWEN
SPRINGS

Old Owen Springs
Homestead

Ewaninga
Fettlers Cottage

Ooraminna

Ewaninga Rock
Carvings Cons Res

SANTA TERESA
ABORIGINAL

LAND TRUST

TODD RIVER

Numery

11

4

12

18

Haunted Tree
Bore

Lawrence
Gorge

Waterhouse Range

21

HIGHWAY

OLD

GHAN

83

Phillipson
Pound

No permits are required
to travel along the Old
Andado Track.

COLLINS RA

24°

Intjarrtnama

Wallace Rock
Station

Redbank
Waterhole

Mt Polhill
Rest Area

87

Polhill (ruin)

Mt Ooraminna
652 m

Ltyentye Apurte
(Santa Teresa)

Mt Pellimore
446 m

Old

Todd River
Downs

Boggy Hole

25

STUART

12

Hugh River

RAILWAY

DEEP
WELL

18

Allambi

Andado

AROOKARA RA

ORANGE CREEK

22

Rainbow Valley
Cons Reserve

36

Ooraminna (ruin)

Deep Well

TRAIN HILLS

RODINGA RA

330

Stuarts Well

15

199

Orange Creek

Rainbow Valley

Canonball Run
Memorial

35

Oak
Valley

Stock
Route

11

Deep Well (private)

ALLAMBI

Old

Finke River
Rest Area

29

CHANDLERS RA

34

Hugh River

19

Rodinga (ruin)

Mt Rodinga
495 m

No permits are required
to travel along the Old
Andado Track.

Henbury
Meteorites
CR

Henbury

FINKE

RIVER

12

HENBURY

Maryvale

14

Titjikala

ANDADO

Old Andado Track

48

37

Mt Breaden
583 m

18

MARYVALE

Mt Charlotte
511 m

Percy Hill

43

Charlotte Ra

228

HORSESHOE

BEND

15

Palmer

The Twins

The Sisters

P

Palmer Valley

18

44

Highway Bore

133° 10' 20' 60 30' 40' 50' 134° 10' 20' 30' 40' 50' 135° 10' 20'

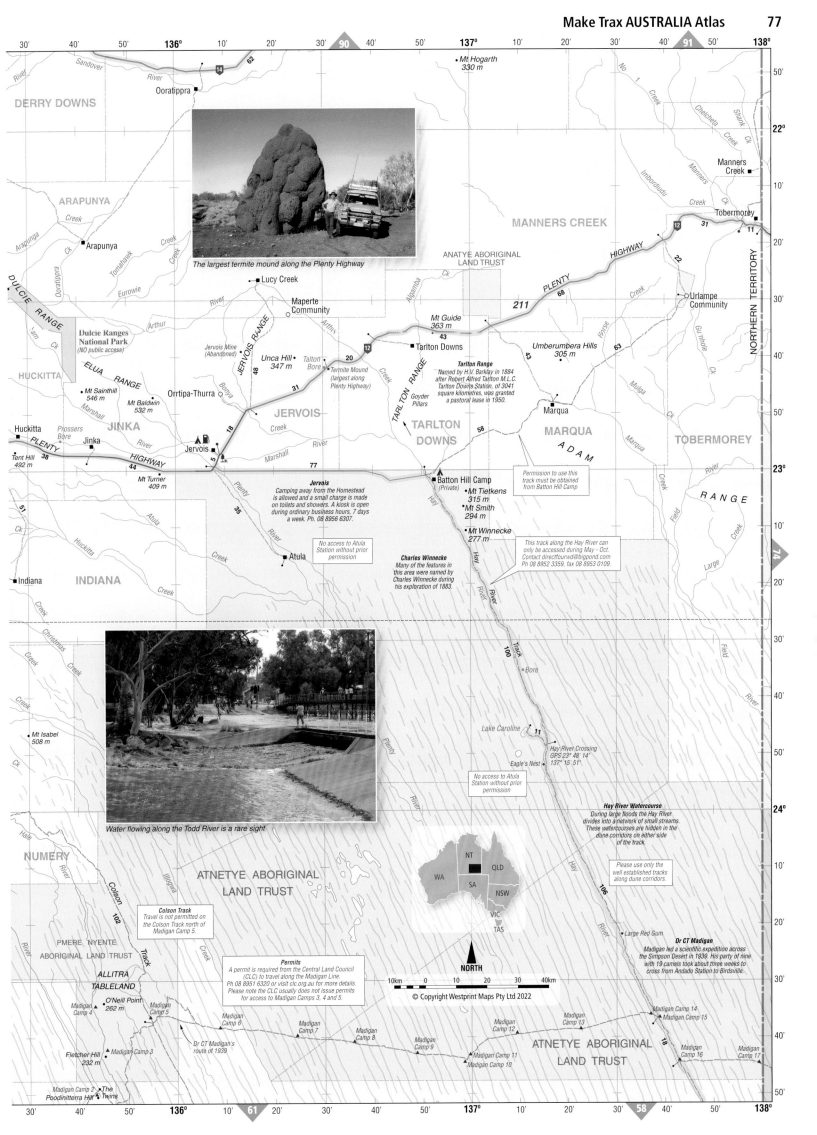

The largest termite mound along the Plenty Highway

Water flowing along the Todd River is a rare sight

DERRY DOWNS

Ooratippra

• Mt Hogarth
330 m

Manners Creek

ARAPUNYA

Arapunya

MANNERS CREEK

Tobermorey

DULCIE RANGE

Dulcie Ranges
National Park
(NO public access)

ANATYE ABORIGINAL LAND TRUST

Lucy Creek

Maperte Community

Urlampe Community

PLENTY   HIGHWAY

211   68

HUCKITTA

Jervois Mine
(Abandoned)

Mt Sainthill
546 m

Mt Baldwin
532 m

Orrtipa-Thurra

Unca Hill
347 m

Talton Bore

Termite Mound
(largest along
Plenty Highway)

Goyder Pillars

Mt Guide
363 m

43

Tarlton Downs

Umberumbera Hills
305 m   63

Tarlton Range
Named by H.V. Barklay in 1884
after Robert Alfred Tarlton M.L.C.
Tarlton Downs Station, of 3041
square kilometres, was granted
a pastoral lease in 1950.

Marqua

JERVOIS

JINKA

Huckitta

Prossers Bore

Jinka

Tent Hill
492 m

PLENTY   38

HIGHWAY   44

Mt Turner
409 m

Jervois

TARLTON DOWNS

58

MARQUA

ADAM

TOBERMOREY

RANGE

Jervois
Camping away from the Homestead
is allowed and a small charge is made
on toilets and showers. A kiosk is open
during ordinary business hours, 7 days
a week. Ph. 08 8956 6307.

Batton Hill Camp
(Private)

• Mt Tietkens
315 m

• Mt Smith
294 m

• Mt Winnecke
277 m

Permission to use this
track must be obtained
from Batton Hill Camp

No access to Atula
Station without prior
permission

Atula

Charles Winnecke
Many of the features in
this area were named by
Charles Winnecke during
his exploration of 1883.

This track along the Hay River can
only be accessed during May - Oct.
Contact directfourwd@bigpond.com
Ph 08 8952 3359, fax 08 8953 0109.

Indiana

INDIANA

Mt Isabel
508 m

Track   100

• Bore

Lake Caroline   11

Hay River Crossing
GPS 23° 48' 14"
137° 15' 51"

Eagle's Nest

No access to Atula
Station without prior
permission

Hay River Watercourse
During large floods the Hay River
divides into a network of small streams.
These watercourses are hidden in the
dune corridors on either side
of the track.

NUMERY

ATNETYE ABORIGINAL LAND TRUST

Please use only the
well established tracks
along dune corridors.

Colson Track
Travel is not permitted on
the Colson Track north of
Madigan Camp 5.

PMERE NYENTE ABORIGINAL LAND TRUST

ALLITRA TABLELAND

O'Neill Point
262 m

Madigan Camp 4

Madigan Camp 5

Madigan Camp 6

Madigan Camp 7

Madigan Camp 8

Madigan Camp 9

Madigan Camp 12

Madigan Camp 13

Large Red Gum

Dr CT Madigan
Madigan led a scientific expedition across
the Simpson Desert in 1939. His party of nine
with 19 camels took about three weeks to
cross from Andado Station to Birdsville.

Madigan Camp 14

Madigan Camp 15

Permits
A permit is required from the Central Land Council
(CLC) to travel along the Madigan Line.
Ph 08 8951 6320 or visit clc.org.au for more details.
Please note the CLC usually does not issue permits
for access to Madigan Camps 3, 4 and 5.

Dr CT Madigan's
route of 1939

Fletcher Hill
232 m

Madigan Camp 3

Madigan Camp 2

The Poodinitterra Hill

The Twins

Madigan Camp 11

Madigan Camp 10

ATNETYE ABORIGINAL LAND TRUST

Madigan Camp 16

Madigan Camp 17

NORTH

10km   0   10   20   30   40km

© Copyright Westprint Maps Pty Ltd 2022

NORTHERN TERRITORY

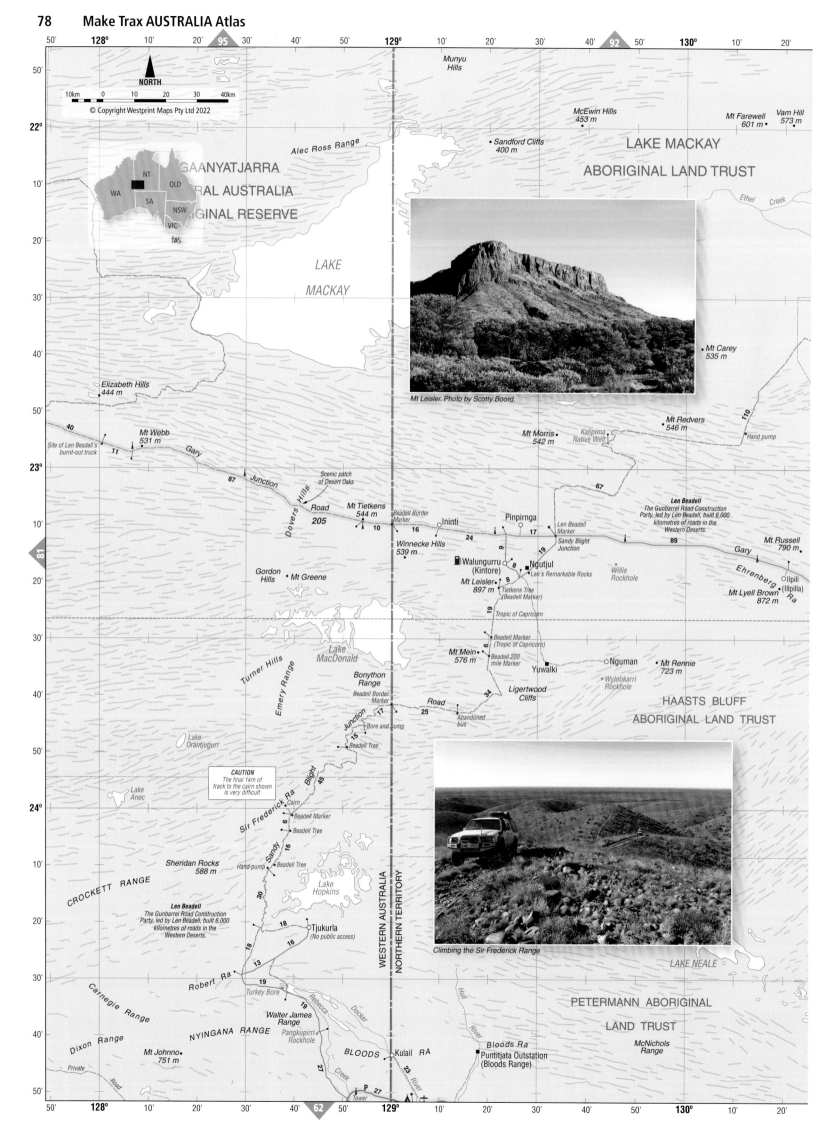

NORTH

10km 0 10 20 30 40km

© Copyright Westprint Maps Pty Ltd 2022

50' **128°** **10'** **20'** 95 **30'** **40'** **50'** **129°** **10'** **20'** **30'** **40'** 92 **50'** **130°** **10'** **20'**

22°

GAANYATJARRA
TRAL AUSTRALIA
RIGINAL RESERVE

Alec Ross Range

Munyu Hills

McEwin Hills 453 m

Mt Farewell 601 m

Vam Hill 573 m

LAKE MACKAY
ABORIGINAL LAND TRUST

Sandford Cliffs 400 m

Ethel Creek

LAKE MACKAY

Mt Leisler. Photo by Scotty Boord.

Mt Carey 535 m

23°

Elizabeth Hills 444 m

Site of Len Beadell's burnt-out truck

40

11

Mt Webb 531 m

Gary

87 *Junction*

Road 205

Dovers Hills

Scenic patch of Desert Oaks

Mt Tietkens 544 m

10

Mt Redvers 546 m

110

Hand pump

Mt Morris 542 m

Kalipima Native Well

Beadell Border Marker

16 *Ininti*

24

9

Pinpirnga

17

Len Beadell Marker

Len Beadell
The Gunbarrel Road Construction Party, led by Len Beadell, built 6,000 kilometres of roads in the Western Deserts.

67

89

Gary

Mt Russell 790 m

Winnecke Hills 539 m

Walungurru (Kintore)

8

19

Sandy Blight Junction

Ehrenberg

Ra

Ilpili (Illpilla)

Gordon Hills

Mt Greene

Ngutjul
Len's Remarkable Rocks

Willie Rockhole

Mt Leisler 897 m

Tietkens Tree (Beadell Marker)

8

Mt Lyell Brown 872 m

19

Tropic of Capricorn

Lake MacDonald

19

Turner Hills

Emery Range

Bonython Range

Beadell Border Marker

17

25 *Road*

Abandoned bus

6

Beadell Marker (Tropic of Capricorn)

Mt Mein 576 m

Beadell 200 mile Marker

Nguman

Mt Rennie 723 m

Yuwalki

Wylookarri Rockhole

Ligertwood Cliffs

HAASTS BLUFF
ABORIGINAL LAND TRUST

34

Junction

15

Bore and pump

Beadell Tree

Lake Orantjugurr

24°

Lake Anec

CAUTION
The final 1km of track to the cairn shown is very difficult

Blight

45

Sir Frederick Ra

Cairn

6 *Beadell Marker*

Beadell Tree

Climbing the Sir Frederick Range

LAKE NEALE

Sandy

16

Sheridan Rocks 588 m

Hand pump

Beadell Tree

Lake Hopkins

CROCKETT RANGE

Len Beadell
The Gunbarrel Road Construction Party, led by Len Beadell, built 6,000 kilometres of roads in the Western Deserts.

30

18

18

16

Tjukurla
(No public access)

PETERMANN ABORIGINAL

LAND TRUST

Carnegie Range

13

Robert Ra

19

Turkey Bore

19

Rebecca

Walter James Range

Pangkupirri Rockhole

NYINGANA RANGE

Docker

Hull River

Bloods Ra

Puntitjata Outstation (Bloods Range)

McNichols Range

Dixon Range

Mt Johnno 751 m

Private

Road

27

Creek

BLOODS

Kulail RA

23

27 P
Tower

WESTERN AUSTRALIA

NORTHERN TERRITORY

50' **128°** **10'** **20'** **30'** **40'** 62 **50'** **129°** **10'** **20'** **30'** **40'** **50'** **130°** **10'** **20'**

81

62

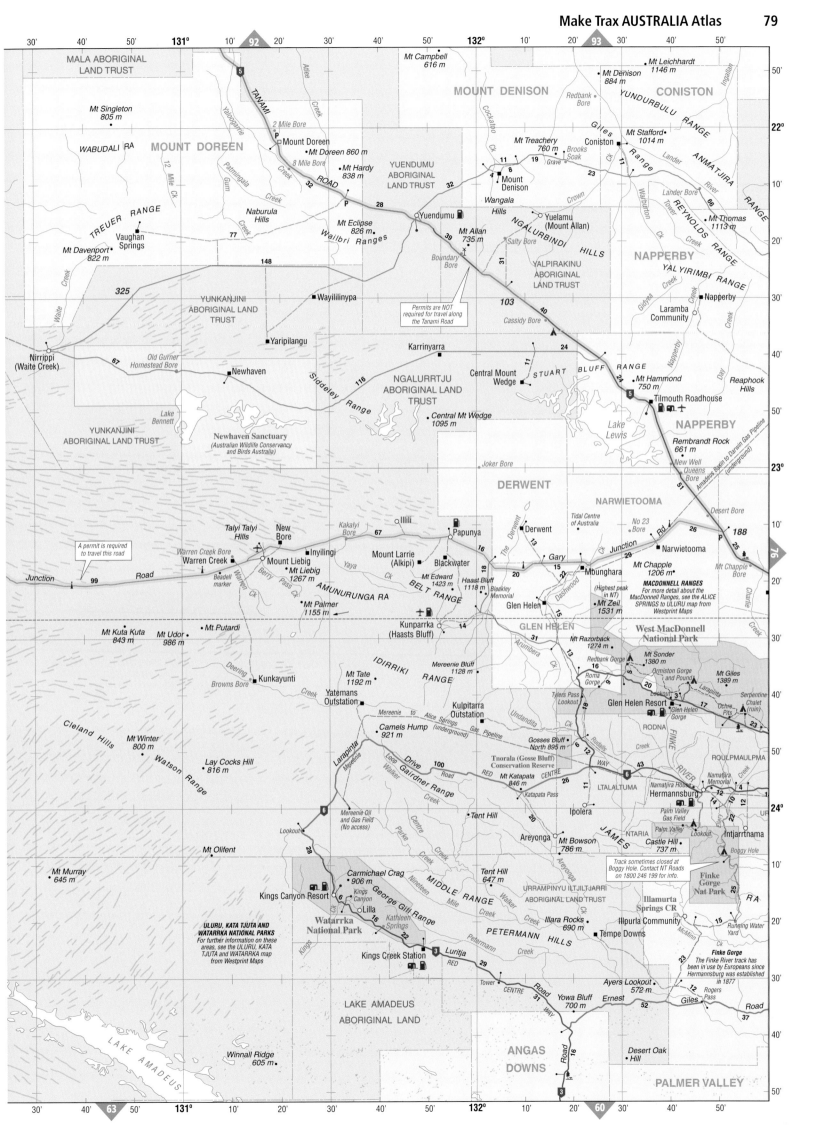

This track to Eighty Mile Beach is in poor condition. It is approximately 500 km to the Great Northern Highway.

Lake Dora viewpoint

Punmu

Lake Dora

(Approximate position)

28

36

35

180 (Kidson

Wapet)

101

Road

Track)

This track is in good condition (to Marble Bar)

8   Rocky outcrops

97

123°   124°   125°

Heavy corrugations along this section

Ph 08 9176 9040

Kunawaritji   19

Telephone

Rudall River National Park

Lake Auld

Lake Blanche

Nangabbittajarra Native Well

Route

Well 30 (Dunda Jinnda)

6   12

Mujingerra Spring

4

Nurgurga Native Well (Difficult to locate)

Well 31

29

162

Well 33 (Gunowaggi)

Mallowa Native Well

Well 32

17

10

129

Bungabinni Native Well (restored)

Well 36 (Wanda)   12

Well 35 (Minjoo)   4   19   10   11   22

Ural Native Well

5   19   Kidson Bluff   9

Callowa   Track   32

Jenkins   Track   54   Gary Junction

Len Beadell Marker

Good travelling between Wells 27 and 30

Well 29   6

31

Well 28

27   6   19

6   King Hill

Thring Rock 318 m

Kidson   55

31   NM F 236 376 m

Kidson Airstrip

Spot Junction

23

High sandhills on this section of track should be easily crossed if tyre pressures are lowered to about 20psi

Lake George

Stock   15

Well 27   15

15   Helen Hill 352 m

Slate Range

Lake Winifred

CANNING STOCK ROUTE
For further information between Wiluna and Halls Gap, see the CANNING STOCK ROUTE map from Westprint Maps

Separation Well

No public access to Separation Well.

Calvert Expedition
Charles Wells and George Jones explored a western route from Separation Well, intending to meet the main party at Joanna Spring.

Len Beadell
The Gunbarrel Road Construction Party, led by Len Beadell, built 6,000 kilometres of roads in the Western Deserts.

Wildlife Well

Veevers Meteorite Crater

28

NM F 239 362 m

Wau Wau Well

16

Canning

15

Well 26 (Tiwa Well) Water available

27

Fuel dump by Dunning Fuel, Newman ph 08 9175 0355

Well 25

21

126

Harbutt Ra

61   23°

Water & toilet available Georgia Bore

Willjabu Track (no access)

Well 22

40

Well 21

9   22   Well 23   14   3

Well 24 (Curara Soaks)

Severe corrugations along this section to Georgia Bore

Nimberra Well

Cronin Hills

Talawana

85   Track

GIBSON DESERT

Cleared Line   HWH   Cleared

Gary

28

13   Rocky outcrops and caves

15   Marker

Calvert Expedition
Larry Wells returned from Midway Well to Harry Johnston Water where he re-provisioned. He then returned to Midway Well and continued north.

Midway Well   6

Aboriginal outstation only.

Tropic of Capricorn 23°26'30"

Surprise Well

Runton Ra

Lake Disappointment

Glynde Hill

Lady Victoria Hills

72

Extensive sand plain - poor camping

46

Tropic of Capricorn 23°26'30"

Len Beadell marker

Windy Corner

359   42

66

Traeger Hills

Woolnough Hills

26   Eagle

NMF 246

49

The Eagle and Gary Highways south of this point are in good condition (at Aug 2000) due to oil exploration maintenance in the mid 1990's

Desert Discovery Camp 1998

67   Highway

10

Lake Cohen

14

NMF 250

5

Blazed tree ?

Lake Hancock

25   McPhersons Pillar

Mulgan Rockhole

A water pump along the Canning Stock Route

NT   QLD
WA   SA   NSW
VIC
TAS

NORTH

10km   0   10   20   30   40km

© Copyright Westprint Maps Pty Ltd 2022

Eagle   Highway

Gary   Highway

Hutton Range

145   64   58

83

GREAT SANDY

DESERT

Well 39 (Murgaga)

Rocky breakaway
& trig point

Well 38
(Wardabunni Rockhole)

Reeves Knoll
389 m

Wandurba
Rockhole (cave)

Billigilli Native Well
Well 37 (Libral)

Bibarrd Aboriginal
Outstation

CANNING STOCK ROUTE
For further information between
Wiluna and Halls Gap, see the
CANNING STOCK ROUTE map
from Westprint Maps

Digging Jupiter Well. Photo by ex-NatMap surveyor Ed Burke (front row on left).

NGAANYATJARRA
AKA MARUWA
ABORIGINAL RESERVE

Sufficiency Knob

Gary
35

NM F 158
381 m

Junction

NGAANYATJARRA
ABORIGINAL RESERVE

Road
84

350

NM F 154
428 m

39

NM F 153
431 m

Hand pump
Jupiter Well

Jupiter Well
Ruin

19

Beadell
Tree

7

Emergency
airstrip

Nyinmy

Contention Heights

42

51

Take care -
dangerous corner

NGAANYATJARRA
KIWIRRKURRA
ABORIGINAL RESERVE

Pollock
Hills

9

6

Kiwirrkurra

40

Jupiter Well
Surveyors from the Department of National
Mapping built Jupiter Well while surveying sites
that would be linked by a road to be built by Len
Beadell. The planet Jupiter was clearly visible when
the water level was first checked at night.

*Jolly
Peaks*

23°

Line

Patience No 2
Oil Well

Patience Well
Several possible sites have been
located but cannot be confirmed by
local Aborigines because David Carnegie
did not record an Aboriginal name when
he used Patience Well in 1897.

Patience Well
(Approx position)

Camping along the Canning Stock Route near Lake Disappointment

Baron Range

NGAANYATJARRA
KURLKUTA
ABORIGINAL
RESERVE

78

Dowling Hills

Hickey
Hills

Gillespie Hills

Lake Cobb

24°

**Gibson Desert
Nature Reserve**

Patjarr Community
Visitors are welcome at
the craft centre. A permit is
required, ph 08 8950 1711
or call on UHF 6.

Patjarr

NGAANYATJARRA
CLUTTER BUCK HILL
ABORIGINAL RESERVE

Ernest Giles
Giles led an expedition into
this area in 1874. He named the
Alfred and Marie Range but
was unable to reach it.

Lake
Christopher

Private

ALFRED AND MARIE RA

Lake Blair

Lake
Newell

56

Lake
Farnham

Beadell
Tree

RAWLINSON RA

16

13

Blazed tree

15

5

Blazed tree

Coolawanyah

Hooley

Mt Margaret
868 m

Mungaroona Range
Nature Reserve

West Yule River

Mulga Downs

Wittenoom

Powellinna Pool

Rio Tinto Gorge

Hammersley Gorge

Range Gorge

Wittenoom Gorge

Old Wittenoom Gorge Mine

Mt Frederick
1235 m

Knox Gorge

Kalamina Gorge

Yampire Gorge

Munjina Road

Wittenoom Road

Auski Roadhouse

Maddina Pool

Fortescue River floodplain

HAMERSLEY RANGE

Karijini National Park

Banjima Drive

Dales Gorge Lookout

Dales Gorge

Fortescue Falls

Dignam Gorge

Munjina East Gorge Lookout

Albert Tongolini

Munjina

Karijini Drive

Mt Bruce
1235 m

Marandoo

Marandoo Mine

Lookout

Tom Price

Tom Price Mine

Milli Milli Spring

Coppin Pool

De La Porte Ck

Juna Downs

Hancock Range

Mt Meharry
1250 m

Karijini National Park

West Angela Hill
1010 m

Mt Robinson (toilets & emergency telephone)

Mt Robinson
1158 m

West Angelas Mine

NORTHERN HWY

GREAT

Open pit mine

Wanna Munna Flats

PILBARA

Shaw

Hesta

Cowra Line Camp

Fort

Roy

CHICHESTER RANGE

Western

Garden Ck

Shaw River

Haunted Hole Ck

Bonney Downs

Nullagine
Garden Pool

Blue Spec Mine

Beaton Gorge

Nullagine Mine

Day Dawn Mine

Quartz Hill
482 m

Bamboo Springs

Mt Maggie
546 m

Noreena

Bonney Downs

Warrie

Noreena Downs

Mt McKay
578 m

Rat Hill
533 m

Fortescue Marsh

Marillana

Weeli

Roy Hill 457 m

Roy Hill

189

Bakers Dam

Coondiner Pool

207 Mile Camp

Sandhill

Mindy

Ethel Creek

Yards

Marillana

Yandi No 2 Mine

Yandicoogina Mine

Yandi Mine open pits

Railway

Corktree Bore

Yandicoogina

Weeli

Weeli Wolli Spring

HAMERSLEY RANGE

Punda Rockhole

Eagle Rock Pool

Rhodes Ridge

164

Kalgan Ck

Kalgan Pool

Kalgan

Shovelanna Hill
805 m

Jimblebar Mine

Jimblebar

McCamey

Ophthalmia Range

Mt Newman
1057 m

Mt Whaleback Mine

Mt Newman Mine

Mt Newman Mines

Newman

Cathedral Gorge

Ophthalmia Dam

Capricorn Roadhouse

Coobina Mine (abandoned)

Sheep Well

Sylvania

No 42 Well

Mundiwindi

Cundlebar

Weelarrana

Spearhole Creek

Yarraloola

to Prairie

Prairie Downs

Turee Creek

Deadman Hill
732 m

GREAT NORTHERN HWY

Warrawanda

Bulloo Downs

161

Ilgarie Hill
672 m

Ilgarari Mine

Gas Station

LOFTY RANGE

Minaritchie Hill
715 m

Collier Range National Park

Box Bluff
831 m

Kumarina Mine

Kumarina Roadhouse

Wonyulgunna Hill
768 m

Beyondie

4 Mile Well

Beyondie

Beyondie Lakes

COLLIER RANGE

Collier Range National Park

Tangadee

Mount Vernon

Woodlands

Mulgul

Urary

ASHBURTON RIVER

Angelo River

Kennedy Creek

Tunnel Creek

Perry Creek

Ashburton River

Monkey Creek

Brumby Creek

Big Spring Creek

Bujundunna Pool

47km of unmaintained station track to Kumarina Roadhouse. Permission required for use.

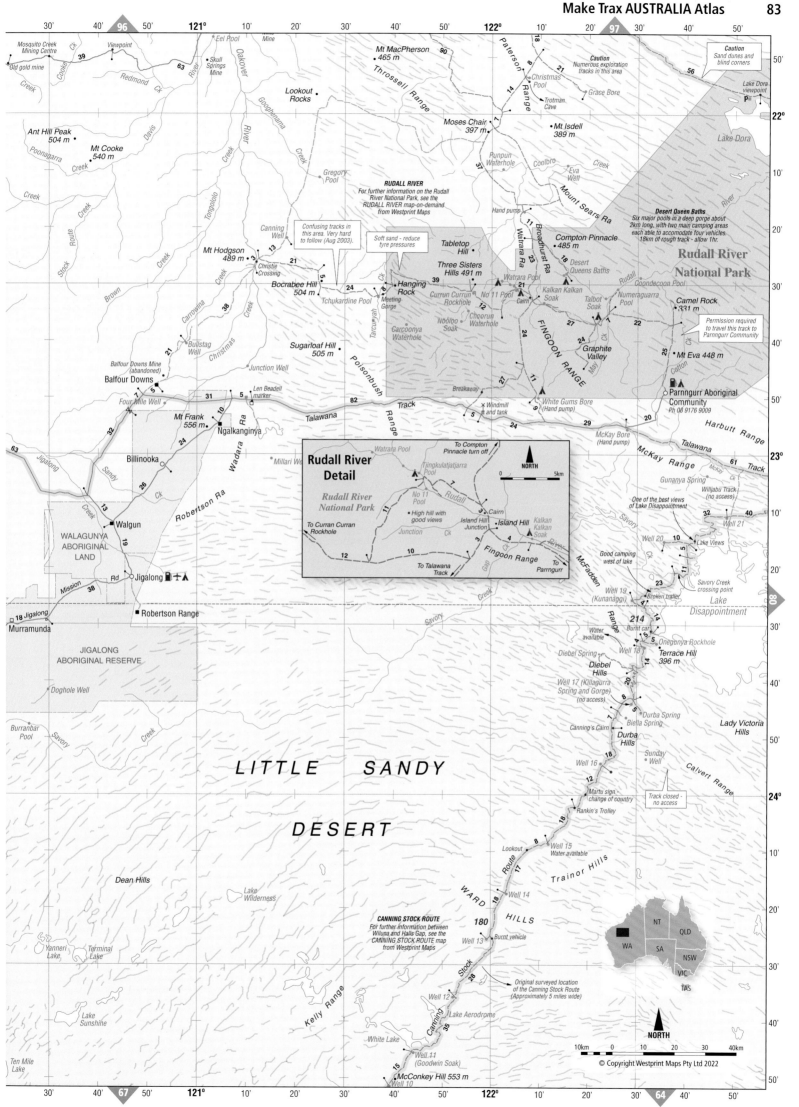

Mosquito Creek Mining Centre
Old gold mine
39
Viewpoint
63
Cooke Ck
Redmond Ck
Creek
Davis Creek
Poonagarra Creek
Ant Hill Peak 504 m
Mt Cooke 540 m
Stock Route
Brown Creek
Carrowina Creek
Bullstag Well
21
38
Balfour Downs Mine (abandoned)
Balfour Downs
7
Four Mile Well
31
5
Len Beadell marker
Mt Frank 556 m
Ngalkanginya
10
24
32
Wadara Ra
Robertson Ra
Billinooka
26
Sandy Ck
13
Walgun
19
WALAGUNYA ABORIGINAL LAND
63
Jigalong Creek
Rd
Jigalong
38
Mission
18 Jigalong
Murramunda
Robertson Range
JIGALONG ABORIGINAL RESERVE
Doghole Well

Oakover River
Eel Pool
White Mine
Skull Springs Mine
Googhennama Creek
Creek
Lookout Rocks
Gregory Pool
Mt Hodgson 489 m
3
13
21
Canning Well
Christie Crossing
Bocrabee Hill 504 m
5
24
8
Tchukardine Pool
Meeting Gorge
Tarculyah
Christmas Creek
Junction Well
Sugarloaf Hill 505 m
Poisonbush Range
Talawana
82
Track
Millari Well
Watrara Pool
Dean Hills
Lake Wilderness

Mt MacPherson 465 m
90
Throssell Range
Paterson Range
Christmas Pool
Grace Bore
Trotman Cave
14
8
21
18
Moses Chair 397 m
7
Punpun Waterhole
Coolbro Creek
Mt Isdell 389 m
Eva Well
Mount Sears Ra
37
Hand pump
11
Watara Ra
23
18
Broadhurst Ra
RUDALL RIVER
For further information on the Rudall River National Park, see the RUDALL RIVER map-on-demand from Westprint Maps
Confusing tracks in this area. Very hard to follow (Aug 2003).
Soft sand - reduce tyre pressures
Tabletop Hill
Three Sisters Hills 491 m
39
Hanging Rock
Compton Pinnacle 485 m
Desert Queens Baths
Watrara Pool
21
Cairn
No 11 Pool
Curran Curran Rockhole
Kalkan Kalkan Soak
Nooloo Soak
Choorun Waterhole
Talbot Soak
Numeraguarra Pool
27
7
22
Camel Rock 331 m
Carcoonya Waterhole
FINGOON RANGE
24
Graphite Valley
24
25
Mt Eva 448 m
24
11
Breakaway
27
11
White Gums Bore (Hand pump)
5
Windmill and tank
9
24
29
McKay Bore (Hand pump)
20
Parnngurr Aboriginal Community Ph 08 9176 9009
Harbutt Range
Talawana
McKay Range
61
Track

Desert Queen Baths
Six major pools in a deep gorge about 2km long, with two main camping areas each able to accomodate four vehicles. 18km of rough track - allow 1hr.
Rudall River National Park
Coondecoon Pool
Rudall River
Cotton Ck
Permission required to travel this track to Parnngurr Community
56
Lake Dora viewpoint
P
Lake Dora

Rudall River Detail
Rudall River National Park
To Compton Pinnacle turn off
Tjingkulatjatjarra Pool
7
No 11 Pool
11
Rudall
Cairn
3
Island Hill Junction
Island Hill
Kalkan Kalkan Soak
To Curran Curran Rockhole
Junction Ck
Fingoon Range
3
4
Gap
To Talawana Track
12
10
To Parrngurr
NORTH
0   5km

Savory Ck
One of the best views of Lake Disappointment
Gunanya Spring
Willjabu Track (no access)
32
40
Well 21
Well 20
10
Lake Views
5
23
11
Broken trailer
4
Savory Creek crossing point
214
Burnt car
14
Lake Disappointment
Good camping west of lake
Well 19 (Kunanaggi)
Water available
Onegunya Rockhole
Well 18
Terrace Hill 396 m
Diebel Spring
Diebel Hills
14
20
Well 17 (Killagurra Spring and Gorge) (no access)
8
5
Canning's Cairn
Durba Spring
Biella Spring
18
Durba Hills
Lady Victoria Hills
Calvert Range
Well 16
Sunday Well
12
Martu sign - change of country
Rankin's Trolley
Track closed - no access

LITTLE SANDY DESERT

Burranbar Pool
Savory Creek
Terminal Lake
Yanneri Lake
Lake Sunshine
Ten Mile Lake

WARD HILLS
Ward Hills
Kelly Range
Lookout
8
Well 15 Water available
17
18
Well 14
180
CANNING STOCK ROUTE
For further information between Wiluna and Halls Gap, see the CANNING STOCK ROUTE map from Westprint Maps
Well 13
Burnt vehicle
Trainor Hills
28
Original surveyed location of the Canning Stock Route (Approximately 5 miles wide)
Well 12
Lake Aerodrome
Canning Stock Route
35
White Lake
Well 11 (Goodwin Soak)
15
Well 10
McConkey Hill 553 m

NT
QLD
WA
SA
NSW
VIC
TAS

NORTH
10km   0   10   20   30   40km

© Copyright Westprint Maps Pty Ltd 2022

NORTH

10km 0 10 20 30 40km

© Copyright Westprint Maps Pty Ltd 2022

WA NT QLD SA NSW VIC TAS

INDIAN OCEAN

Vlaming Head Lighthouse
North West Cape
Point Murat
Jurabi Coastal Park
Ningaloo Reef
'Bundegi Coastal Park
Fly Island
Locker Point
Urala
Tubridgi Gas Field
Tubridgi Point
Brown I.
Chinty Pool
Onslow
Ningaloo Marine Park
Exmouth
Nature Reserves
Victor I.
Rivoli Islands
Y Island
Coastal salt flats
Minderoo
ASHBURTON RIVER
Ned's Camp, Mesa Camp
Milyering (Ranger)
Cape Range National Park
CAPE RANGE
Tent Island Nature Reserve
Proposed Conservation Area (formerly Mount Minnie Station)
Tulki Beach
Shothole Canyon
Burnside I. Nature Reserve
Simpson I.
Ningaloo Reef
North Mandu
Charles Knife Canyon
Mt Hollister 310 m
EXMOUTH GULF
Hope Point
Kurrajong Camp
Pilgramunna Camp
Learmonth Aerodrome
Sandy Bay
Osprey Bay
Learmonth
Heron Point
Bay of Rest
Point Lefroy
Rest Bay
Yardie Creek
Yardie Gorge
Boat Harbour
Exmouth Gulf
Whitmore I.
Sandy Point
Gales Bay
Roberts I.
Giralia Bay
Defence Reserve (No access)
Nature Reserve
Sandalwood Peninsula
Doole Island
Coastal salt flats
Ningaloo Reef
Winderabandi Point
Lefroy Bay
Point Billie
Point Edgar
Norwegian Bay
Old whaling station
Yanrey
Whisky Pool
Beacon Point
Frazer I.
Ningaloo Station
Basic bush campsites along the coast can be accessed through Ningaloo Station. Ph 08 9942 5936 for details.
Ningaloo
Point Cloates
Burkett
Bullara
Giralia
Proposed Conservation Area (formerly Giralia Station)
NORTH WEST COASTAL
Ningaloo Marine Park
Jane Bay
GIRALIA RANGE
Marrilla
Netting Dam
Woggola
Emu Creek
Cardabia Station
Basic bush campsites (including 9 Mile Camp) along the coast can be accessed through Cardabia Station. Ph 08 9942 5935 for details.
Chabjuwardoo Bay
Bruboodjoo Point
9 Mile Camp
Five Mile Bay
Bateman Bay
Maults Landing
Point Maud
Cardabia
Coral Bay
Turtle Cliffs
Cardabia Pool
Winning
Towera
Yannarie River
Warroora Station
Basic bush campsites (including 14 Mile and Black Moon Cliff) along the Ningaloo Coast can be accessed through Warroora Station. Ph 08 9942 5920 for details or visit www.warroora.com.au
14 Mile
Chinkia Ck
Mia Mia
Maluwarra Pool
Kiolowibri
Pelican Point
Lyndon
Pleiades Hills
Warroora
Alison Point
Black Moon Cliff
Lyndon River (24 hr camping)
Ningaloo Marine Park
Bulbarli Point
Lake Macleod
Lyndon
Gnaraloo Station
A working pastoral station with accommodation and wilderness camping adjacent Ningaloo Reef. www.gnaraloo.com
Cape Farquhar
Permission may be required to use this track
Lyndon
Minilya River
Wandagee
Williambury
Ningaloo Reef
Gnarraloo Bay
Minilya
Minilya Roadhouse
Middalya
Gnaraloo
3 Mile
HMAS Sydney Memorial
Red Bluff
Manberry
Proposed Conservation Areas (formerly Middalya Station)
(formerly Williambury Station)
Lake Macleod
Hutton Creek
KENNEDY RANGE
Salt Loading Facility
Cape Cuvier
Salt Haul Road (No access)
Proposed Conservation Area (formerly Boolgoroo Station)
Trybaroo
Hill Springs
(formerly Mardathuna Station)
(formerly Lyons River Station)
Quobba
Lake Macleod Saltworks
Salt Evaporators
Cooralya
Mardathuna
Kennedy Range National Park
Blowholes
Point Quobba
NORTH WEST COASTAL HIGHWAY
GASCOYNE RIVER
Binthalya
Geographe Channel
Blowfish Banks
Blowholes Road
Boolathana
Rocky Pool
Lyons River
Bernier and Dorre Islands Nature Reserve
Cape Ronsard
Wedge Point
Miaboolya Beach
Brick House
Carnarvon
Mullewa
Doorawarrah
Proposed Conservation Area (formerly Mooka Station)
KENNEDY RANGE
Bernier Island
Ingada Village

P I L B A R A

HAMERSLEY RANGE

CAPRICORN RANGE

Minnierra Range

Godfrey Range

High Range

Barlee Range Nature Reserve

Cane River Conservation Park

Proposed Conservation Area (formerly Nanutarra Station)

Proposed Conservation Area (formerly Wanna Station)

Proposed Conservation Areas

Proposed Conservation Areas

Proposed Conservation Area (formerly Cobra Station)

Proposed Conservation Area (formerly Waldburg Station)

Proposed Conservation Area

Proposed Conservation Area (formerly Mount Phillip Station)

BURRINGURRAH (MOUNT JAMES) ABORIGINAL LAND

Burringurrah (Mount Augustus) National Park

Peedamulla
Mount Minnie
Mount Minnie Road
Cane River
Red Hill
Cardo Outstation
Nanutarra
Mount Stuart
Duck Creek
Mt Murray 255 m
Nanutarra Roadhouse
Mt Alexander 410 m
Uaroo
Glen Florrie
Wyloo
Kooline
Goorderman Pool
Pamprunnah Pool
Kohlbing-Karrung Pool
Maroonah
Ullawarra
Edmund
Star of Mangaroon Mine
Mangaroon
Mt Thomson 367 m
Minnie Creek
Wongarrie Pool
Gifford Creek
Wanna
Edithana Pool
Woolshed Bore
Bangemall
Cobra "Bangemall Inn" Farmstay
Mount Phillips
Mount Sandiman
Eudamullah
Morrissey Hill Mining Centre
Yinnetharra
Police Station Woolshed
Emu Hill Lookout
Cattle Pool
Mt Augustus 1106 m
Mount Augustus
Burringurrah Community
Gramma Hole
Waldburg
Five Mile Well
Dooley Downs
Pingandy
Mininer
Ashburton Downs
Baring Downs
Koonong Pool
Kazput Pool
Woongarra Pool
Rocklea
Mt Truchanas 1154 m
Tom Price
Mt Reeder Nichols 1111 m
Tom Price Mine
Paraburdoo
Paraburdoo Mine
Channar Mine
Mt McRae 1028 m
Mount Brockman
Mt Brockman 1132 m
Brockman Mine
Donkey Hole
Mt Sheila 1006 m
Hamersley
Hamersley
Mt Margaret 868 m
Camp Anderson
Coolawanyah
Upper Walloona Pool
Mootana Pool
Cockies Soak
Lookout
Attack Pool
Barliyunnu Pool
Roolaloo Pool
Metawandy
FORTESCUE RIVER
Iron Railway

Cane River
Red Hill Creek
Underground
Gas Pipeline
Duck Creek
Ashburton River
Henry River
Wannery Creek
Wongide Creek
Mountain Ck
Cain Spring
Caraline Ck
Yannarie Creek
Cunyoo Creek
Discovery Ck
Yijinna Pool
Doolgarrie Creek
Yulawarra Creek
Irregully Creek
Septennio Creek
Boolgeeda Creek
Pinnara Creek
Brolgeeda Creek
Beasley River
Hardey River
Six Mile Ck
Seven Mile Creek
Turee Creek
Stockyard Ck
Wandarry Creek
Fords Creek
Koorabooka Creek
Frederick Creek
Lyons River
Lyons River North
Thomas River
Three River
Morrissey Creek
Thirty Mummil Pool
Twenty Four Mile
Onslow Creek
Ullawarra Creek
Gifford Creek
Little Minnie Ck
Mucalana Creek
Pirraburdu Ck
Tableland Ck
Price
Tom Price Rd
Paraburdoo
Wachilura Ck
Barnett Road
Weelumurra Creek
Tom Price Railway
Camp Price
Caves Creek
Kumina Creek
Robe River
Bungaroo Creek
Hill River
Wittenoom Road
Augustus Woodlands Road
Mount Augustus Road

HIGHWAY

Tropic of Capricorn

116° 117°
22° 23° 24°

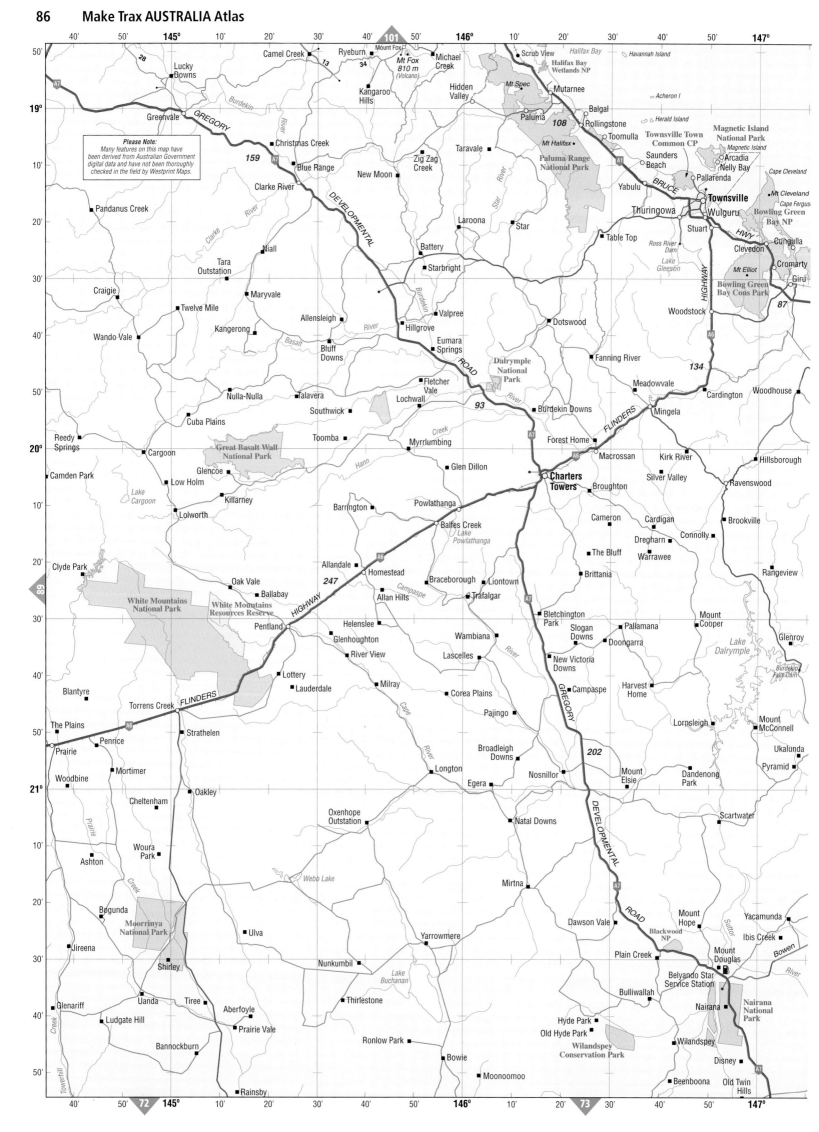

PARK AND RESERVE ABBREVIATIONS
CP — Conservation Park
CA — Conservation Area
Cons — Conservation
FFR — Flora & Fauna Reserve
NP — National Park
NCR — Nature Conservation Area
Res — Reserve
Reg — Regional
RP — Regional Park
WPA — Wilderness Protected Area

CORAL SEA

Broadhurst Reef
Bowden Reef
Shrimp Reef
Darley Reef
Stanley Reef
Old Reef

Great Barrier Reef Marine Park (Central Section)

Bait Reef
Hardy Reef
Hook Reef
Black Reef East
Hewitt Reef
Ross Reef
Round Reef

NORTH
10km 0 10 20 30 40km
© Copyright Westprint Maps Pty Ltd 2022

Cape Bowling Green
Bowling Green Bay
Bowling Green Bay National Park
Jerona
Alva
Brandon
Ayr
Jardine
Rita Island
Home Hill
Peters Island
Clare
BRUCE
Upstart Bay
Cape Upstart
Cape Upstart National Park
Byrne Valley
Rocky Ponds
Gumlu
114
HWY
Abbot Bay
Abbot Point Coal terminal
Guthalungra
Plumtree
Range More
Merinda
Inveroona
Bowen
Stone I
Millaroo
Bogie River
Port Bowen
Gloucester Island
Gloucester Island National Park
George Point
Hayman Island
Hook Island
Whitsunday Group
Strathalbyn
Strathbogie
Mount Abbot National Park
Mount Aberdeen National Park
Earlando
Whitsunday Passage
Border Island
Whitsunday Islands National Park
Dalbeg
McGregor Peak
Mount Aberdeen
Binbee
61
Dryander National Park
Cannonvale
Airlie Beach
North Molle I.
Whitsunday Island
Haslewood Island
Table Mtn
Crystal Brook
Foxdale
Shutehaven
59
Hamilton Island
Pretty Bend
Peter Faust Dam
Mount Julian
Proserpine
Conway NP
Long Island
Lindeman Group
Lindeman Island
Lake Proserpine
Dittmer
Conway Beach
Wilson Beach
Mansell Island
Shaw Island
Strathbowen
Scottville
Collinsville
Mt Flat Top
Mt Hector
Lethebrook
Cape Conway
Lindeman Islands National Park
Heidelberg
Birralee
Mount Hector
Repulse Bay
Repulse Nat Park
Blacksmith I.
Smith Islands National Park
Midge Point
Goldsmith Island
Linne Island
Tinsmith Island
Wigton Island
Cumberland Islands
Emu Plains
Mt Marion
Bloomsbury
BRUCE
120
Carlisle Island
Cockermouth Island
Calder Island
Broken River
Elaroo
Yalboroo
Wagoora
Newry Islands National Park
Rabbit I.
Newry I.
Brampton Island Nat Park
South Cumberland Islands National Park
Scawfell Island
Hidden Valley
Exmoor
Urannah
Pindi Pindi
Calen
Seaforth
Ball Bay
Cape Hillsborough NP
St Bees Island
Dicks Tableland
Eungella National Park
Mount Ossa
Buthurra
Pioneer Peaks NP
Sand Bay
Shoal Point
Mt Black Jack 330 m
Weetalaba
Byerwen
Blenheim
Bluff Hill NP
Aminungo
Bucasia
Eimeo
Blacks Beach
Slade Point
Hibiscus Coast
Redcliffe Vale
Lake Eungella
Eungella
Finch Hatton
Mount Martin NP
Marian
Mackay
Bungobine
Newlands
Newlands Coal Mine
Turrawalla
Pinnacle
Mirani
Walkerston
Sandringham Bay
Cerita
Credition
North Eton
36
Whynot
Mount Lookout
Wollombi
Suttor Creek
Glenden
Exevale
Homevale Resources Reserve
Eton
Homebush
Half Tide Beach
Prudhoe Island
Mount Coolon
Talwood
Lancewood
Mt Andrew
Oakenden
Alligator Creek
Grasstree Beach
Sarina Beach
Kenilworth
Glen Eva
Eaglefield
Lenton Downs
Mount Robert
Homevale National Park
70
Sarina
Armstrong Beach
Knight Island
Police
Warrigal
Wards Well
Fort Cooper
DOWNS
120
Blue Mountain
Koumala
Mt Funnel
Ince Bay
Cape Palmerston
Gunjulla
Glenavon
Chesterfield
Burton Downs
Kemmis Creek
Bolingbroke
Hatfield
Cape Palmerston National Park
North Goonyella Coal Mine
Red Hill
St Albands
Nebo
Ilbilbie
Connor Islet
Pasha
Old Pasha
Riverside
Ellensfield
Strathfield
PEAK
West Hill Island
Avon Downs
Goonyella/Riverside Coal Mine
Wyena
Hamilton Park
Tierawoomba
Undercliff
Carmila
Yarrawonga Point

40' 50' **140°** 10' 20' 30' 40' △103 50' **141°** 10' 20' 30' 40' 50' **142°**

19° 13
Wills 26
Lorraine
10
Coolibah
Tower
84 36
Road
Myally Jacks Waterhole
31
13
14
Burke and Wills Roadhouse
23
Cowan Downs
B&W Camp 114
B&W Camp 113
Wurung
B&W Camp 112
Iffley
11
14
12
Norman Bore
Cudgee
Momba
Earls Camp Waterhole
Myola
30
33

10'
18
Blue Bush Swamp Waterhole
Kamileroi
33
83
P
1
27
Mistake Camp
Gleeson
Kingfield
White Hills
White Hills Outstation
18
20
Black Mtn 215 m
Boomarra
B&W Camp 111 Seaward WH
Canobie
B&W Camp 110
Wills 12
Madcap Ck
35
Byway
84
Gateway to the Gulf
Monstraven
Violet Vale
16
Lyrian Waterhole
Lyrian
Arizona
Taldora
18 Mile Waterhole
Twelve Mile Ck
Savannah Downs
Mundjuro Waterhole
Numil Downs
28
28
Boorabin
Crooked Ck

20°
Quail
189
24
Burke
7
30
Dobbyn
Mt Stanley
32
19
Tower
P
P
The Nobbies
Bellman
B&W Camp 107
Illistrin
Palmer Lagoon
Numerous channels and waterholes
Etta Plains
Baalootha
Millungera
51
Saxby River
Spear Creek

20°
Mt Cuthbert
Kajabbi
31
26
18
12
Developmental
Granada
35
23
Koolamarra
Jessievale
Cotswold
B&W Camp 105
Glen Isla
B&W Camp 104
Clonagh
B&W Camp 106
34
Byrimine
RIVER
15
10
6
20
232
Zingari
Williams River was named by McKinlay in April, 1862
Dalgonally
Cabanda
52
31
Manfred Downs
21
Fairlea
Flers
84
35
Werrina
16
Alva Downs
Lindfield
13

Lake Julius
14
Lake Julius
Mt Remarkable 475 m
73
Naraku
16
40
Round Mtn 355 m
Quamby
9
Urquhart
B&W Camp 103
21
Hillside
83 1
Ginburra
19
Fort Constantine
Mt Eliza Ck
Margaret River
Mt Douglas 277 m

30'
Lake Moondarra
West Leichhardt
MT GODKIN RANGE
Mt Isa
Old Cloncurry Road
B&W Camp 102
17
Mindie
Courtenay Ck
Fisher Ck
Ernestina Plains
Caiwarra
18
23
25
Julia Ck
32
HIGHWAY 50
FLINDERS

BARKLY
20
9
29
P P
B&W Camp 101
HWY 35
123
Mary Kathleen
19
A2
Lake Corella
Burke & Wills Memorial
P
11
Cloncurry
A
14
Oonamurra
Pymurra
A2
34
FLINDERS
137
Oorinda
Bookin
Undina
Tibarri
17
29
Gilliat
Eddington
A6
Belgravia
Eureka
37
38
Yorkshire Downs

50'
The Three Sisters
Rifle Creek Reservoir
Dolomite
Marimo
37
Roxmere
A2
LANDSBOROUGH
Arrolla
49
51
Levuka
Ivellen
Holy Ck
Carrum
Kamerooka
Coolreagh
21

21°
Kabayah
Malbon Vale
Mt Philp
Mt Tabletop 346 m
Marraba
10
Malbon
Black Mtn 565 m
32
Woonigan
Wammutta
Kennedy Memorial
Dronfield
Devoncourt
B&W Camp 99
B&W Camp 98
38
Kurialda
Mt Tracey
Mt Boorama
Mayfields
15
16
Rutchillo
11
180
Lagaven
30
27
Eulolo
Glenbervie
43
21

10'
Bushy Park
Myubee
18
Bungalien
Duchess
10
8
B&W Camp 97
Mt Collis 404 m
Farley
Strathfield
McKinlay
29
5
36

20'
McPhee Hills 441 m
Ashover
19
The Brothers
B&W Camp 96
Mt Birnie 445 m
Mt Alpin 496 m
SELWYN
Selwyn
8
Beaudesert
Dingading
Wolseley Downs
27
HIGHWAY
Mimong
Crendon
Glenagra
11
9
4
Kynuna
Belfast
Combo Waterhole

30'
Butru
34
Garden Creek
The Monument
12
39
Big Red Bluff
29
RANGES
B&W Camp 95
B&W Camp 94
Limestone Creek
8
RANGE
52
Gin Creek
Glenholme
Ranges Valley
Cannington Mine
Cannington
48
DIAMANTINA
SWORDS RA
Frensham

40'
50'
40' 50' **140°** △74 10' 20' 30' 40' 50' **141°** △75 10' 20' 30' 40' 50' **142°**

Seek local advice prior to using minor roads in this area

NORTH

10km 0 10 20 30 40km

© Copyright Westprint Maps Pty Ltd 2022

Please Note:
Many features on this map have been derived from Australian Government digital data and have not been thoroughly checked in the field by Westprint Maps.

Esmeralda
Prospect
North Head
South Head
Robinhood
Kidston
The Lynd Junction Roadhouse
The Lynd
Glenora
Spring Valley
Lyndhurst
Fog Creek
Mount Hogan
Gilberton
Ten Mile
Oak Park
Pandanus Creek
Perryvale
Werrington
Victoria Vale
Bellfield
Blackbraes National Park
Black Braes
Malpas Hut
Strathpark
Cheviot Hills
Gregory Springs
Clarke Hills
Chudleigh Park
Middle Park
Riellys Gully Mill
Gregory Springs
Etheldale
Mount Norman
Reedy Springs
Bunda Bunda
Pialah
Pretty Plains
Camden Park
Mount Sturgeon
Mount Emu Plains
Somerville
Stawellton
Beeantha
Walkers Park
Ronald Plains
Coalbrook
Stawell
Trivalore
Bylong
Burleigh
Gallipoli
Runnymede
Boonderoo
Clyde Park
Doncaster
Charlotte Plains
Strath-Stewart
Colindale
Porcupine Gorge National Park
Rockvale
Kenmac
Dunraven
Artesian Downs
Gracedale
Hazlewood
Rainscourt
Wallegege
Jones Valley
Wongalee
Yan Yean
Acton Downs
Nelia Ponds
Ranmoor
Villa Dale
Soda Valley
Harrogate
Torver Valley
New Glendower
Blantyre
Nelia
Nonda West
Molesworth
Boree Park
Lucerne
Stewart Park
Telemen
Rokeby
Koon Kool
Glenmoan
The Plains
Tower
Maxwelton
Malvern Park
Richmond
Marathon
Nindi
Gunnerside
Hughenden
HIGHWAY
Prairie
Alexmere
Maxwelton
Allaru
Riverdale
FLINDERS
Gairloch
Rose Downs
Marvada
Hazelwood
Woodbine
Langdale
Merriula
Patroy
Tweedsmuir
Hilltop
Edith Downs
Lucindale
Clare Valley
Glenalvon
Redcliff
Lonsdale
Arjuna
Illalong
Moonby Downs
Hillview
Arrara
Tarbax
Clareborough
Wolston
Essex Downs
Terranburby
Ashton
Coleraine
Dalmuir
Limbri
Zara
Dimora
Bora
Hanworth
Abbotsford
Stamford
Braemar
Barragunda
Plainby
Dundee
Nottingham Downs
Vuna
Maranie
Cameron Downs
Ensay
Hamilton Downs
Minerva
Cracrin
Elvira
Airewoth
Jireena
Albion Downs
Wetherby
Kiriwina
Sesbania
Katandra
Sutton Downs
Glenariff
Clio
Raelee Downs
Anrod Downs
Conamore
Glenelg
Ballater
Barenya
Moreena
Maidavale
Ingle Downs
Camberwarra
Corfield
Woolfield
Broadford
Jindaroo
Tangorin
Rockwood
Wongan
Brooklyn
Akunam
Wirilla
Coralton
Cressy
Glenreigh
Dagworth
Werna
Wyora
Olio
Escombe
Malboona
Burnside
Catumnal
Broadfield

Prospect
20
41
Victoria Vale
Creek
Gilbert River
Saxby River
Sandy Creek
Creek
Creek
22
10
P
Nelia
A6
147
51
Alick Creek
44
17
27
27
17
12
164
Kennedy Developmental Road
Wokingham Creek
Kate Creek
Rupert Creek
Ck
Alick
Flinders River
Dutton River
Stawell River
Stamford
214
113
A6
204
Porcupine
Ck
Kerr Creek
Towerhill Ck
72
143°
144°

ROCKHAMPTON DOWNS

Lake Sylvester

Lake DeBurgh

Lake Sylvester

MITTIEBAH
Connells Lagoon
Connells Lagoon

Mitiebah Range

BRUNCHILLY

Boree

Creek

Tower

Emu Waterhole

Tower

Alexandria

19°

WARUMUNGU
ABORIGINAL
LAND TRUST

Lignum
Waterhole

HIGHWAY

184

Playford River

Playford

Buchanan

Buchanan
Dam

Buchanan
Bore

White

Hole

10°

BARKLY HIGHWAY

41 Mile Bore
Rest Area

27

34

187

Lower Amazon
Lagoon

Upper Amazon
Lagoon

Alroy Downs

ALROY
DOWNS

77

77

22

23

Creek

30

25

EAST
RANKEN

20°

66

KURNTURLPARA
ABORIGINAL LAND TRUST

Frewena Rest Area

55

55

Prentice
Lake

TABLELANDS

DALMORE
DOWNS

Barkly Tableland
Huge black-soil plains covered with waving
Mitchell grass caused problems for drovers bringing
cattle over from the Kimberley to eastern markets.
Although the scarcity of trees caused problems for
cooks trying to provide meals it was the lack of surface
water that caused the most difficulty when moving or
stocking cattle. Underground water and road transport
has made cattle handling much easier
on the Barkly Tableland.

Ranken

Ranken

42

33

Road

Ranken

30°

NORTH

10km 0 10 20 30 40km

© Copyright Westprint Maps Pty Ltd 2022

WA NT QLD
SA NSW
VIC
TAS

Barkly Homestead
Roadhouse

11

31

88

266

Kerringnew
Swamp

Boorodo
Waterhole

Olgoolgarri
Swamp

WEST
RANKEN

40°

50°

Purukuwurru Community

WAKAYA ABORIGINAL
LAND TRUST

20°

WARUMUNGU
ABORIGINAL LAND TRUST

81

Creek

Wunara

66

33

Soudan

15

BARKLY

20

Lorne

Ranken

10°

KURUNDI

Mosquito
Creek

Kurundi
Creek

EPENARRA

Walkabout

Creek

Frew

River

EPENARRA

93

Quarry Ck

10 Mile Bore

18

52

Epenarra
Wutunugurra

River

15

Hanlon

Creek

Teatree

Creek

Yaddanilla

Creek

20°

Kurundi

24

Mt Cairns
609 m

Injandan
Rockhole)

SINGLETON

Whistleduck

Whistleduck
Waterhole

Frew River

50

Canteen Creek

KURUNDI

19

8

20

Bull Ck

30°

Skinner
Pound

Iytwelepenty /
Davenport
Ranges NP

Old Police Stn
Waterhole
Frew River Camps

15

13

Hatches Creek
Mine Ruins

Hatches Creek

21

Long
Pound

ANURRETE ABORIGINAL
LAND TRUST

40°

Kaidwalla
Waterhole

Skinner

Ck

Amelia

Errolola Waterhole

Davenport Range

Gastrolobium

Creek

50°

21°

Murray
Downs

25

21

36

Elkedra
Pound

Pound Ck

Elkedra

Elkedra

River

Annitowa

139

407

10°

MURRAY DOWNS

ELKEDRA

75

59

George

Creek

Trew

Creek

Creek

ANNITOWA

ARGADARGADA

20°

AMMAROO

24

Atcherie

95

Arganara Bore

Floodout Area
(Sandover River)

10

30°

Antarrengenge

ALAYAWARRA
ABORIGINAL
LAND TRUST

Ampilatwatja
(Aherrenge)

Honeymoon
Bore

Ammaroo

28

Ck

floodout

Bundey

Sandover

River

Sandover

SANDOVER

River

OORATIPPRA

Ooratippra

14

HIGHWAY

62

Irraman
(Ermarne)

Floodout Area
(Sandover River)

Argadargada

Mt Hogarth
330 m

40°

Urapuntja

No 8
Bore

18

Corella Bore

DERRY DOWNS

50°

Ruins of the Hatches Creek Tungsten Mine

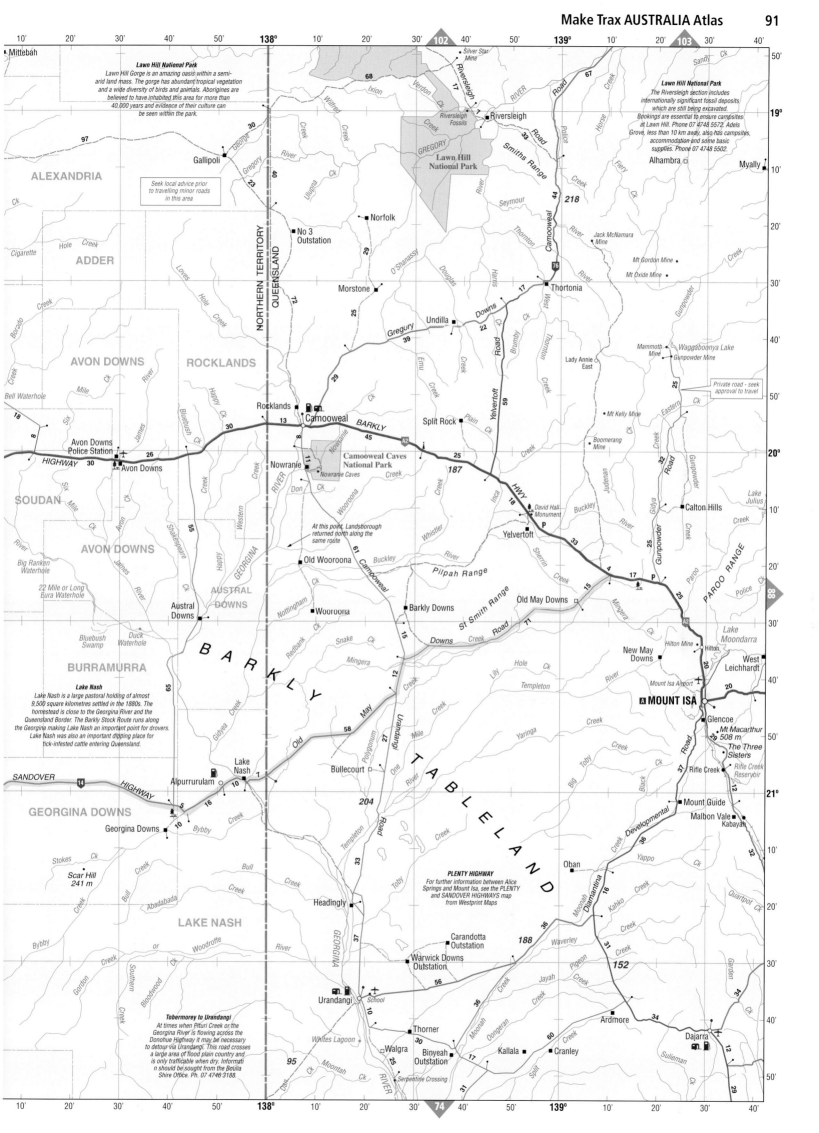

Mittebah

102

Silver Star Mine

Lawn Hill National Park
Lawn Hill Gorge is an amazing oasis within a semi-arid land mass. The gorge has abundant tropical vegetation and a wide diversity of birds and animals. Aborigines are believed to have inhabited this area for more than 40,000 years and evidence of their culture can be seen within the park.

Lawn Hill National Park
The Riversleigh section includes internationally significant fossil deposits which are still being excavated. Bookings are essential to ensure campsites at Lawn Hill. Phone 07 4748 5572. Adels Grove, less than 10 km away, also has campsites, accommodation and some basic supplies. Phone 07 4748 5502.

68

Riversleigh

Riversleigh Fossils

67

GREGORY

Lawn Hill National Park

Smiths Range

Alhambra

Myally

ALEXANDRIA

97

Gallipoli

30

Seek local advice prior to travelling minor roads in this area

23

40

Norfolk

218

44

Camooweal

Jack McNamara Mine

Mt Gordon Mine

Mt Oxide Mine

ADDER

Cigarette

Hole Creek

No 3 Outstation

29

O'Shanassy

Douglas

Harris

West

Thornton River

76

Thortonia

Morstone

72

25

Gregory

39

Undilla

Downs Ck

22

Brumby Ck

17

Mammoth Mine

Waggaboonya Lake

Gunpowder Mine

AVON DOWNS

ROCKLANDS

29

Emu

Creek

Lady Annie East

Private road – seek approval to travel

Loves

Hole Creek

Bluebush Ck

Rocklands

13

Camooweal

BARKLY

Split Rock

Plain Ck

59

Yelvertoft

Mt Kelly Mine

25

Boomerang Mine

Bell Waterhole

18

8

James

Avon Downs Police Station

26

30

Avon Downs

HIGHWAY

30

Six Mile Ck

Nowranie

8

11

Nowrane

Camooweal Caves National Park

45

A2

25

187

Inca

18

David Hall Monument

Buckley

Calton Hills

Lake Julius

SOUDAN

Six Mile

Avon

Nowranie Caves

Don Ck

At this point, Landsborough returned north along the same route

P

Yelvertoft

33

Gidyea

Gunpowder Road

25

Judenan

32

AVON DOWNS

55

Shakespeare

AUSTRAL DOWNS

Old Wooroona

61

Buckley

Whistler

River

Sherrin Creek

15

4

17

P

Paroo

PAROO RANGE

Police

88

Big Ranken Waterhole

22 Mile or Long Eura Waterhole

Austral Downs

Nottingham

Wooroona

Barkly Downs

St Smith Range

Old May Downs

Mingera

71

New May Downs

Hilton Mine

Hilton

Lake Moondarra

West Leichhardt

BURRAMURRA

Bluebush Swamp

Duck Waterhole

15

Downs Creek Road

Snake Ck

12

Mingera

Lily Hole Ck

Templeton

Mount Isa Airport

20

Lake Nash
Lake Nash is a large pastoral holding of almost 9,500 square kilometres settled in the 1880s. The homestead is close to the Georgina River and the Queensland Border. The Barkly Stock Route runs along the Georgina making Lake Nash an important point for drovers. Lake Nash was also an important dipping place for tick-infested cattle entering Queensland.

B A R K L Y

65

Gidyea Creek

Old May

58

27

Urandangi Road

One Mile River

Yaringa

River

20

MOUNT ISA

Glencoe

Mt Macarthur 508 m

The Three Sisters

37

Rifle Creek

Rifle Creek Reservoir

Lake Nash

204

Bullecourt

Polygonum

Toby Ck

Black Ck

12

Alpurrurulam

10

1

Mount Guide

SANDOVER

14

HIGHWAY

Malbon Vale

Kabayah

32

GEORGINA DOWNS

5

16

Georgina Downs

10

Bybby

Creek

Templeton

33

T A B L E L A N D

Oban

Creek Developmental Road

36

16

Stokes Ck

Scar Hill 241 m

Bull Creek

Abadabada

Headingly

Toby Creek

PLENTY HIGHWAY
For further information between Alice Springs and Mount Isa, see the PLENTY and SANDOVER HIGHWAYS map from Westprint Maps

Diamantina

Moonah

LAKE NASH

Gordon

Southern

Bloodwood

GEORGINA

37

Carandotta Outstation

188

Waverley

31

152

Ardmore

34

Garden Ck

Bybby

Woodroffe

River

Warwick Downs Outstation

56

Pigeon Creek

Jayah Ck

Quartpot Ck

34

Tobermorey to Urandangi
At times when Pituri Creek or the Georgina River is flowing across the Donohue Highway it may be necessary to detour via Urandangi. This road crosses a large area of flood plain country and is only trafficable when dry. Information should be sought from the Boulia Shire Office. Ph. 07 4746 3188.

Urandangi

School

10

Thorner

30

Moonah Ck

36

Kahko Ck

60

Kallala

Cranley

Dajarra

12

95

Walgra

Binyeah Outstation

17

Oongeran Ck

Spill Ck

Sulleman

29

Whites Lagoon

Serpentine Crossing

31

74

139°

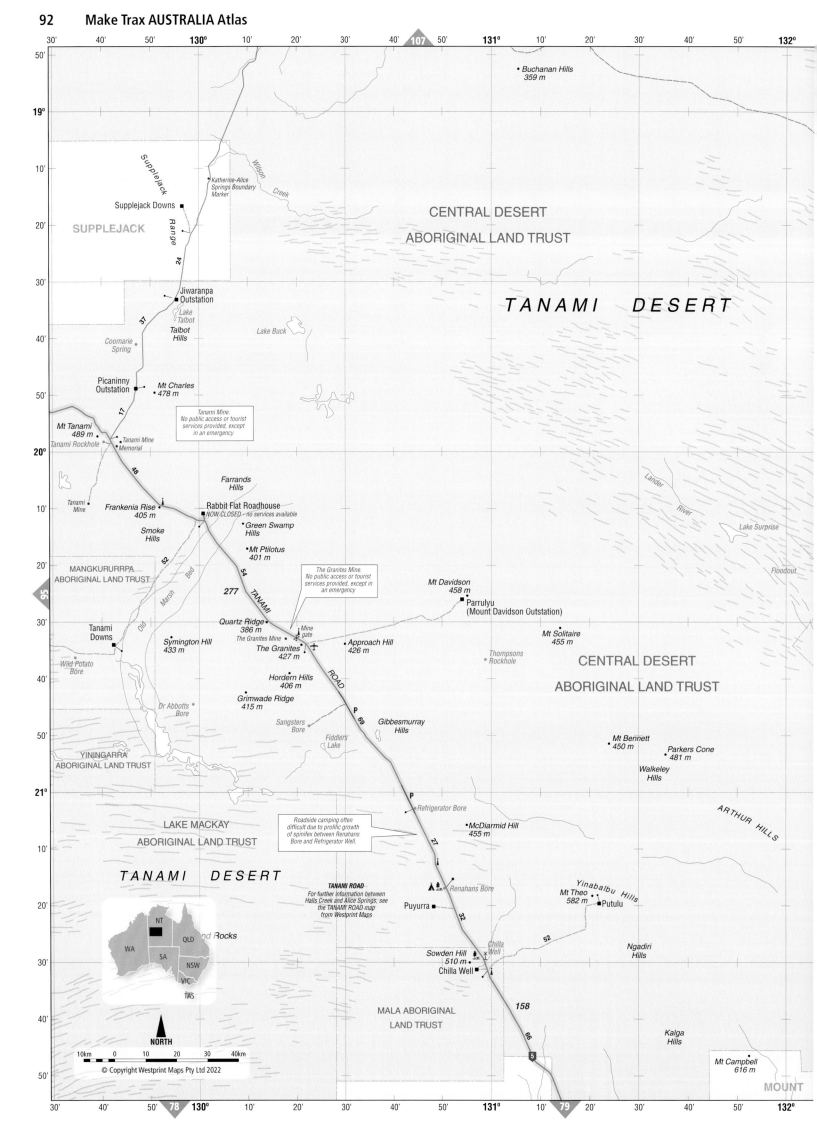

CENTRAL DESERT
ABORIGINAL LAND TRUST

T A N A M I   D E S E R T

• Buchanan Hills
359 m

Supplejack

Wilson Creek

Katherine-Alice
Springs Boundary
Marker

Supplejack Downs

SUPPLEJACK

Range

24

Jiwaranpa
Outstation

37

*Lake
Talbot*

Talbot
Hills

Lake Buck

Coomarie
Spring

Picaninny
Outstation

Mt Charles
• 478 m

17

Tanami Mine.
No public access or tourist
services provided, except
in an emergency

Mt Tanami
489 m •

Tanami Rockhole
Tanami Mine
Memorial

48

Farrands
Hills

Tanami
Mine

Frankenia Rise •
405 m

Rabbit Flat Roadhouse
NOW CLOSED - no services available

Smoke
Hills

• Green Swamp
Hills

52

Old Marsh Bed

MANGKURURRPA
ABORIGINAL LAND TRUST

54

277

TANAMI

• Mt Ptilotus
401 m

The Granites Mine.
No public access or tourist
services provided, except in
an emergency

Mt Davidson
458 m •

• Parrulyu
(Mount Davidson Outstation)

Quartz Ridge •
386 m

Mine
gate

Mt Solitaire
455 m

Tanami
Downs

Symington Hill
433 m

The Granites Mine

• Approach Hill
426 m

Thompsons
• Rockhole

CENTRAL DESERT

95

The Granites •
427 m

Wild Potato
Bore

Hordern Hills
406 m

ABORIGINAL LAND TRUST

ROAD

Dr Abbotts
Bore •

Grimwade Ridge
415 m

Mt Bennett
• 450 m

Parkers Cone
• 481 m

YININGARRA
ABORIGINAL LAND TRUST

Sangsters
Bore

P

69

Gibbesmurray
Hills

Walkeley
Hills

Fiddlers
Lake

21°

P

ARTHUR HILLS

LAKE MACKAY

Refrigerator Bore

Roadside camping often
difficult due to prolific growth
of spinifex between Renahans
Bore and Refrigerator Well.

• McDiarmid Hill
455 m

ABORIGINAL LAND TRUST

27

Yinabalbu Hills

T A N A M I   D E S E R T

TANAMI ROAD
For further information between
Halls Creek and Alice Springs, see
the TANAMI ROAD map
from Westprint Maps

Renahans Bore

Mt Theo
582 m •

Putulu

NT

QLD

d Rocks

Puyurra

32

WA

SA

NSW

Chilla
Well

52

Ngadiri
Hills

VIC

Sowden Hill
510 m •

TAS

Chilla Well

MALA ABORIGINAL

LAND TRUST

158

Kalga
Hills

NORTH

66

10km   0   10   20   30   40km

5

Mt Campbell
616 m •

© Copyright Westprint Maps Pty Ltd 2022

MOUNT

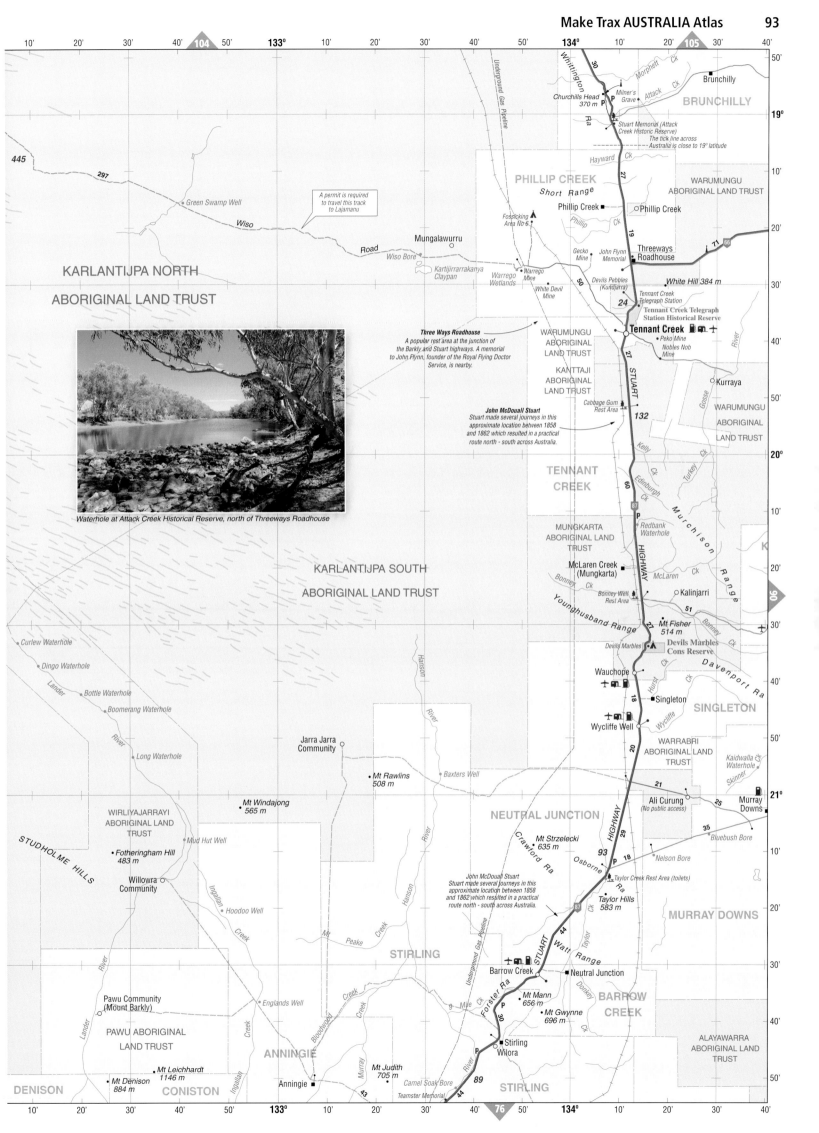

Waterhole at Attack Creek Historical Reserve, north of Threeways Roadhouse

BRUNCHILLY

Brunchilly

Churchills Head 370 m
Milner's Grave
Stuart Memorial (Attack Creek Historic Reserve)
The tick line across
Australia is close to 19° latitude

Whittington Ra

Morphett Ck
Attack Ck
Hayward Ck

PHILLIP CREEK
Short Range

Phillip Creek
Phillip Creek
Phillip Ck

WARUMUNGU
ABORIGINAL LAND TRUST

Threeways Roadhouse

A permit is required
to travel this track
to Lajamanu

Mungalawurru

Wiso

Road

Wiso Bore

Green Swamp Well

445
297

KARLANTIJPA NORTH
ABORIGINAL LAND TRUST

Kartijirrarrakanya
Claypan

Fossicking
Area No 6

Gecko Mine
John Flynn Memorial

Devils Pebbles
(Kundjarra)

White Hill 384 m

Warrego Wetlands
Warrego Mine
White Devil Mine

Tennant Creek
Telegraph Station
**Tennant Creek Telegraph
Station Historical Reserve**

Three Ways Roadhouse
A popular rest area at the junction of
the Barkly and Stuart highways. A memorial
to John Flynn, founder of the Royal Flying Doctor
Service, is nearby.

WARUMUNGU
ABORIGINAL
LAND TRUST

Tennant Creek

Peko Mine
Nobles Nob Mine

KANTTAJI
ABORIGINAL
LAND TRUST

Kurraya

John McDouall Stuart
Stuart made several journeys in this
approximate location between 1858
and 1862 which resulted in a practical
route north - south across Australia.

Cabbage Gum
Rest Area

132

WARUMUNGU
ABORIGINAL
LAND TRUST

STUART
Gosse River
Murchison Ra

Kelly Ck
Edinburgh Ck
Turkey Ck

**TENNANT
CREEK**

60

HIGHWAY

KARLANTIJPA SOUTH
ABORIGINAL LAND TRUST

Curlew Waterhole

Dingo Waterhole

Bottle Waterhole

Boomerang Waterhole

Lander River

Long Waterhole

MUNGKARTA
ABORIGINAL LAND
TRUST

Redbank
Waterhole

McLaren Creek
(Mungkarta)

Bonney Ck
McLaren Ck

Kalinjarri

Bonney Well
Rest Area

Younghusband Range

Mt Fisher
514 m

Bonney Ck

51

Devils Marbles
**Devils Marbles
Cons Reserve**

Davenport Ra

Wauchope

Hanson River

Jarra Jarra
Community

Mt Rawlins
508 m

Baxters Well

Hurst Ck
Wycliffe Ck

18
Singleton

SINGLETON

Wycliffe Well

WARRABRI
ABORIGINAL LAND
TRUST

Kaidwalla
Waterhole
Skinner Ck

Mt Windajong
565 m

WIRLIYAJARRAYI
ABORIGINAL LAND
TRUST

Mud Hut Well

NEUTRAL JUNCTION

21

Ali Curung
(No public access)

25

Murray
Downs

STUDHOLME HILLS

Fotheringham Hill
483 m

Willowra
Community

Mt Strzelecki
635 m

Crawford Ra

Osborne Ra

HIGHWAY

29

93
18

Nelson Bore

Bluebush Bore

35

Taylor Creek Rest Area (toilets)

John McDouall Stuart
Stuart made several journeys in this
approximate location between 1858
and 1862 which resulted in a practical
route north - south across Australia.

Taylor Hills
583 m

Hanson River

MURRAY DOWNS

Ingallan Creek

Hoodoo Well

87

Taylor Ck

Watt Range

STUART
44

STIRLING

Underground Gas Pipeline

Mt Peake Ck

Pawu Community
(Mount Barkly)

**PAWU ABORIGINAL
LAND TRUST**

Englands Well

Bloodwood Creek

9 Mile Ck

Forster Ra

30

Barrow Creek
Neutral Junction

Mt Mann
656 m

Mt Gwynne
696 m

**BARROW
CREEK**

Donkey Ck

ALAYAWARRA
ABORIGINAL
LAND TRUST

DENISON

Mt Leichhardt
1146 m

Mt Denison
884 m

CONISTON

Anningie

ANNINGIE

Mt Judith
705 m

Murray Ck

Camel Soak Bore
Teamster Memorial

Stirling
Wilora

River

89
44

43

STIRLING

Lander River

Ingallan Creek

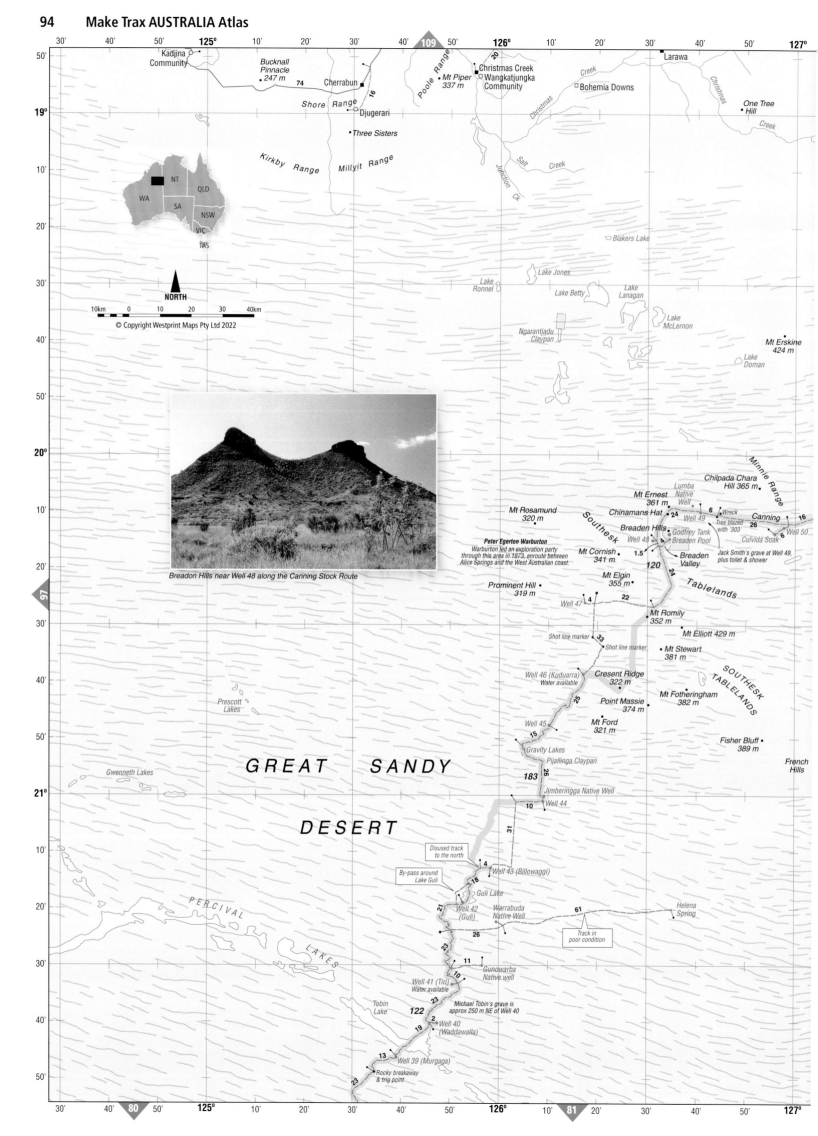

Kadjina
Community

Bucknall
Pinnacle
• 247 m

74

Cherrabun

16

109

Poole Range

• Mt Piper
337 m

20

Christmas Creek
Wangkatjungka
Community

Christmas   Creek

Larawa

□ Bohemia Downs

One Tree
• Hill

Christmas   Creek

Shore   Range

Djugerari

19º

• Three Sisters

Salt   Creek

Junction   CK

Kirkby   Range

Millyit   Range

NT

QLD

WA

SA

NSW

VIC

TAS

10'

NORTH

10km   0   10   20   30   40km

20'

20º

Blakers Lake

Lake Jones

Lake
Ronnel

Lake Betty

Lake
Lanagan

Lake
McLernon

30'

Ngarantjadu
Claypan

Mt Erskine
424 m

40'

Lake
Doman

Breadon Hills near Well 48 along the Canning Stock Route

Minnie   Range

Chilpada Chara
Hill 365 m

50'

Mt Rosamund
320 m

Mt Ernest
361 m

Lumba
Native
Well

6

6

Wreck

24

Well 49

Canning

16

Chinamans Hat

24

Tree blazed
with '303'

26

Well 50

Peter Egerton Warburton
Warburton led an exploration party
through this area in 1873, enroute between
Alice Springs and the West Australian coast.

Breaden Hills
Well 48

Godfrey Tank
Breaden Pool

Culvida Soak

Jack Smith's grave at Well 49,
plus toilet & shower

10'

Mt Cornish
341 m

1.5

Breaden
Valley

Mt Elgin
355 m

120

24

Tablelands

Prominent Hill
319 m

Well 47

4

22

Mt Romily
352 m

Mt Elliott 429 m

30'

97

Shot line marker

33

Shot line marker

Mt Stewart
381 m

SOUTHESK

Well 46 (Kuduarra)
Water available

Cresent Ridge
322 m

Mt Fotheringham
382 m

TABLELANDS

40'

25

Point Massie
374 m

Well 45

15

Mt Ford
321 m

Fisher Bluff
389 m

50'

Gravity Lakes

Pijallinga Claypan

183

26

French
Hills

GREAT   SANDY

Jimberingga Native Well

21º

Gwenneth Lakes

10

Well 44

DESERT

31

10'

Disused track
to the north

4

Well 43 (Billowaggi)

By-pass around
Lake Guli

18

Guli Lake

20'

PERCIVAL

21

Well 42
(Guli)

Warrabuda
Native Well

61

Helena
Spring

26

Track in
poor condition

LAKES

23

11

Gunowarba
Native well

30'

10

Well 41 (Tiri)
Water available

23

Michael Tobin's grave is
approx 250 m NE of Well 40

Tobin
Lake

122

2

Well 40
(Waddawalla)

40'

19

Well 39 (Murgaga)

13

23

Rocky breakaway
& trig point

50'

10' 20' 30' 40' 50' **128°** 10' 20' 30' 40' 50' **129°** 10' 20' 30'

50'

19°

10'

20'

30'

40'

20°

10'

20'

30'

40'

21°

10'

20'

30'

40'

50'

71
Wolfe

• Taylor Lookout
542 m

Creek

CANNING STOCK ROUTE
For further information between
Halls Creek and Wiluna, see the
CANNING STOCK ROUTE map
from Westprint Maps

Kundat Djara
Community

168

**Wolfe Creek Meteorite
Crater National Park**

Deep creek crossing
at Carranya

16
▲ Wolfe Creek
Meteorite Crater

■ Carranya

Sturt Creek ■

Bindi Bindi Waterhole

Jawilga Pool

Mt Lane
694 m •

Brophy   Ck

Lewis

Creek

YINGUALYALYA
ABORIGINAL
LAND TRUST

PURTA ABORIGINAL
LAND TRUST

Purta
Co-management
Area

41

Weedy
Waterhole

Wowaljarrow
Pool
Ima Ima Pool

Junction Waterhole

Knobby
Hills

Creek

DENISON   RA

Bramall
Hills

Slatey

GARDNER

Creek

RANGE

Mallee Hill
511 m •

MOUNT
FREDERICK
ABORIGINAL
LAND TRUST

• Skeen Hill

Fuel available from Billiluna
Mon to Fri 8 - 11am and 2 - 4pm.
Sat 8 - 10:30am.
After hours call out fee applies.

Mt Bannerman
449 m •

Sturt

Billiluna (Mindibungu) ○
Myarra Pool •

Road may occasionally
be closed due to flooding
of Sturt Creek

TANAMI

10

• No 3 Bore

Mt Frederick
• 529 m

Mount Frederick
Outstation

MINDIBUNGU
ABORIGINAL
RESERVE

6 2

Bloodwood Bore •   7 5 3
Stretch Lagoon
Lake Stretch
(Nyarna) Campsite

101

48

Elsey

ROAD

Killi Killi Hills
470 m •

BILLILUNA
ABORIGINAL
LAND

52
Ck
Gingerally
Waterhole

Bowshed Waterhole

Hills

Permits are NOT
required for travel along
the Tanami Road

BILLILUNA
ABORIGINAL
LAND

Mt Mueller
417 m •

Selby

24

Mine
gate
☒

84

156

Coyote Gold
Project •

21

58

Sections of the Tanami Road
between Tanami Mine and the
border may be heavily corrugated

Billiluna
Pool

Back

58

Track

Hills

52 Road

Three
Ways

Durbal

39

37

Route

Overflow

Ck

Sturt

13

44

Balgo Hill
333 m •

Ck

Warlayirti Art Centre is
located at Balgo,
ph (08) 9168 8960.

Lewis   Range

Tanami
Mine

MOUNT FREDERICK
(No 2) ABORIGINAL
LAND TRUST

Flood
by-pass

Well 51 Stock

17

4

Mulan •
Condren
Pinnacles
330 m

11

✛
Wirrimanu (Balgo)

Point Nelligan
515 m •

Guda
Plain

Handover
Campsite

23

Yunpu
Campsite
▲

8

Bulbi
Plain

Weriaddo
Yard

Lens Bore

Mt Wilson
359 m •

31

McGuire
Gap

McGuire
Bore •

75

○ Killi Killi

Pussycat
Bore •

40

Wilson   Ra

MANGKURURRPA
ABORIGINAL LAND TRUST

9

MULAN
ABORIGINAL
RESERVE

27

23

12

23

Stafford Bore

Small stone
hill

23

Gunawarrawarra
Rockhole

Flood by-pass

Point Alphonse

75

Bloodwood Bore •

Wilsons
Cave Bore •

Lake
Sarah

34

Lake Alec

Bullocks Head
Lake

Ferdies Bore •

Luckies Bore •

60

Wild Potato
Bore

Djaluwon
Well

Cleared lines -
no through roads

WARNING
Much of the flood bypass between
Balgo and Well 51 is along disused
seismic lines. Extra fuel may be
required if this route is followed.

KEARNEY

Ngulupi ■

WESTERN AUSTRALIA   NORTHERN TERRITORY

Mt Hughes
• 463 m

Phillipson   Range

Lake
Jeavons

YININGARRA
ABORIGINAL
LAND TRUST

ABORIGINAL   RESERVE

BM 338 •

89

Yagga Yagga ■

Thomas Peak
• 414 m

Lake Dennis

Lake Lucas

Lake White

Bishop   Range

Roberts Ra

Stretch Range

Powell

Ck

Talapanpta Claypan •

Tirriparri
Claypan

Wantitjatra Claypan •

Weston
Basin

Sidney Margaret
Range

Farewell
Lakes

93

Lamanbundah ■

STANSMORE   RANGE

Warri
Peak
505 m •

Warri   Creek

HIDDEN
BASIN

Lake Willis

Lake Hazlett

Murraba   Ranges

Lake
White

Nicker

Brookham

Ck

Mt Russell
400 m •

Jangga Bluff
450 m •

Nardudi Hill
450 m •

Yapparu
Claypan

Tingaritjatja
Claypan

Murraba   Ranges

Brookham   Creek

Wilbrunga   Range

Laka Claypan

Munyu
Hills

10'

20'

30'

40'

50'

INDIAN   OCEAN

Cape Frezier
Geoffroy Bay
Cape Jaubert
Desault Bay

108
47
288
Stony Hill 127 m
Parda Hill 127 m •

Cape Missiessy

Willara Hill •

18
Nita Downs

Anna Plains ■

14

Mt Phire
• 92 m

52

Baker Bore

Beach

1

Lyngett Well

Mile

Mandora ■

Eighty Mile Beach
Caravan Park
Wallal
Downs

6

22

20

23

Sandfire
Roadhouse

Eighty

Tower

Wapet

48

138

Ironstone Hill
127 m

HIGHWAY

Coastal Reserve
Cape Keraudren

45

61

Road

Track

20°

Red
Point

This track to the Canning Stock
Route is in poor condition. It is
approximately 620 km to
Kunawaritji Community.

NORTHERN

Pardoo Roadhouse ■

Pardoo ■

32

Shay

Road

The Old Telegraph Track
is mainly overgrown
and best avoided

99

15

GREAT

1

Gap

41

Boreline

Telegraph

102

19

(old gold town)
Goldsworthy

Rd

Old

Pardoo

Cattle

47

Mount Goldsworthy
Mines (abandoned)

28

Ck

Mulyie

Carleecarleethong Pool

Creek

Nimingarra
Mine

Shay Gap
Mines

Shay Gap
(dismantled town)

75

Coongan

Ck

25

Shay
Gap

Eel

Warralong ■

Coongan ■

Pear

Soda

Muccanoo Pool

Muccan ■

27

Yarrie ■

Yarrie Mine
and Camp

Callawa ■

Kimberley
Gap

Ck

Woodie

152

40

River

Eginbah ■

17

Talga Peak
296 m

Coppin Gap

Warrawagine

Warrawagine ■

Oakover

Ulalling
Hills

Isabella Range

GEORGE RANGE

Creek

24

Eight

Mile

Ck

Bamboo Creek ■
• Bamboo Creek
Mines

Ck

River

Road

21°

Panorama ■

26

Moolyella Mines
(abandoned)

Talga

Proposed
Conservation Area
(formerly Meentheena Station)

Koongaling Hill
387 m •

Muttarbarty Hill
316 m •

41

Marble Bar

8

14

Ripon

River

Bullgarina Hill
• 342 m
Hills

Nullagine

Coonanbunn

• Mt Newgate

Braeside □

Creek

Barnicarndy Hills
281 m •

Chinaman Pool

17

Limestone

Salgash

Yandicoogina

Tumbinna Pool

Gregory

Rabbit Proof
Fence Memorial

Lake
Waukarlycarly

14

Brockman

Meentheena
Outcamp

134

156

Road

Range

Telfer

Camel

Sandy

Ck

Mount Edgar ■

Marble

Creek

□ Pelican Pool

Proposed
Conservation Area
(formerly Meentheena Station)

Yilgalong

9

Midgengadge

16

Woodie

Mine

107

38

Glen Herring
Gorge

Corunna Downs
WWII Airfield

Corunna
Downs

Emu

Stony

Blue Bar Pool

Elsie

Ck

Carawine Gorge •

Two Sisters 301 m •

Woodie Rd

28

247

Ck

P I L B A R A

Bar

Mt Elsie
• 502 m

Boodarrie

Upper Carawine Gorge •

Warri

Woodie Woodie
Mining Centre

Mt Crofton
352 m •

115

Lionel Mining
Centre

Nullagine

Mt Olive
485 m

Ck

Tooncoonaragee Pool •

9

45

Nifty
Mine

Coongan

White Quartz
Knob •

Blue Spec
Mine

Mill

Mosquito Creek
Mining Centre

Viewpoint •

McPhee

Skull

Running
Waters WH

Woodie
Woodie Mine

7

Mike Mine •

90

Mt MacPherson
465 m •

Old Eleys Mine •

River

20

Ck

Depot

Springs

Road

39

Cooke

63

Skull
Springs
Mine

Eel Pool

Old Hillside Mine •

Beaton Gorge

Nullagine
Mine

Old gold
mine •

Creek

Ck

Warri

Mt MacPherson
465 m •

45

82

120°

Nullagine ■

32

83

247

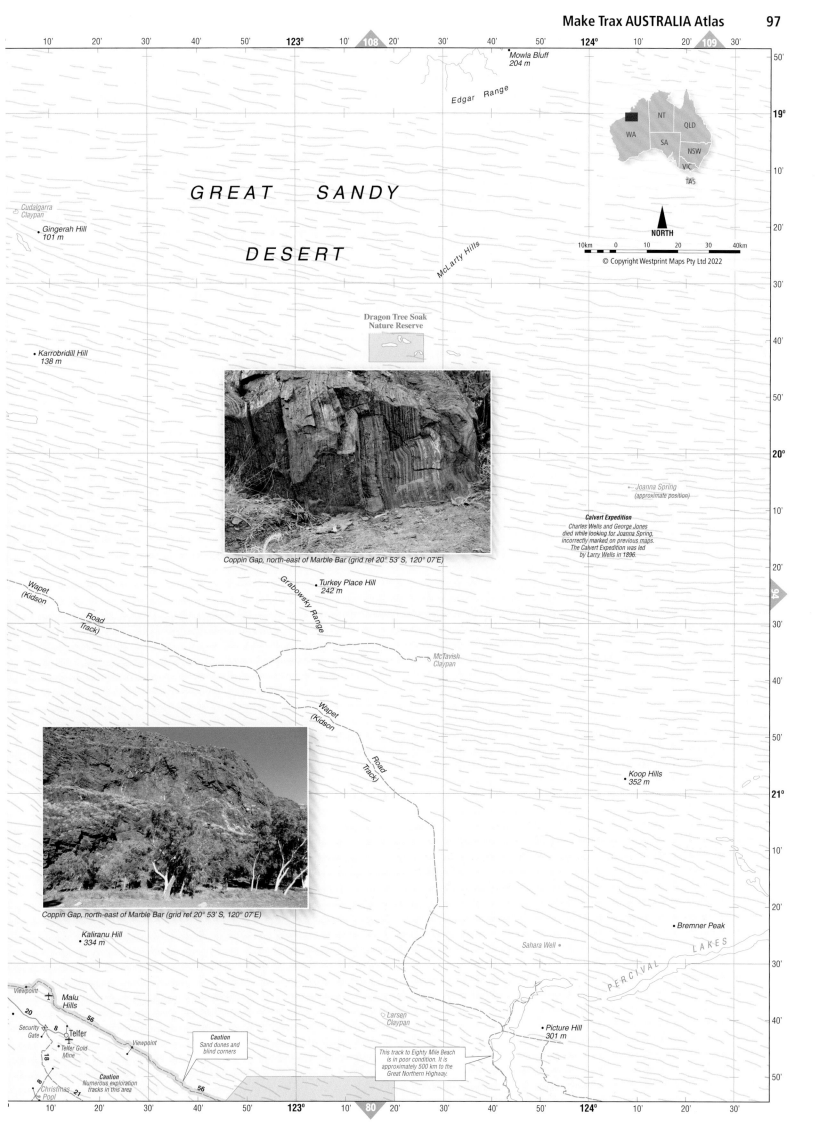

10'   20'   30'   40'   50'   **123⁰**   10'   **108**   20'   30'   40'   50'   **124⁰**   10'   20'   **109**   30'

Mowla Bluff
204 m

Edgar Range

NT
QLD
WA
SA
NSW
VIC
TAS

NORTH

10km   0   10   20   30   40km

© Copyright Westprint Maps Pty Ltd 2022

Cudalgarra
Claypan

Gingerah Hill
101 m

G R E A T   S A N D Y

D E S E R T

McLarty Hills

**Dragon Tree Soak
Nature Reserve**

Karrobridill Hill
138 m

*← Joanna Spring
(approximate position)*

Calvert Expedition
*Charles Wells and George Jones
died while looking for Joanna Spring,
incorrectly marked on previous maps.
The Calvert Expedition was led
by Larry Wells in 1896.*

Coppin Gap, north-east of Marble Bar (grid ref 20° 53' S, 120° 07'E)

Wapet
(Kidson

Road
Track)

Turkey Place Hill
242 m

Grabowsky Range

McTavish
Claypan

Wapet
(Kidson

Road
Track

Koop Hills
352 m

Coppin Gap, north-east of Marble Bar (grid ref 20° 53' S, 120° 07'E)

Bremner Peak

Kaliranu Hill
334 m

Sahara Well

P E R C I V A L   L A K E S

Viewpoint

Malu
Hills

Security
Gate

Telfer

20

56

8

Telfer Gold
Mine

Viewpoint

Caution
Sand dunes and
blind corners

Larsen
Claypan

Picture Hill
301 m

*This track to Eighty Mile Beach
is in poor condition. It is
approximately 500 km to the
Great Northern Highway.*

18

8

Christmas
Pool

21

Caution
Numerous exploration
tracks in this area

56

19⁰
20'
30'
40'
50'
20⁰
10'
20'
30'
40'
50'
21⁰
10'
20'
30'
40'
50'

94

10'   20'   30'   40'   50'   **123⁰**   10'   **80**   20'   30'   40'   50'   **124⁰**   10'   20'   30'

19°
19°

20°

NORTH

10km 0 10 20 30 40km

© Copyright Westprint Maps Pty Ltd 2022

20°

I N D I A N   O C E A N

Montebello Islands Marine Park

Montebello Islands

North West I.

Bluebell I.
Alpha I.
Trimouille Island
South East I.

Hermite I.
Montebello Islands Conservation Park
Ivy I.

Ah Chong I.

Barrow Island Marine Management Area

Parakeelya I.
Lowendal Islands
Varanus I.

Cape Dupuy
Surf Point

Flacourt Bay

■ Wapet Landing
Double I.

Barrow Island Marine Park

Barrow Island
● Gorgon Gas Plant

Barrow Island Nature Reserve
■ Wapet Camp

Eagles Nest
South End

Stokes Point
Middle Island

Boodie, Double, Middle Islands Nature Reserve
Boodie Island

21°
21°

Barrow Island Marine Management Area

Barrow Island Shoals

North Sandy I.

Passage Islands *Angle I.*

Great Sandy Island Nature Reserve
Pup I.

Great Sandy Island

Cowle I.

Mary Anne Passage

Lightfoot Reef

Rosily Islands

Taunton Reef

Mary Anne I.
Airlie Island
Mary Anne Group
West Island *Large I.*
Great Sandy Island Nature Reserve
East I. *Robe Point*

Weld Island Nature Reserve

Thevenard Island Nature Reserve

Mangrove Islands
North I.

Bessieres (Anchor) I. Nature Reserve

Direction I.
South I.

Coolgra Point
Mangrove Passage
Yardie Landing

Flat Island
Tortoise I.
Serrurier (Long) I. Nature Reserve
Ashburton I.

Beadon Point
Onslow ■
Onslow Saltfield

Entrance Point

Sunday I.

Baresand Point
Old Onslow
Proposed Wheatstone Gas Plant

Locker Island Nature Reserve

Observation I.
Urala ■
15
Tubridgi Gas Field
19

Fly Island

Locker Point
16
6

Tubridgi Point
17

Brown I.
Chinty Pool
41

Cane River
64

Peedamulla ●
121

Cape Legendre
Legendre Island

Keast Island
Nature Reserve

Rosemary Island Nature Reserve
Gidley I.
Hauy I.
Malus Islands
Angel I.
Dolphin Island

Goodwyn Island
West Lewis I.
Burrup Peninsula

Enderby Island Nature Reserve
Nature Reserve East Lewis I.
NW Shelf and Pluto Gas Plants

Mermaid Sound

Eaglehawk I.
West Intercourse Island
Dampier ○
Sloping Point

Karratha Aerodrome
Nickol Bay
13
6
9

Karratha ●

North East Regnard I.
South West Regnard I.
Gnoorea Point

Steamboat Island
Regnard Bay

Preston I.
Maitland River
Roadhouse
13
6
9
31

Cape Preston
28
Cockatoo Ck
21
42

Karratha ■
Miaree Pool

Great Sandy Island Nature Reserve
Fortescue I.
Potter I.
Carey I.

Sholl Island
Round Island

Mardie I.
Fortescue River Mouth

Long Island

25
Yannare
Devil Creek
Byong Creek

Armstrong Creek
Brill Creek

Toorare Pool
Radio Hill Mine
36
Iron Ore Railway

23
139
1

32
FORTESCUE

Mardie ●
22

Chuerdoo Pool
Mungowarra Pool

Fortescue Roadhouse ■
Tarda Pool

Minderoo Pool
Booyeema Pool Creek

Curramuna Waterhole
RIVER
Munni Munni

Robe River

Peter Creek

41
HIGHWAY

Portland Pool
Cooribin Pool

Yarraloola ●
Pannawonica Road

27
Pannawonica
Pannawonica ●
18
Mine
Yalleen ■
Pannawonica
55
Millstream
Robe River - Deepdale Mining Area
Mine
Mine
38
Road

Mine
Pannawonica ●
Mine

85
Kumina Creek

Robe River

NORTH WEST COASTAL HIGHWAY
1
43

PILBARA

Port Hedland
South Hedland
Boodarrie
Wedgefield
Redbank
Carpill Salt Farm
Cooke Point
Hot Briquetted Iron Plant
Finucane Island
Downes Island
Cape Thouin
Geographe Shoals
Reefs Island
Cape Cossigny
Ronsard Island
Mundubullangana
Balla Balla Harbour
Balla Balla Fishing Access
Depuch Island
West Moore I.
Forestier Bay
Sherlock Bay
Bezout Island
Cape Lambert
Point Sampson
Dixon Island
Cleaverville Mine
Cossack
Wickham
Roebourne
Woodbrokk
Warambie
Harding Dam
Lake Poongkaliyarra
Pyramid
Bottom Pool
Kangan Pool
Langwell Gorge
Caralowana Pool
Red Dog Gorge
Python Pool
Camp Curlewis
Millstream Chichester National Park
Crossing Pool
Deep Reach Pool
Coolawanyah
Upper Wallopna Pool
Mootana Pool
Hooley
HAMERSLEY RA
FORTSCUE RIVER
CHICHESTER RANGE
Mungaroona Range Nature Reserve
Mungaroona Range
YANDEYARRA ABORIGINAL LAND
Cheearra Hill • 425 m
Yandeyarra
Yandeyarra Pool
Kangan Pool
Old Wodgina Mine
Walla Siding
Indee Station stay
Gillam
Turner
Abydos
Old Pinga Mine
Woodstock
Red Granite Hill 430 m •
Coon
Tambourah
Hillside
Old Eleys Mine
Old Hillside Mine
White Quartz Hill
Old Spear Hill Mine
Panorama
Cooke Bluff Hill
North Pole Mine (abandoned)
Fey Hill
Lalla Rookh
Pilgangoora Mine
Wallareenya
Carlindie
Warralong
Mulyie
Strelley
De Grey
Goldsworthy (old gold town)
Pardoo
Cartaminia Point
Condini Landing
Shellborough
Poissonnier Point
Larrey Point
Spit Point
Mystery Landing
Ripon Island
Salt Pool
Salt Evaporators
Ridley River
De Grey River
GREAT
NORTHERN
HIGHWAY
GREAT NORTHERN HIGHWAY
COASTAL HIGHWAY
NORTH WEST COASTAL HIGHWAY
GEORGE RA
Marble Bar
Shaw River
Strelley River
Tabba Tabba Creek
East Strelley River
North Pole Creek
Coongan Ck
Coolyia Ck
Paddy Market Ck
Miralga
Six Mile Creek
Chinnamon Creek
Newman
Mount Newman
Beebingarra Creek
Patermater Ck
Jinparinya Mine
Turner River
Yule River
West Turner River
Herbert Parker
Peawah
Sherlock River
Balla Balla R
Poverty Creek
Peawah (toilets)
Mallina
Yirrakulanha Hills
Sherlock (toilets)
Sherlock
Madabarena Pool
Wonda Wokatena Pool
Coppermine Hills
Croydon Outstation
Coorbelbie
Pilbara Creek
Spring Creek
Grant Creek
Pillingini Ck
Harding River
Roebourne Wittenoom Road
Cherratta Rd
Western Ck
Delambre Island Nature Reserve

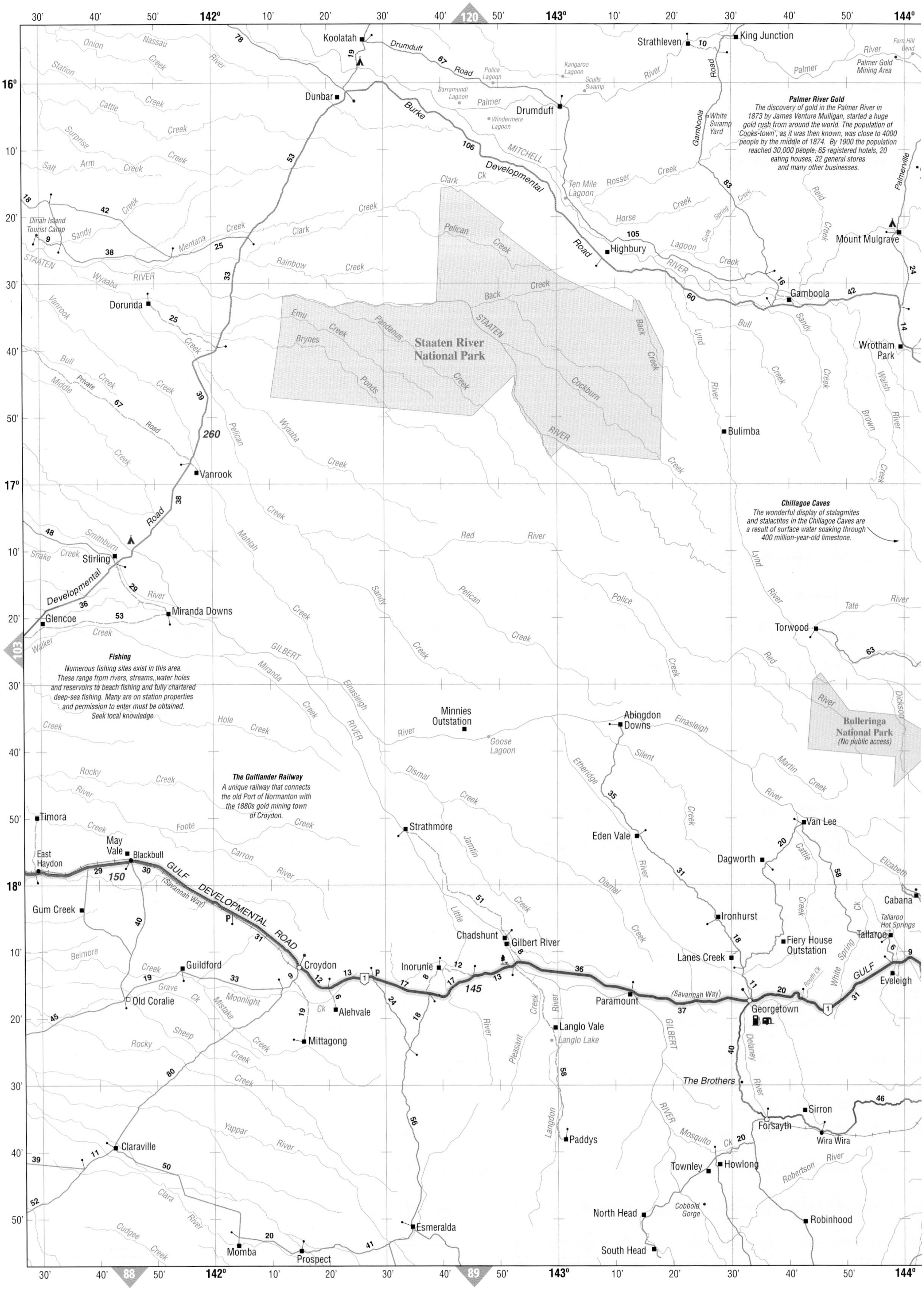
142°
143°
144°
16°
17°
18°
120
103
88
89
Koolatah
Drumduff Road
Strathleven
King Junction
Fern Hill Bend
Palmer Gold Mining Area
Police Lagoon
Kangaroo Lagoon
Sculls Swamp
Dunbar
Barramundi Lagoon
Windermere Lagoon
Drumduff
Burke Developmental Road
MITCHELL
White Swamp Yard
Gamboola Road
Palmer River Gold
The discovery of gold in the Palmer River in 1873 by James Venture Mulligan, started a huge gold rush from around the world. The population of 'Cooks-town', as it was then known, was close to 4000 people by the middle of 1874. By 1900 the population reached 30,000 people, 65 registered hotels, 20 eating houses, 32 general stores and many other businesses.
Palmerville
Ten Mile Lagoon
Rosser Creek
Horse Creek
Soda Spring
Mount Mulgrave
Highbury
Dinah Island Tourist Camp
Sandy
Mentana Creek
Clark Creek
STAATEN
Wyaaba
RIVER
Rainbow Creek
Gamboola
Dorunda
Staaten River National Park
Emu Creek
Brynes
Pandanus
Ponds
Back Creek
Cockburn
Wrotham Park
Bull Creek
Private Road
Middle Creek
Pelican Creek
Bulimba
Vanrook
Chillagoe Caves
The wonderful display of stalagmites and stalactites in the Chillagoe Caves are a result of surface water soaking through 400 million-year-old limestone.
Red River
Smithburn
Stirling
Snake Creek
Developmental Road
Mahlah
Sandy Creek
Lynd River
Tate River
Miranda Downs
Glencoe
Walker Creek
Police Creek
Torwood
Fishing
Numerous fishing sites exist in this area. These range from rivers, streams, water holes and reservoirs to beach fishing and fully chartered deep-sea fishing. Many are on station properties and permission to enter must be obtained. Seek local knowledge.
GILBERT
Miranda Creek
Einasleigh RIVER
Minnies Outstation
Goose Lagoon
Abingdon Downs
Einasleigh River
Bulleringa National Park
(No public access)
Dickson
Hole Creek
Etheridge
Silent Creek
Martin Creek
Rocky River
The Gulflander Railway
A unique railway that connects the old Port of Normanton with the 1880s gold mining town of Croydon.
Dismal Creek
Timora
Foote Creek
Strathmore
Jamtin
Eden Vale
Van Lee
May Vale
Blackbull
East Haydon
Carron Creek
Dagworth
Cattle Creek
Elizabeth
GULF DEVELOPMENTAL ROAD
(Savannah Way)
Gum Creek
Little Creek
Ironhurst
Cabana
Tallaroo Hot Springs
Tallaroo
Chadshunt
Gilbert River
Fiery House Outstation
Belmore
Guildford
Croydon
Inorunie
Lanes Creek
White Spring Ck
Eveleigh
Grave Ck
Moonlight
Mistake
Alehvale
Paramount
Georgetown
Old Coralie
Langlo Vale
Langlo Lake
Pleasant Creek
Sheep Creek
Mittagong
Rocky Creek
The Brothers
Delaney River
Sirron
Forsayth
Wira Wira
Yappar River
Langdon
Paddys
Mosquito Ck
Claraville
Townley
Howlong
Robertson River
Clara River
Cobbold Gorge
North Head
Robinhood
Cudgee Creek
Esmeralda
Momba
Prospect
South Head

CORAL SEA

NORTH

10km 0 10 20 30 40km

© Copyright Westprint Maps Pty Ltd 2022

WA

NT

QLD

SA

NSW

VIC

TAS

Great Barrier Reef

Marine Park

GREAT BARRIER REEF

Palmerville
Logan Jack Memorial
Palmer Goldfield Resources Reserve
Maytown Ruins
Old Louisa Mine
Maytown Monument
Mt Musgrave 468 m
The Granite
Maitland Downs
Palmer River Roadhouse
Hamilton Peak 644 m
Lakeland
Honey Dam
Mt Boolbun North 921 m
Ayton
Wujal Wujal
Permit required
Weary Bay
Bloomfield Track
Cowie Point
Donovan Point
Cape Tribulation
Myall Beach
Noah Head
Thornton Beach
Daintree National Park
Undine Reef
St Crispin Reef
Bailey Point
Cape Kimberley
Snapper Island Nat Park
Daintree
Daintree National Park
Bellevue
Mount Windsor National Park
Mount Elephant 1046 m
Bobs Lookout
Mareeba Mining Field
Mount Spurgeon NP
Mt Carbine Mine
Mount Carbine
Mount Lewis NP
Daintree NP
Wonga Beach
Dayman Point
Low Islets
Mossman
Port Douglas
Craiglie
Mowbray National Park
Pebbly Beach
Macalister Range NP
Rex Lookout
Julatten
Miallo
Newell
Black Mtn
Rudder Reef
Opal Reef
Tongue Reef
Batt Reef
Hastings Reef
Oyster Reef
Michaelmas Reef
Trinity Bay
Nychum
Mount Mulligan
Kingsborough
Thornborough
Old Tyrconnell Gold Mine
Hann Tableland National Park
Mount Molloy
Kuranda NP
Ellis Beach
Palm Cove
Smithfield CP
Green Island National Park
Arlington Reef
Yalkula
Koah
Kuranda NP
Trinity Beach
Yorkeys Knob
Holloways Beach
Barron Gorge NP
Bare Hill CP
Biboohra
Mareeba
Davies Creek NP
Dinden NP
CAIRNS
Yarrabah
Cape Grafton
Wide Bay
Fitzroy Island National Park
Deception Point
Moore Reef
Sudbury Reef
Edmonton
YARRABAH
Grey Peaks NP
Scott Reef
Rookwood
Ryan Imperial Cave
Kays Mtn
Wolfram
Chillagoe-Mungana Caves NP
Mungana
Chillagoe
Calcifer
Royal Arch Cave
Dimbulah
Atherton Tableland
Watkamin
Danbulla NP
Little Mulgrave NP
Gordonvale
Mt Massey 1258 m
Deeral
High I.
Frankland Islands National Park
Normanby I.
Hamils
Flurospar
Crooked Creek
Almaden
Lappa
Petford
Kooboora
Atherton
Herberton Range National Park
Tinaroo Falls
Lake Tinaroo
Crater Lakes NP
Yungaburra
Gadgarra NP
Malanda
Bellenden Kerr 1561 m
Bellenden Ker NP
Russell River NP
Babinda
Bartle Frere 1622 m
Bramston Beach
Cooper Beach
Eubenangee Swamp NP
Ella Bay NP
Crystal Brook
Bolwarra
Fischerton Homestead
Tate Tin Mine
Shebas Breasts
Irvinebank
Watsonville
Herberton
Kalunga
Tarzali
Zillie Falls
Ellinjaa Falls
Innisfail
Moresby Range NP
Weepen
Ord
Opah
Emuford
Evelyn Creek CP
Millaa Millaa
Wooroonooran National Park
Mourilyan
Moresby
Lindquist I.
Adelaide Reef
Hall-Thompson Reef
Barwidgi
Gingerella
Mount Garnet
Innot Hot Springs
Makan NP
Ravenshoe
Crawfords Lookout
Wangan
Basilisk Range NP
Double Point
Kent I.
Potter Reef
Round Mtn
Amber
Burlington
Lyndbrook
Sundown
Morecambe
Tumoulin
Millstream Falls NP
Tully Falls National Park
Cardstone
Tully Gorge NP
Japoon NP
Silkwood
Kurramine Beach NP - Stephens i.
Cowley Beach
Kurrimine Beach
Maria Creek NP
Farquarson Reef
Frewhurst
Springfield
Tirrabella
Gunnawarra
Lake Koombooloomba
Tully River Station
El Arish
Bingil Bay
Mission Beach
Djiru NP
Mount Mackay NP
South Mission Beach
Dunk Island
Family Islands National Park
Outer Reef
O'Briens Creek Gemfield
Mt Surprise
Brooklands
Mount Surprise
Undara Resort
Kalkani Crater
Yarramulla (Ranger)
Forty Mile Scrub National Park
Native Wells
Wombinoo
Glen Ruth
Kirrama National Park
Cashmere
Bilyana
Tully
Lower Tully
Tully Heads
Girramay National Park
Girramay NP
Smith (Kurrambah) I.
Hudson I.
Coombe Is
DEVELOPMENTAL
Rosella Plains
Mount Rosey Resource Reserve
Undara Volcanic National Park
Commissioners Cap 1028 m
Boomerang Crater
Minnamoolka
Wyoming
Meadowbank
Glen Harding
Walters Plains Lake
Burdekin
Herbert River Falls
Blencoe Falls Lookout
Murray Falls
Girrungun National Park
Gool Island NP
Brook Islands National Park
Cape Richards
Cape Sandwich
Missionary Bay
Einasleigh
Red Rock
Kinrara National Park
Mt Kinrara
Glen Dhu
Kinrara
Lava Plains
Gemfields
Wairuna
Wairuna Plain
Kennedy
Cardwell
Hinchinbrook Island National Park
Ramsay Bay
Zoe Bay
Hillcock Point
Pelorus (North Palm) Island
Spring Creek
Marionvale
Conjuboy
Reedy Brook
Valley of Lagoons
Lake Lucy
Wallaman Falls are situated in some of the oldest rainforests on earth and at 268 metres are the highest, permanent, single-drop falls in Australia.
Abergowrie
Long Pocket
Bemerside
Lucinda Point
Lucinda
Orpheus I. NP
Carpentaria Downs
Mywyn
Wyandotte
Jervoise
Rhonella Park
Trebonne
Halifax
Victoria Mill
Taylors Beach
Fantome I.
Palm Island
The Oaks
Kidston
The Lynd Junction Roadhouse
The Lynd
Lucky Downs
Camel Creek
Ryeburn
Mt Fox 810 m (Volcano)
Michael Creek
Ingham
Forrest Beach
Upper Stone
Pombel
Halifax Bay Wetlands NP
Scrub View
Halifax Bay Wetlands NP
Mutarnee
Mt Spec
Great Palm Island
Havannah Island

Fishing
Numerous fishing sites exist in this area.
These range from rivers, streams, water holes
and reservoirs to beach fishing and fully chartered
deep-sea fishing. Many are on station properties
and permission to enter must be obtained.
Seek local knowledge.

Crocodiles and Box Jellyfish
Saltwater crocodiles inhabit coastal waterways
especially river estuaries. Swimming is not recommended.
Highly venomous box jellyfish infest these waters between
October and May. Swimming is not recommended.

The Great Top Road
The original coach road connecting Port Douglas
to Darwin, it was named by thousands of travellers
making their way from the east coast to Darwin
or the Kimberley during the 1880s.
(See Stock Routes information overleaf).

Private track.
Ph (08) 8975 9904
for permission.

Private track to coast.
For permit enquiries
Ph (08) 8975 9944.

Private track to coast.
Permit enquiries to
Hells Gate (07) 4745 8258.

Road Conditions
Many roads shown on this map will
flood during the Wet Season and become
completely impassable. Contact NT recorded
road report on 1800 246 199 or Queensland
recorded road report on 1300 130 595
for current information.

Connells Lagoon
This Reserve preserves an area of the
Mitchell grass, black-soil plains of the Barkly Tableland.
A 4WD track provides access to the reserve but there
are no visitor facilities. Connells dip near the southern
boundary was one of several cattle dips on
the Barkly Stock Route.

MANANGOORA
GREENBANK
SEVEN EMU
GARAWA
ABORIGINAL
LAND TRUST
PUNGALINA
WOLLOGORANG
KIANA
CALVERT
HILLS
CRESSWELL
DOWNS
WAANYI - GARAWA
ABORIGINAL LAND TRUST
CHINA WALL
DOOMADGEE
ABORIGINAL
LAND
BENMARRA
Lawn Hill
National Park
CARRARA RANGE
MITTIEBAH
MT DRUMMOND
Connells Lagoon
Conservation
Reserve
Lawn Hill
National Park
CONSTANCE RANGE

NORTHERN TERRITORY
QUEENSLAND

Batten Point
King Ash Bay
Pelican Spit
Manangoora
Spring Creek
Greenbank
Seven Emu
Scrutton Lagoon
Robinson River
Pungalina
Calvert Hills
Redbank Mine &
Mastertons Cave
Echo Gorge
Wollogorang
Westmoreland
Hells Gate
Benmarra
Kingfisher Camp
Corinda
Doomadgee
Community
Bowthorn
Accident
Mt Oscar
115 m
Stockyard
Camp
Musselbrook
Mining Camp
Mt Caroline
Lawn Hill
Lawn
Hill
Yeldham
Adels Grove
New
Century
Mine
Silver Star
Mine
Mt Drummond
Mittebah
Connells Lagoon

(Savannah Way)
Great Top Road
The Great Top Road
(Savannah Way)
Calvert Road
Bluey Road

NORTH

10km   0   10   20   30   40km

© Copyright Westprint Maps Pty Ltd 2022

Matthew Flinders
Matthew Flinders completed a marine survey of these waters in 1802 during his voyage around Australia.

Mornington Island
An Aboriginal Council is responsible for the administration of Mornington and a cluster of surrounding islands. Permits are not required for access to Birri Lodge or Sweers Island Resort where fishing holidays are a speciality. Sweers Island Resort is built on the site of the old town of Carnarvon where survivors of the 1866 Gulf Fever epidemic were housed. Several historic sites are marked on the island.

Crocodiles and Box Jellyfish
Saltwater crocodiles inhabit coastal waterways especially river estuaries. Swimming is not recommended. Highly venemous box jellyfish infest these waters between October and May. Swimming is not recommended.

So close…
Burke and Wills reach the mangrove-lined coast of the Gulf of Carpentaria on 11 Feb 1861, but cannot set foot on the beach due to the impenetrable nature of the trees.

Road Conditions
Many roads shown on this map will flood during the Wet Season and become completely impassable. Contact NT recorded road report on 1800 246 199 or Queensland recorded road report on 1300 130 595 for current information.

WELLESLEY ISLANDS

White Cliffs
Birri Lodge
Lingnoonganee Island
Mornington Island
Cape Van Diemen
Charlie Bush Bay
Gee Wee Point
Gununa
Denham Island
Sydney Island
Bountiful Islands
Tulburrerr Island

WELLESLEY ISLANDS ABORIGINAL LAND

Forsyth Island
FORSYTH ISLANDS
Bayley Island
Bayley Point

SOUTH WELLESLEY ISLANDS

Horseshoe Island
Allen Island
Bentinck Island
Sweers Island Resort

Tarrant Point

Inkerman
18
Dinah Island Tourist Camp
9
Macaroni Outstation

Rocky Creek

GILBERT RIVER

Spring Ck
Van Diemen Inlet
Point Burrowes
Point Austin
Smithburn
River
Delta Downs
Lotus Vale
Myra Vale
48
Snake Ck
Accident Inlet
Crooked Fitzmaurice
48 Ck
Double Lagoon
Glencoe
Brannigan
32 (Mitchell Byway)

Pascoe Inlet
Kangaroo Point
Gore Point
Disaster Inlet
Morning Inlet
Finucane Island NP
Truganini Landing
Cadell Landing
The Lake
LEICHHARDT

Karumba Point
Alligator Point
Karumba
41   70
Maggieville
Mutton Hole Wetlands NP
18
NORMAN
11
Mutton Hole
Wills Creek
Walker Ck

Escott Lodge   11
Burketown   6
Yarrum   6
Floraville   28
NICHOLSON
20
Armraynald
Beames Brook
Brookdale
Brinawa
Almora
119
84 (Barra)
Wills
Gregory Downs
26
76
Kamarga
67
Nardoo   13
84
Devel Rd   26

Magowra
FLINDERS RIVER
Bynoe River
Normanton
Road   25
B&W Camp 119
Old Glenore Station
Glenore Crossing   P
The   17
Gulflander Railway
1   35
East Haydon
Timora

Shady Lagoon
Station stay
8
Carron River
Broadwater
Silverfish Creek
Campbells Creek

Inverleigh
Normanton   32
Burketown   34   232
(Savannah Way & Barra Byway)
Ten Mile   Rd
B&W Camp 118
Lena Tank
19
Milgarra   8
B&W Camp 117
The Forty Mile Waterhole
Wynard
Jumble Ck Hole Creek

Gap Dam
Manooka Dam
Wernadinga   33
New Armraynald   18
Leichhardt Falls
Floraville
Walker Memorial
Pokino Dam
McAllister
Two Tree Hill
Mt Victoria
Neumayer Valley
Augustus Downs
Talawanta   44
30

Punchbowl Ck
M Lagoon
M Creek
L Creek
30
40
26   200
Warren Vale
B&W Camp 116
Paddys Lagoon
Bang Bang Jumpup   P
Bang Bang
12   45
Wondoola
Donors Hill   P
32
Ten Mile Tank
B&W Camp 114
Burke (Matilda Hwy)

Iffley   42
Yappar River
Surveyors
Surveyors Waterhole
22
Vena Park
20
Clara River
Muggera Waterhole   52
Iffley   22
11   14   12
Norman Bore

GREGORY Beames Road (Barra Byway) Developmental RIVER
Wills
Macadam Ck
Sandy Ck   Road   26
Planet Downs   17
Augustus
LEICHHARDT RIVER
Floraville Road
Wills Ck   143
Cartridge Ck
Fiery Ck
Nardoo Ck
Sandy Ck
Woodbine
Millar Creek
Twelve Mile Creek
Gidya Ck
Alexandra Ck
Collien Ck
Armstrong Creek
Wondoola Creek
Saxby River
Developmental Road
39
17
15   1
83
Peters Creek
Tabba Creek
FLINDERS RIVER
200
45

Delamere

Dillinya

DILLINYA ABORIGINAL LAND TRUST

166

16°

96

33

P

Killarney

Moolooloo Outstation

23   80

AVAGO

SUNDAY CREEK

Sunday Creek

Kalala

KALALA

86

24

10

Highway

10'

BIRRIMBA

HIDDEN VALLEY

Historic Hotel and Airfield

Daly Waters

Stuart Tree

11

Buntine

37

20

Birrimba

20'

CARPENTARIA

83

Hi-Way Inn Motel

Top Springs

30'

Montejinni

Yingawunarri

15

YINGAWUNARRI MUDBURA ABORIGINAL LAND TRUST

55

Hidden Valley

John McDouall Stuart
Stuart made several journeys in this approximate location between 1858 and 1862 which resulted in a practical route north - south across Australia.

Dingo Hill Rest Area

36

SHENANDOAH

MONTEJINNI WEST

77

P

MONTEJINNI EAST

Buchanan

Dungowan

71

No 13 Bore

No 12 Bore

Highway

23

31

8

87

Dunmarra

Shenandoah

Milner Lagoon

12

BUCHANAN DOWNS

Buchanan Downs

96

40'

Mt Wallaston
222 m

17°

No 11 Bore

80

15

147

Todd Memorial
Robert Charles Patterson joined the Overland Telegraph Line near Frews Ponds at noon, Thursday August 22, 1872. Charles Todd was superintendent of telegraphs, responsible for the success of this huge project.

DUNGOWAN

MURRANJI ABORIGINAL LAND TRUST

MURRANJI

Murranji

HAYFIELD

Sir Charles Todd Memorial

Frew Ponds Historical Reserve

P

P   23

BEETALOO

CAMFIELD

Bullock   Ck

10'

38

28

Newcastle

George Redmond Crossing

Beetaloo

43

Historic site

Newcastle Waters (Marlinja)
Newcastle Waters

15

107   68

CATTLE CREEK

Cattle   Creek

20'

Cattle Creek

WAMPANA - KARLANTIJPA ABORIGINAL LAND TRUST

30'

NEWCASTLE WATERS

20

Elliott

10

TANDYIDGEE

Longreach Waterhole

Longreach Waterhole Protected Area

19

POWELL CREEK

Lake Woods

30

Barkly

Longreach Waterhole (see campsite 25, west of Elliott)

18°

Junction Reserve

42   92

P

10'

STUART

Powell   Ck

Powell Creek

Alice Springs to Darwin Railway

Hunter   Ck

ASHBURTON

31

87

20'

Renner Springs

Lubras Lookout

Mt Willieray
361 m

Burke   Ck

18

Koo

Nara

Helen Springs

MUCKATY ABORIGINAL LAND TRUST

RANGE   HWY

20

Tomkinson

Muckaty

Ck

Church

Duck Ponds Waterhole

NT
WA
QLD
SA
NSW
VIC
TAS

NORTH

10km 0 10 20 30 40km

© Copyright Westprint Maps Pty Ltd 2022

135

Banka Banka

Underground Gas Pipeline

134°   10'   20'   30'   40'   110   50'   135°   10'   20'   30'   40'   50'   136°   10'   111   20'   30'

NUTWOOD DOWNS

Minamia
(Cox River)

53

O'Connor
Pocket

147

13

King Ash Bay

22   7

16°

BROADMERE

45

Top

Ck

Campbell
Spring

12   14   9   18   8   Borroloola

68

10'

TANUMBIRINI

**BAUHINIA
DOWNS**

**BILLEN-
GARRAH**

Ryan Bend
Waterhole

**NARWINBI
ABORIGINAL LAND
TRUST**

Tanumbirini

Bauhinia Downs

24

11   Billengarrah

51

Cowlagoon
(Tawallah)

13

**Caranbirini
Cons Res**

**SPRING
CREEK**

1

HIGHWAY

56   (Savannah Way)

**JANDANKU
ABORIGINAL LAND
TRUST**

Batten Creek
Rest Area

Tower

Starvation Hill 118 m

20'

Amungee
Mungee

272

30

Broadmere

**Limmen
National
Park**

44

109

22

McArthur River
Mine

Spring Creek

30'

**Bullwaddy
Conservation
Reserve**

October

Ck

Barney   Ck

34   HIGHWAY

**AMUNGEE
MUNGEE**

45

Favenc   Range

38

**CARPENTARIA
DOWNS**

Leila
Tower   Ck

**McARTHUR
RIVER**

40'

BEETALOO

17   CARPENTARIA

41   OT Downs

14   McArthur River

Cape Crawford

Cape Crawford
Cape Crawford is a geological
feature at the northern end of the
Abner Range, on McArthur
River Station.

Balbirni

Top
Crossing

BALBIRINI

The exact location
and condition of this
track is unknown

**MAMBALIYA RRUMBURRIYA
WUYALIYA ABORIGINAL
LAND TRUST**

37   HIGHWAY

Abner   Range

50'

Newcastle

Tower

Mallapunyah

17°

Road Conditions
Many roads shown on this map will
flood during the Wet Season and become
completely impassable. Contact NT recorded
road report on 1800 246 199 or Queensland
recorded road report on 1300 130 595
for current information.

71

**ABORIGINAL
LAND**

UCHARONIDGE

11

Kiana

Kiana

10'

MUNGABROOM

**MALLAPUNYAH
SPRINGS**

171

TABLELANDS

102

20'

30'

Barkly Tableland
Huge black-soil plains covered with waving
Mitchell grass caused problems for drovers bringing
cattle over from the Kimberley to eastern markets.
Although the scarcity of trees caused problems for
cooks trying to provide meals it was the lack of surface
water that caused the most difficulty when moving or
stocking cattle. Underground water and road transport
has made cattle handling much easier
on the Barkly Tableland.

Ucharonidge

WALHALLOW

28

**CRESSWELL
DOWNS**

40'

52

Mungabroom

Walhallow

Creek

50'

21

17

Cresswell Road   103

Route   70

39

32

Cresswell
Downs

15

16

18°

Stock

11

Anthony
Lagoon

Puzzle

79

18

Eva Downs

Calvert   36

10'

EVA DOWNS

Creek

Cresswell   Creek

Anthony Lagoon
Taken up in the early 1880s, Anthony
Lagoon is one of the great cattle stations
of the Barkly Tablelands and an important
point on the old Barkly Stock Route.

TABLELANDS

B A R K L Y

Tarrabool
Lake

ANTHONY LAGOON

Tower

39

11

20'

Harry Redford
The man who stole 1000 head of
cattle and drove them down Strzelecki
Creek, drowned in Corella Creek and
is buried on Brunette Downs.

Corella Creek
Community

HIGHWAY

24

HELEN SPRINGS

Cameron
Lagoon

Hole
Creek

Munkaderry
Waterhole

Dingo
Waterhole

Long Waterhole

30'

T A B L E L A N D

No public
access

Bootu
Manganese
Mine

BANKA BANKA

Brunette Downs
One of the largest cattle stations in the
Northern Territory, (12,250 square kilometres),
closely followed by Victoria River Downs and Andado
stations. Brunette Downs was taken up by John
and Tom MacAnash in 1883 and is now regarded
as one of Australia's top properties.
Brunette Downs has almost 5,000 kilometres of
roads, 2,500 kilometres of fencing, more than 100
bores and about 50,000 cattle. Visitors should
contact station management prior to arrival.

**BRUNETTE
DOWNS**

10

13   10

Brunette Downs   9

Ranken

62

Tower

40'

21

Corella   Lake

Road

30

BRUNCHILLY

**ROCKHAMPTON
DOWNS**

Lake
Sylvester

Connells Lagoon

MITTIEBAH
Connells Lagoon

50'

Brunchilly

Lake
DeBurgh

Boree   Creek

77

134°   10'   20'   30'   135°   90   10'   20'   30'   40'   50'   136°   10'   20'   30'

Map coordinates (top margin)

30'   40'   50'   **127°**   10'   20'   30'   40'   **115**   50'   **128°**   10'   20'   30'   40'   50'

16°

336

26

Ellenbrae   *5*   Mosquito Hills   New York Jump Ups   Palmer Ck   River   Emma Gorge Resort   Noble Memorial   *87*

24

21

Oomaloo Falls   Nimberline Valley   *16*   Tier Ra   *30*

16°   *47*   *49*   Royston   Salmond   El Questro Wilderness resort   El Questro Gorge   *45*   Lake Argyle Resort   Historic Durack Family Homestead

40   *108*   Gibb Range   Dunham Pilot Dam   *LAKE ARGYLE*

River   Horse   Salmond Gorge   Mt Throssell   Saw Ranges   Dunham   River

Gibb River (Ngallagunda)   Karunjie (Pentecost Downs)   Elgee Cliffs   DOON DOON ABORIGINAL RESERVE   Doon Doon Roadhouse   *16*   Carr Boyd Ranges

Karunjie   Ck   Dunham Hill 346 m   *152*   *38*   Argyle Downs   *147*

K I M B E R L E Y   FACE   Chapman   BLUFF   Salmond   Jerry   Ck   Mandangala (Glen Hill)   Ragged Range   Spring Creek

Blackfellow   RANGE   Cabbage   O'Donnell Ra   GLEN HILL ABORIGINAL RESERVE   Rugan   Argyle Aerodrome   Lissadell   Spring Hill 384 m   *19*

Siddins Creek   Gordons Gorge   Wilson   *19*   Argyle Village   Argyle Mine   *10*   Wandarrie Hill Village   Darlu   *22*

17°   Wood   DURACK   RIVER   Wilson   Creek   Castlereagh   O'Donnell   Bow   Bow River   *24*   Turkey   Cattle   *DARLU ABORIGINAL RESERVE*

Tablelands   Road   Tableland   RANGE   *56*   *29*   Bedford Downs   Survey   *21*   Warmun (Turkey Creek) Roadhouse and Visitor Centre   *Purnululu Conservation Reserve*   Mt Elder 271 m

Warton Range   *100*   *75*   Private road   VIOLET VALLEY ABORIGINAL RESERVE   Mabel Downs   Osmand Ra   Buchanan   Ck   New Ord River

109   FITZROY   RIVER   Private road   Spring   Violet Hill 518 m   *12*   Wurrenranginy   Allow 3hrs to campsites   *53*   Kurrajong Camp   *19*   Echidna Chasm   Bungle Bungle Range   Malangan (Illengirri)   *17*

Landsdowne   Little   Gold   ORD   *19*   *7*   Frank   *10*   Piccaninny Gorge   **Purnululu National Park**   Ord Hill 230 m   *151*

Tunganary Gorge   Sandy   *43*   *160*   Mt Ranford 479 m   McKenzie Bore   Wilfs   Walardi Camp   *16*   Cathedral Gorge   Ord   Duncan   *81*

Leopold   Little   Gold   O'Donnell River Gorge   *82*   road   Mabel Hill 520 m   Edle   Ck   Bungle Bungle Wilderness Camp   Dixon Ra   ORD

18°   Springvale   *16*   *17*   Alice Downs   Panton   CHINAMAN'S GARDEN YURUNGA   Nicholson

Little   Gold   O'Donnell   Watery   *36*   Alice Hill 506 m   Panton R   Little   Albert Edward Ra   Turner   Emu Springs   Marella Gorge   Nicholson   *12*

Neville Gorge   Mt Barrett 692 m   HIGHWAY   *22*   Sophie Downs   Elvire   Marella Hole   Great Antrim Plateau

Collett Cliffs and Crowhurst Gorge   Mt Amhurst   Moola Bulla   Caroline Pool Old Halls Creek   Stallion Yard   Oaks Mtn 436 m   *80*   *187*   *39*

MUELLER   RANGES   **Halls Creek**   *16*   China Wall   Elvire Gorge   Old Flora Valley (Wungu)   Road   Lilly Dam

Mount Amhurst   Station Ck   NORTHERN   *16*   Palm Springs Mines   *31*   Leedawooloo   Duncan   *66*   Alice Ck

Eagle Hawk Crossing Gorge   Mt Angelo 449 m   Lamboo Gunian   *31*   Palm Spring   Foster   Denison Plain

Pannikin Springs   Mt Ramsay 421 m   Ramsay Ra   Lamboo   Ruby Queen Mine   Sawpit Gorge   Mt Wittenoom 428 m

Margaret River   GREAT   Old Lamboo   *29*   *40*   Black   **TANAMI ROAD** For further information between Halls Creek and Alice Springs, see the TANAMI ROAD map from Westprint Maps   Rocky Waterhole

Mt Bertram 375 m   Yiyili   Savannah Way   *48*   Ruby Plains   Albert Edward Ra   TANAMI   Gordon Downs

Ganinyi   *35*   Mary Pool Rest Area   Mt Dockrell 500 m   MC CLINTOCK RANGE   Wolfe   ROAD   *168*   Kundat Djara Community

Larawa   *17*   *301*   Taylor Lookout 542 m   *71*

Map coordinates (bottom margin)

30'   40'   **94**   50'   **127°**   10'   20'   30'   40'   **95**   50'   **128°**   10'   20'   30'   40'   50'

129°
10'
20'
30'
40'
50'
130°
10'
20'
30'
40'
50'
131°
10'
20'
30'

16°
10'
20'
30'
40'
50'
17°
10'
20'
30'
40'
50'
18°
10'
20'
30'
40'
50'

NEWRY

Gurrandalng

Cockatoo Lagoon

Newry Station

Newry (Dumbaral)

VICTORIA HWY 185

12 7 Saddle

35

19

AUVERGNE

Drovers Rest

Saltwater Creek

Stock Route

East Baines Crossing

Bullita 70

Limestone Gorge

Spring Creek Yard

Bullita Outstation

11 4

Fig Tree Yard

Buchanan

Charles Crossing 80

Jasper Gorge

21

WANIMIYN ABORIGINAL LAND TRUST

WAMBARDI ABORIGINAL LAND TRUST

RIVER

Cow Ck

DELAMERE

VICTORIA RIVER DOWNS

Victoria River Research Station

20

35 Highway

Waterbag Creek

Dashwood Crossing

Inoculation Yard

Moolooloo Outstation

ROSEWOOD

Keep River Road 45

Kildurk Ck

Gum Ck

Blackfellow Creek

NAGURUNGURU ABORIGINAL LAND TRUST

Kildurk (Amanbidji)

Judbarra / Gregory National Park

Baines River

East Baines River

Track

Humbert 46

Humbert

Top Humbert Yard

Wickham Track

21 Humbert River

28

Humbert River

47 Yarralin

YARRALIN ABORIGINAL LAND TRUST

Victoria River Downs

14

Buchanan 45 80 23

Fisher Creek

MONTEJINNI WEST

Rosewood

WATERLOO

Cattle Creek

Waterloo Ck

Waterloo

Niger Creek

West Creek

Baines River

Bamboo Springs

Mistake Ck

MALNGIN 2

Mistake Creek (Moondabijerra) 7

15

Negri River

Bareback

Stirling

27

Nelson Springs

19

MALNGIN ABORIGINAL LAND TRUST

Leichhardt Ck

LIMBUNYA

Uindait Creek

Campbell Creek

Broadarrow Track

Broadarrow Creek

Wickham River

Broadarrow Depot

Limbunya

Fish Hole Yard (private property)

Gregorys Remarkable Pillar

HUMBERT RIVER

Wickham Ck

Globie Track 65 Globie

Paperbark Yard

Mount Sandford

Gordon Creek

VICTORIA RIVER DOWNS

Fever Ck

Stevens Creek

Gill Creek

BILINARA ABORIGINAL LAND TRUST

Armstrong Ck

Townsend Ck

Pigeon Hole Outstation

64 Spring Creek

Kalumbulani

35 Camfield

Mt Wallaston 222 m 96

Camfield

CAMFIELD

KIRKIMBIE

Moonbool Ck

Breakaway views

75

Swan Creek 50 GB 221

55

Kirkimbie

Buntine Highway 96 54

17

WESTERN AUSTRALIA / NORTHERN TERRITORY

BUNDA

Bunda

Maud Bore

Bauhinia Bore

Mt Archie 478 m

INVERWAY

Inverway (Mamadi)

Laura Ck

Sturt Creek

Matud Ck

Track 39 10

221

44

Riveren

Giles Creek

Hughie Ck

DAGURAGU ABORIGINAL LAND TRUST

McDonald Ck

Mt Barton 388 m

Horse Ck

Daguragu 9

Kalkarindji (Wave Hill)

75 96

75 8

Buntine 22 11 Wave Hill

P

Blackgin Bore

56

Lochart Creek

Gidyea Ck

Bilyanarri Hill 235 m

VICTORIA RIVER

48

Chungari Ck

68

CAMFIELD

Cattle Creek

WAVE HILL

CATTLE CREEK

Mt Possum 276 m

Lookout

Camfield Ck

Gordy Creek

106

WALLAMUNGA

Eya Ck

No 17 Bore

Birrindudu Waterhole

Wallamunga

Birrinduc

Mt Reid 338 m

Spring Ck

Victoria River

HOOKER CREEK ABORIGINAL LAND TRUST

Hooker Creek

Nongra Lake

Styles Creek

Creek

153

Winnecke Creek

Lajamanu

Wiso

A permit is required to travel this track to Tennant Creek

NORTH

Parnta

Winnecke Creek

Mt Winnecke 436 m

Road 55

43

Merrina Waterhole

Duck Ponds Waterhole

Duck Ponds Outstation (Mirirrinyunga)

Buchanan Hills 359 m

YINGUALYALYA ABORIGINAL LAND TRUST

Lajamanu Gorge

WA NT QLD SA NSW VIC TAS

10km 0 10 20 30 40km

© Copyright Westprint Maps Pty Ltd 2022

129°
10'
20'
30'
40'
50'
130°
10'
20'
30'
40'
50'
131°
10'
20'
30'

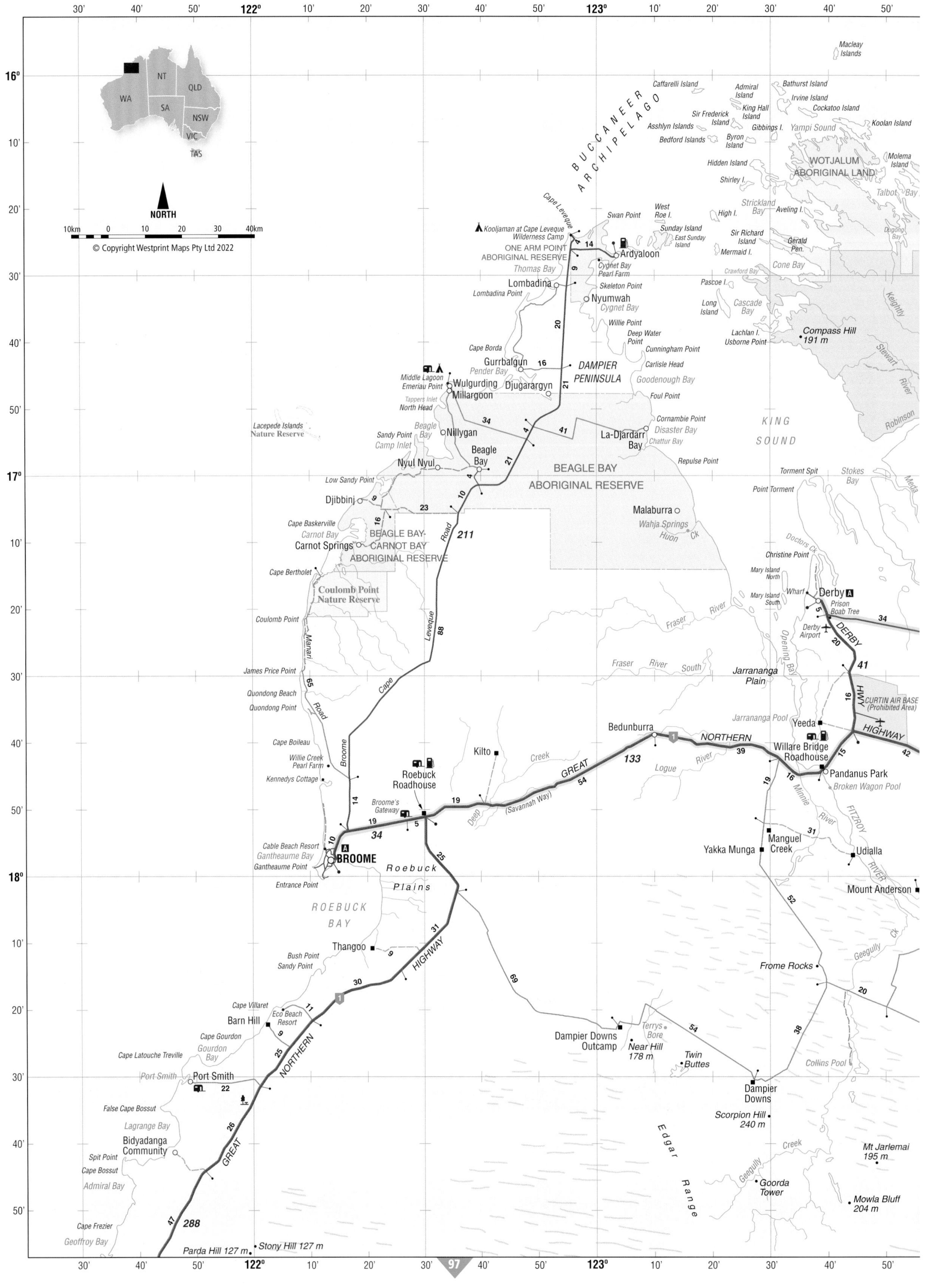

30'
40'
50'
122°
10'
20'
30'
40'
50'
123°
10'
20'
30'
40'
50'
16°
10'
20'
30'
40'
50'
17°
10'
20'
30'
40'
50'
18°
10'
20'
30'
40'
50'
WA
NT
QLD
SA
NSW
VIC
TAS
NORTH
10km 0 10 20 30 40km
© Copyright Westprint Maps Pty Ltd 2022
BUCCANEER ARCHIPELAGO
Macleay Islands
Caffarelli Island
Admiral Island
Bathurst Island
Irvine Island
King Hall Island
Cockatoo Island
Sir Frederick Island
Asshlyn Islands
Gibbings I.
Yampi Sound
Koolan Island
Bedford Islands
Byron Island
Hidden Island
WOTJALUM ABORIGINAL LAND
Molema Island
Shirley I.
Talbot Bay
Cape Leveque
Swan Point
West Roe I.
High I.
Strickland Bay
Aveling I.
Dugong Bay
Kooljaman at Cape Leveque Wilderness Camp
Sunday Island
East Sunday Island
Sir Richard Island
Gerald Pen.
ONE ARM POINT ABORIGINAL RESERVE
Ardyaloon
Mermaid I.
Thomas Bay
Cygnet Bay Pearl Farm
Crawford Bay
Cone Bay
Lombadina
Skeleton Point
Pascoe I.
Lombadina Point
Nyumwah
Cygnet Bay
Long Island
Cascade Bay
Keightly
Willie Point
Deep Water Point
Lachlan I.
Usborne Point
Compass Hill 191 m
Cape Borda
Cunningham Point
Stewart
Gurrbalgun
DAMPIER PENINSULA
Carlisle Head
Pender Bay
Middle Lagoon
Emeriau Point
Wulgurding
Djugarargyn
Goodenough Bay
River
Tappers Inlet
Millargoon
North Head
Foul Point
Cornambie Point
Robinson
Lacepede Islands Nature Reserve
Beagle Bay
Nillygan
La-Djardarr Bay
Disaster Bay
Chattur Bay
KING SOUND
Sandy Point
Camp Inlet
Beagle Bay
Nyul Nyul
Repulse Point
BEAGLE BAY ABORIGINAL RESERVE
Torment Spit
Stokes Bay
Meda
Low Sandy Point
Point Torment
Djibbinj
Malaburra
Wahja Springs
Huon Ck
Cape Baskerville
Carnot Bay
BEAGLE BAY-CARNOT BAY ABORIGINAL RESERVE
Carnot Springs
Road
211
Doctors Ck
Christine Point
Cape Bertholet
Mary Island North
Coulomb Point Nature Reserve
Mary Island South
Wharf
Derby
Prison Boab Tree
Coulomb Point
Fraser River
Derby Airport
DERBY
Manari
Leveque
James Price Point
Fraser River South
Opening Bay
41
Jarrananga Plain
Quondong Beach
Quondong Point
Cape
HWY
CURTIN AIR BASE (Prohibited Area)
Jarrananga Pool
Yeeda
Cape Boileau
Broome
Bedunburra
NORTHERN
HIGHWAY
Kilto
Willare Bridge Roadhouse
Willie Creek Pearl Farm
Creek
Kennedys Cottage
Roebuck Roadhouse
GREAT
133
Logue River
Pandanus Park
Broken Wagon Pool
Broome's Gateway
Deep
(Savannah Way)
Minnie River
FITZROY
34
Manguel Creek
Yakka Munga
Udialla
Cable Beach Resort
Gantheaume Bay
Gantheaume Point
BROOME
Roebuck Plains
RIVER
Entrance Point
Mount Anderson
ROEBUCK BAY
Thangoo
Geegully Ck
Bush Point
Sandy Point
HIGHWAY
Frome Rocks
Cape Villaret
Eco Beach Resort
Barn Hill
Cape Gourdon
Gourdon Bay
NORTHERN
Dampier Downs Outcamp
Terrys Bore
Near Hill 178 m
Twin Buttes
Cape Latouche Treville
Collins Pool
Port Smith
Dampier Downs
False Cape Bossut
Scorpion Hill 240 m
Lagrange Bay
Edgar Range
Creek
Bidyadanga Community
Mt Jarlemai 195 m
Spit Point
Cape Bossut
Geegully
Goorda Tower
Admiral Bay
Mowla Bluff 204 m
Cape Frezier
288
Geoffroy Bay
Stony Hill 127 m
Parda Hill 127 m

97

124° 10' 20' 30' 40' 50' 125° 10' 114 20' 30' 40' 50' 126° 10' 20' 30'

The Breakwater
KUNMUNYA ABORIGINAL LAND
Montgomery Reef
Montgomery Islands
Storr I.
Creek
Pitta Creek
58
16°
10'

Viney I.
Station Reef
Raft Point
Doubtful Bay
Sale River
GARDNER PLATEAU
Caroline Ranges
Road
40

Kingfisher I.
Wood Islands
Melomys I.
Eagle Point
Onad I.
Walcott Inlet
EDKINS RANGE
HARDING RANGE
MUNJA ABORIGINAL LAND
Calder River
Ashton Ck
BLYTHE CREEK ABORIGINAL LAND
Maddie Ck
Charnley River
Hann River
Mt Elizabeth 667 m
Gibb River (Ngallagunda)
108
20'

Collier Bay
Walalam Island
Fletcher Islands
Yule Entrance
Traverse I.
Charnley River
Isdell River
Mount Elizabeth
30
Gibb River
30

Horizontal Waterfall
Secure Bay
Proposed Conservation Area (formerly Charnley River Station)
MAURICE CREEK ABORIGINAL LAND
Barnett River Gorge
9
Gibb
30'

McLarty Range
Mangrove Creek
Poulton Creek
Humbert Creek
The Dromedaries 334 m
Synnot Range
Donkey Yard
7
Manning River
Mt Barnett
Manning Gorge
Mt Barnett Roadhouse
Maurice Ck
Barnett Range
29
Police Valley

MILITARY TRAINING AREA (Public Access Prohibited)
Tarraji River
King Creek
Munboon Plateau
Forbes Hill
Charnley River
Walker Hill 483 m
Beverley Springs Rd
Isdell River
PHILLIPS
Hann River
40'

Oobagooma
River
Spригg Creek
Mount Hart Wilderness Lodge
Mt Bartlett 391 m
29
13
Moses Bore
49
RANGE
Moll Gorge
50'

KIMBERLEY
Alexander Creek
Hawkstone Creek
Mount Hart Rd
50
KING Rd
Bell Gorge
Silent Grove Ranger
Isdell Gorge
Mount House
Mt House 547 m
25
176
10
Mornington
Urquhart River
Tablelands
17°

Kimbolton
May River
Napier Range Road
Barker River
Macs Jumpup
Stumpys Jumpup
Inglis Gap
34
7
Lennard River Gorge
8
Imintji
22
Satans Pass
Mt House
44
Old Glenroy Meatworks
11
Road
7
Warton Range
10'

No public access along this road
Meda
May River Crossing
Kimberley Downs
Gibb
113
Napier Downs
Yammera Gap
21
Wombarella Creek
Barker Gorge
Mt Herbert 762 m
LEOPOLD
King Leopold Ranges Conservation Park
Mt Ord 947 m
Glenroy
Mt Brennan 529 m
Sir John Gorge
20'

29
No public access
River
45
Fairfield
Windjana Gorge
Lillimilura Police Station (ruin)
Lennard River
RANGES
Lady Forrest Ra
19
Mornington
Sir John Ra
30'

Blina Oil and Gas Field
Oil pipeline (underground)
Windjana Gorge NP
21
Leopold Road
36
Tunnel Creek National Park
Millie Windie Gap
RIVER
Mt Leake 700 m
Bluebush Yard
Spider Creek
40'

Debesa
34
Erskine Oil Terminal
20
Jimbalakudunj
216
Fairfield
Fairfield Valley
Oscar Plateau
Devonian Reef Conservation Park
Tunnel Ck
36
Oscar Range
35
Wamali
Leopold Downs
Hooper Creek
Sandy Creek
Davidsons Yard
Dimond Gorge
FITZROY
Cowendyne Creek
50'

Blina
13
9
29
Ellendale
Wynne Creek
(Savannah Way)
49
5
Brooking Gorge CP
Geikie Gorge Conservation Park
Le Lievre Ridge 356 m
Biridu Ck
Stony Creek
18°

Camballin
27
7
Calwynyardah
Mount Creek
14
17
Brooking Gorge
Geikie Gorge National Park
Geikie Gorge
Boab Creek
Barramundi Pool
10'

Looma
12
Myroodah
Mt Wynne 148 m
12
Laurel Downs
23
Brooking Springs
21
Fossil Downs
Muludja
Collett Cliffs and Crowhurst Gorge

Luluigui
25
Lake Daley
Seventeen Mile Dam
Hardman Creek
96
26
Fitzroy Crossing
Margaret Gorge
Mt Ball 554 m

36
Woolabudda Pool
50
95
Mt Hardman 133 m
Walgidgee Hills 121 m
6
Quanban
Jubilee Downs
FITZROY CROSSING ABORIGINAL RESERVE
11
Ngurtuwarta
31
Bayulu
Karnparrni
PILLARA RANGE
Margaret River
20'

Nerrima
64
Machell Pyramid 133 m
RIVER
Mt Huxley 537 m

Kalyeeda
Noonkanbah
Yungngora
15
St George Ranges
Cunningham Creek
42
Pillara
GREAT
Sparke Range
Louisa Creek
Mt Fairbairn 338 m
30'

60
Duckhole Billabong
Rock Hole Pool
Dukes Dome 306 m
Minnie Creek
18
NORTHERN
Emanual Range
Pierre Creek
40'

32
Tullock Peak 228 m
Bucknall Pinnacle 247 m
74
Cherrabun
Cherrabun Ck
9
Ngalingkadji
32
HIGHWAY
51
301

Kadjina Community
Mt Piper 337 m
Poole Ra
20
NGUMPAN ABORIGINAL RESERVE
Christmas Creek
Wangkatjungka Community
Bohemia Downs
50'

124° 10' 20' 30' 40' 50' 125° 94 10' 20' 30' 40' 50' 126° 10' 20' 30'

20'   30'   40'   50'   134°   10'   20'   30'   116   40'   50'   135°   10'   20'   30'   40'

13°

River

Alligator

East

Mann

River

McCaw

Creek

River

Shadforth Hills

Wilton

McKay Hills

River

River

West

Branch

Bulman Gorge

River

Wilton

ARNHEM LAND
ABORIGINAL LAND TRUST

Creek

Snowdrop

Central

Waterhouse

Flying

Fox

Creek

Maiwok

River

Mainoru

Weemol

13

Bulman (Gulin Gulin)

Tower

22

46

24

Horse   Ck

MAINORU

Mainoru

Mt Bridges
• 225 m

Mainoru Roadhouse

Wilton River Crossing

Mount Catt

31   14

Rocky Bottom Creek

Djapingapu

24

Ramingining Turn-off

8   Barrapunta Outstation

Emu Springs

86

Guyuyu

Annie

Road

Arnhem

Creek

Goyder

Sheridan

Creek

MITCHELL RANGES

• Mt Parsons
301 m

• Mt Fawcett
244 m

PARSONS   RANGE

Numerous pools
and waterholes

Walker

Marrkalawa

BATH   RANGE

Latrie Ck

River

ARNHEM   LAND

Jasper

River

Rose

Washaway

Creek

Zamia

River

Harris

Ck

Anbali

14°

113

River

Maiwok

Dil Jin Hill
341 m

Mountain Valley

MOUNTAIN VALLEY

8

22

18

19

18

Mainoru

River

Mainoru

Mt Poiziers
224 m

18

Wongalara

WONGALARA

Strangemans Range

Wilton

ARNHEM LAND
ABORIGINAL LAND TRUST

Phelp

Rose

River

Wukayiwanyu

Numbulwar Community

Nyinpinti Point

13   Tower

Leekout

Tower

Road

Arnhem   71

63

Flying

Fox

Maiwok   Creek

LONE-
SOME
DOVE

Jalbol

BIG
RIVER

River

URAPUNGA
ABORIGINAL
LAND TRUST

Turkey

River

Lagoon

Creek

Ck

Wanmarri

Edward Island
Wilipili Island

Wiyakipa Beach

Warrakunta Point
Yilikukunyiyanga Islet

GOON-
DOOLOO

MOROAK

High   Black   Range

Creek

FLYING
FOX

Chambers

River

Goondooloo

ROPER

Moroak

Bringung

Flying
Fox

24

20

32

MOUNT
McMINN

Buddawarka
Community

Rittarangu
(Urapunga)

7

Roper Bar

21

Boat
Ramp

31

Ngukurr

22

25

St Vidgeon

18

Ck

RIVER

ROPER

Wukoinyarra Plains

Aquafarm
(abandoned)

Port Roper

LIMMEN
BIGHT

Eagle Bay

Maria Island

Limmen Bight
Marine Park

Beatrice Island
(Yumunguni)

HIGHWAY

Elsey

P

20

33

P

179

P

46

P

Roper Valley

YUTPUNDJI-DJINDIWIRRITJ
ABORIGINAL LAND TRUST

NAMUL
NAMUL

River

Mt Eclipse 165 m

Queensland Crossing

Rocky Bar
Crossing

Limmen
National Park

Mountain

Creek

41

Childer

The

31

Great

River

Towns Crossing

188

Top

37

Road

MARRA
ABORIGINAL
LAND TRUST

15°

MANGARRAYI
ABORIGINAL
LAND TRUST

ELSEY

Creek

Cattle

River

Strangways

Mt Davidson
205 m

44

46

Maryfield

ALAWA 1
ABORIGINAL LAND
TRUST

HODGSON DOWNS

Miniyeri Community
(Hodgson Downs)

Hodgson

River

Arnold

ST VIDGEON

Fishing
Numerous fishing sites exist in this area.
These range from rivers, streams, water holes
and reservoirs to beach fishing and fully chartered
deep-sea fishing. Many are on station properties
and permission to enter must be obtained.
Seek local knowledge.

Cox

Towns

(Little

Creek

Towns

River

Yumanji

NATHAN
RIVER

Limmen

Bight

22

Maria Lagoon

21

Limmen
River

Lily Waterhole

The Four Archers
(Barrkuwirriji)

Limmen River
Crossing

Park Ranger

13

6

Nathan River

Butterfly Springs

YIYINTYI   RANGE

LORELLA

Limmen Bight Fishing Camp

VERMELHA

Maryfield   River

HODGSON RIVER

COX RIVER

ALAWA ABORIGINAL
LAND TRUST

Hodgson   River

Magarrayi

Cox

Limmen
National Park

Soda
Waterhole

Limmen National Park
Formerly Nathan River station, Limmen National
Park was declared in July 2012. Limited 4WD
access to several sites including Butterfly Gorge
and the Southern Lost City. Roads may be
impassable for long periods between
December and May.

O'Keefe
Valley

Southern
Lost City

29

The

Great

Lorella
Springs

WWII Hospital

Birdum

36

166

1

Maryfield

Alexander Forrest
Memorial

Ck

33

16

Hodgson

Nutwood Downs

53

River

Minamia
(Cox River)

River

O'Connor
Pocket

147

30

Buffalo

Little   Rosie

Ck

Approx.
Position

147

20'   30'   104   40'   50'   134°   10'   20'   105   30'   40'   135°   10'   20'   30'   40'

50' **136⁰** 10' 20' 30' 40' 50' **137⁰** 10' 117 20' 30' 40' 50' **138⁰** 10' 20'

13⁰

Trial Bay
Cape Grey
Bald Point

Myaoola Bay
Bagbiringula Point
Wardarlea Bay

Grindall Bay
Jalma Bay
○Baniyala
Point Blane
Point Arrowsmith

Round Hill Island
○Djarrakpi
Cape Sheild

Haddon Head
Isle Woodah

Morgan Island
Nicol Island

Crocodiles and Box Jellyfish
Saltwater crocodiles inhabit coastal waterways especially river estuaries. Swimming is not recommended. Highly venemous box jellyfish infest these waters between October and May. Swimming is not recommended.

10km 0 10 20 30 40km
NORTH
© Copyright Westprint Maps Pty Ltd 2022

30'

Coast Ra

BLUE MUD BAY

Burney Island
Hawknest Island
Chasm Island
North Point *Island*
North East Isles
Lane Island

Cape Barrow
Bustard Island
Marble Point
Jagged Head
Hawk Island

North Bay
Bickerton Island
Winchelsea Island
Port Langdon
Scott Point

Donnet Bay
Ck
○Milyakburra
Bartalumba Bay
Thompson Bay

Wurindi Swamp
South Bay
○Bardelumba
○Alyangula
○Umbakumba

Lowrie Channel
Warwick Channel
Connexion I.
Mamalimandja Point

Connexion Channel
●Angurugu
Angurugubira Lake

14⁰

Hart R
Gemco Mines
Groote Eylandt
Ilyungmadja Point

Groote Eylandt Mine
Dalumbu Bay
Adilyagba Point
Ungwariba Point

Rantyirrity Point
Armada Lake

Tasman Point
South Point

Inamalamandja Point
Marangala Bay
Marangala Point
Cape Beatrice

Sandy Island

ARNHEM LAND ABORIGINAL LAND TRUST (ANINDILYAKWA LAND COUNCIL)

G U L F   O F

30'

C A R P E N T A R I A

Crocodiles and Box Jellyfish
Saltwater crocodiles inhabit coastal waterways especially river estuaries. Swimming is not recommended. Highly venemous box jellyfish infest these waters between October and May. Swimming is not recommended.

15⁰

Yarnarndu Inlet

Private track. Ph (08) 8983 3728 for permission.

Rosie Creek Fishing Camp

WURRALIBI ABORIGINAL LAND TRUST
SIR EDWARD PELLEW GROUP

Creek
Barranyi (North Island) National Park
North Island

Rosie
Ck
West Island
Craggy Islands
Watson Island

Bing Bong
Bing Bong Loadout Facility
Skull Island
Cape Vanderlin

Pine
Bing
35
Mule Ck
Centre Island

Wada Warra
McARTHUR RIVER
South West Island
Vanderlin Island

WURRALIBI ABORIGINAL LAND TRUST

Warramana
Bong Ck
Port McArthur
Cora Point
Webinger Point

Fishing
Numerous fishing sites exist in this area. These range from rivers, streams, water holes and reservoirs to beach fishing and fully chartered deep-sea fishing. Many are on station properties and permission to enter must be obtained. Seek local knowledge.

Galah
Ck
14
22
7
Batten Point
Goat Point

Batten
McArthur
River
King Ash Bay
Pelican Spit

50' **136⁰** 10' 20' 30' 40' 50' **137⁰** 10' 102 20' 30' 40' 50' **138⁰** 10' 20'

NORTH

10km 0 10 20 30 40km

© Copyright Westprint Maps Pty Ltd 2022

DELISSAVILLE/WAGAIT/LARRAKIA
ABORIGINAL LAND TRUST

Point Blaze

Finniss River

Bamboo Creek
Tin Mine

Woolaning

La Belle
Downs

Florence
Falls
Buley
Rockhole

Litchfield
Safari Camp

Wangi
Falls

Peron Island North

Reynolds River

Welltree

The Lost City

Peron Island South

Tjaynera Falls
(Sandy Creek)

Palmerston Island

Anson Bay

Litchfield

Cape Ford

Red Cliff

Mt Litchfield
203 m

Cape Scott

DALY RIVER / PORT KEATS
ABORIGINAL LAND TRUST

MALAK MALAK
ABORIGINAL
LAND TRUST

DALY RIVER

Wooliana on
the Daly

Dooley Point

Dinggirriyet
(Browns Creek)

Deleye
Community

Elizabeth
Downs

Nauiyu

Daly
River

Docherty Creek

Woodycupaldiya
Community

Nacoolya
Hills

Cape Dombey

Docherty
Hills

Bank Shoal

Hyland Bay

Tree Point

Cape Hay

Kuy
Community

Perrederr
Community

Dorcherty Island

Movie

Tom

Hermit

Chilling

Muldiva Creek

Munda Beach

Injin Beach

Port Keats
(Wadeye)

Wudapull
Community

Peppimenarti
Community

Yelcher Beach

Palumpa
Community

Ditji Beach

Pearce Point

Treachery Bay

Fossil Head
Community

New Moon Inlet

DALY RIVER / PORT KEATS
ABORIGINAL LAND TRUST

Swamp Point

Whale Flat

MACADAM RANGE

Cul-Eci Creek

Alligator Creek

Laurie Creek

River

JOSEPH BONAPARTE
GULF

Keyling
Inlet

Fitzmaurice River

Lacrosse
Island

Cape
Dussejour

Clump
Island

Quoin
Island

Fitzmaurice

Cape Domett

Shakespeare Hill
134 m

King Gordon
Spring

Turtle
Point

Queens
Channel

Cambridge
Gulf

Extensive areas of
mangroves, tidal creeks
and coastal flats

Ord River
Nature Reserve

BRADSHAW FIELD TRAINING AREA
(PROHIBITED AREA)

Opik Hill
102 m

KEEP RIVER

Forsyth Ck

VICTORIA RIVER

Yambarran Range

Ikymbon River

Ord River
Nature
Reserve

Station Ck

Emu Ck

LEGUNE

Legune

Langgang Creek

Lobby Creek

Onslow
Hills

Skull Ck

Oakes Ck

Sandy Ck

Springs Ck

Nadpn Ck

VICTORIA

Angalarri River

Whirlwind
Plains

Point Spring
Nature Reserve

Kneebone

Marralum
Community

Bullo River

Spirit Hill

Sandy River

(Macka's Barra Camp)

Carlton Hill

Keep River
National Park
Extension
(Proposed)

Gregory's Tree
Historic Reserve

Big Horse
Creek

Bradshaw Bridge
(no entry to traing area)

BULLO
RIVER

Spencer Range

Policeman Point
Lookout

Parry

Mambi
Island

Ord River
Irrigation Scheme

SPIRIT HILLS

Bullo River

Nakeroo WWII
Memorial

Lookout

Timber Creek

Parry Creek
Farm

Black Rock Falls
Middle Springs
Waterfall
Ivanhoe Crossing

Pinkerton Range

Auvergne

(Savannah Way)

Durack Memorial

Parry Lagoons
Nature
Reserve

Mirima
(Hidden Valley)
National Park

Newcastle Ra

Kuwang
Lookout

Kununurra

Zebra Rock
Gallery

Big Police
Hole

Jarnem

Keep River
Nat Park

VICTORIA HWY

East Baines

Baines River

Bullita Stock
Route

Jinumum
Walk

Noble
Memorial

Tier Ra

Deception Range

Dunham River

ORD RIVER

Gurrandalng

Cockatoo
Lagoon

NEWRY

Saddle

AUVERGNE

Drovers
Rest

East Baines
Crossing

WESTERN AUSTRALIA
NORTHERN TERRITORY

Knox Ck

Eighh Mile Ck

Keep River

Saltwater Creek

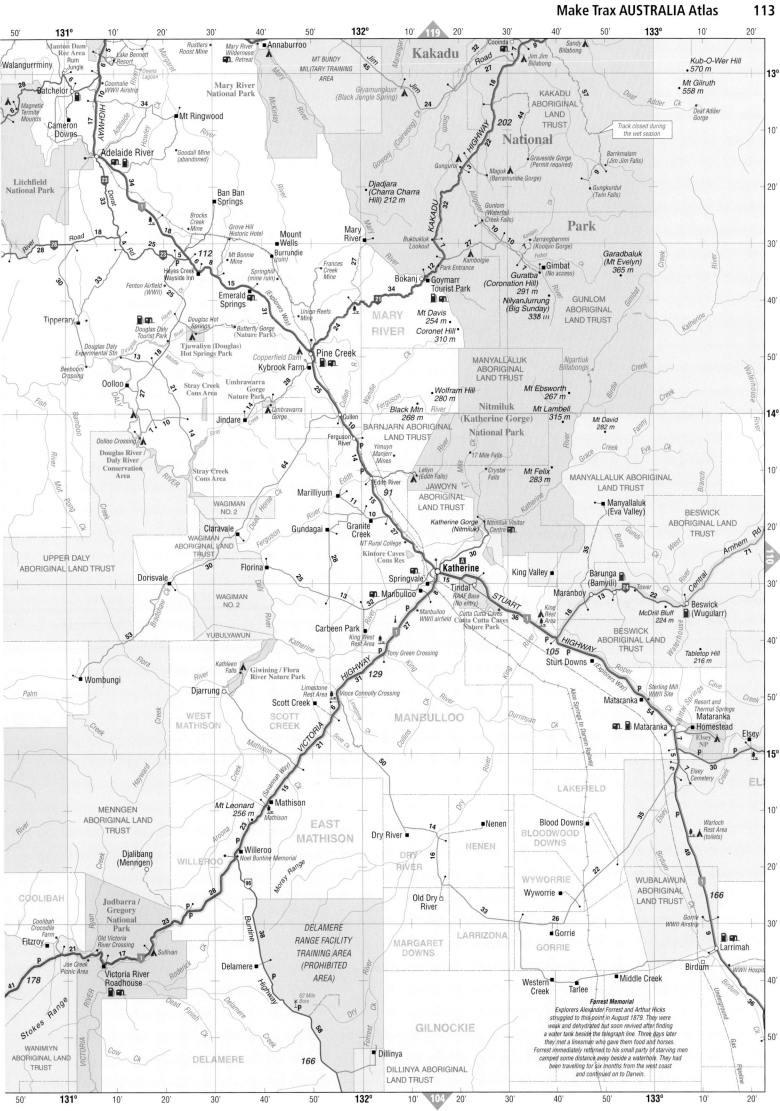

13°
10°

NT
QLD
WA
SA
NSW
VIC
TAS

NORTH

10km 0 10 20 30 40km

© Copyright Westprint Maps Pty Ltd 2022

124° 125°

West Holothuria Reef

14°

Long Reef

Cassini Island

Browse Island
Nature Reserve

BONAPARTE   ARCHIPELAGO

Fenelon I.
Fenelon Passage
Descartes I.
Voltaire Passage
Davidson Point
Cape Voltaire

West Montalivet I.
East Montalivet I.

MONTAGUE

Walmesly Bay

Maret I. *Maret Islands*
South Maret I.

Prudhoe Islands
Cape Chateaurenaud

SOUND

Katers I.

Wollaston I.

Swift Bay

Berthier Island

Boomerang Bay

Capstan I.

Mudge Bay

Bigge Island

Scott Strait

ADMIRALTY GULF
ABORIGINAL RESERVE

River

Surveyor's Pool

Mitchell

Cape Pond

INDIAN OCEAN

Lamarck I.

Mitchell Falls

15°

A R C H I P E L A G O

Colbert I.

D'Arcole Islands *Buffon I.*
Hedley I.

Coronation Islands
Museums I. *Coronation I.*

York Sound

Kartja I.

Hardy Point *Cape Torrens*

Mt Anderson
• 484 m

Mitchell River National Park

Bernouilli I.
Desfontaines I.

Grey I.

Port Nelson

Prince Frederick Harbour

Boongaree Island

Tanpanmirri Island

• *Enid Falls*

BONAPARTE

BRUNSWICK

BAY

Cape Brewster

Cape Wellington

Hunter R.

Laseron I.

Vulcan Islands

Adieu Point

Hanover Bay

Unwins Island

Rothsay Water

Marigui Promontory

Mt Brookes
• 279 m

Roe

Marigui Gorge

Champagny Islands

Jungulu Island

Camden Sound

Heywood I.

Byam Martin I.

Augustus Island

Port George IV

Mt Trafalgar
• 391 m

St Andrew Island

Prince Regent

Nature Reserve

Princess May Ranges

Garimbu *Ck*

River

Moran

Kannamatju I.

Battery Point

Kunmunya Hill
• 192 m

Breaknock Harbour

Augustus Water

St George Basin

MacDonald Range

Mt York
• 528 m

Beagle reef

GARDNER PLATEAU

Churchill Reef

Mavis reef

Albert Reef

Deception Bay *Hope Point*

Hall Point
Parin Peninsula

Prior Point

KUNMUNYA

ABORIGINAL LAND

Wedge Hill
• 286 m

George Water

Prince

Regent

River

Montgomery Reef

The Breakwater

Macleay Islands

Montgomery Islands

KUNMUNYA ABORIGINAL LAND

Storr I.

Elizabeth and Catherine Ra

Pitta

Creek

50' **126º** 10' 20' 30' 40' 50' **127º** 10' 20' 30' 40' 50' **128º** 10' 20'

13º

10'

20'

30'

East Holothuria
Reef

40'

Cape
Londonderry

Cape Talbot

Lesueur Island

50'

Sir Graham
Moore Islands

Glycosmis
Bay

Koolama
Bay Cape Rulhieres

OOMBULGURRI
ABORIGINAL
RESERVE

Napier
Broome
Bay

North Eclipse I.

Eclipse
Islands

Hat Point
Parry Harbour

Bougainville
Peninsula

Geranium Harbour

Anjo Pt

Cape Bernier

14º

Gibson Point

Long I.

Mary I.

Anjo
Peninsula

Galley Pt

Bertram Cove

Seaplane Bay

Freshwater Bay

Kingsmill
Islands

Vansittart
Bay

June Point

Jar I.

Low I.

CAPE
BOUGAINVILLE
ABORIGINAL
RESERVE

Trusgott
Airfield

Honeymoon
Beach

Deep Bay

McGowans
Island

9

8

17

Mission
Bay

Honeymoon Bay

Pago

Placid

KALUMBURU
ABORIGINAL
RESERVE

Beta Creek
Mining Camp

King

George

Cape Whiskey

Elsie Island

Cape St Lambert

Mt Casuarina
221 m

Reveley Island

Buckle Head

10'

ADMIRALTY
GULF

Middle
Osborn I.

South West
Osborn I.

Borda I.

Monger

Ck

Kalumburu

DRYSDALE

19

Mool Mool
Lagoon

Casuarina

Ck

Seppelt Range

20'

Pickering Point

Crystal Head

Port
Warrender

Warrender Hill
243 m

16

8

20

Wade

Ck

King

Edward

Road

River

16

Carson River

Beta

River

Berkeley

Campbell

Range

Thurburn Bluff

Faith Hill
167 m

30º

14

Lawley River
National Park

Lawley

Noolawayoo

Ck

Deep
Gorge

50

Mt Leeming
281 m

Carson

River

Johnson

Creek

OOMBULGURRI

ABORIGINAL RESERVE

De Lancourt

Cape
Dussejour

Dome Hill
215 m

Myrmidon
Ledge

40'

Camp Creek Cons Park

DOONGAN
ABORIGINAL
RESERVE

Laterite
Cons Park

River

70

264

26

Morgan

Theda

37

Kalumburu

River

Carson

Ck

Glider Gorge and
Dulcis Falls

Hudson
Spring

Palmoondoora

K I M B E R L E Y

Drysdale River

National Park

Berkeley

River

Slab Hill
325 m

Cambridge
Gulf

Hardman
Point

15º

Mitchell
River

35

King

Edward

Worriga Gorge and
Morgan Falls

Couchman Range

Laurie

Ck

Carson

River

Foster Range

Ashton Range

Carson Escarpment

Tadarida Scarp

Nicholls Point

FORREST RIVER
ABORIGINAL RESERVE

Oombulgurri

Forrest

River

Agnew Pt

Adolphus
Island

Fairfax

Barnes I.

Ord River
Nature
Reserve

10'

Mitchell

River

Doongan

Crossland

Ck

Banjo

Creek

Ernest

River

Milligan Ranges

Canal

WEST

ARM

East Arm

ORD

RIVER

20'

39

Kalumburu

GARDNER PLATEAU

Damper

RIVER

Creek

RIVER

Anthon Landing

The Gut

Five Rivers
Lookout

Wyndham

Moochalabra
Dam

24

Prison Boab
Tree

Parry
Creek
Farm

18 13

30'

Woodhouse

River

Drysdale
River

DRYSDALE

Road

58

Russ

Gibb

Ellenbrae

Creek

336

5

Ellenbrae

Durack River

Jacks Waterhole

Gibb

26

Mosquito
Hills

New York
Jump Ups

Oomaloo Falls

Gibb

River

Bimdoola

80

Ck

Home Valley

Station stay

Pentecost Range

Palmer

Ck

DURACK

River

9

Cockburn Range

56

Diggers
Rest

35

King

River

59

Emma Gorge
Resort

16

21

Nimberline
Valley

13

8

40'

50'

Mt McCrann
658 m

50' **126º** 10' 20' 30' 40' 50' **127º** 10' 20' 30' 40' 50' **128º** 10' 20'

20'   30'   40'   50'   **134°**   10'   20'   30'   40'   50'   **135°**   10'   20'   30'   40'

10°

NT
QLD
WA
SA
NSW
VIC
TAS

NORTH

10km   0   10   20   30   40km

© Copyright Westprint Maps Pty Ltd 2022

11°

A R A F U R A   S E A

Wudbud Point   *North Goulburn Island*
Cone Point
Sand Point   *South Goulburn Island*
Warruwi   Mangrove Point
Aurari Bay   *Anuru Bay*   Barclay Point
Macquarie Strait   *Waminari Bay*   Turner Point   Guion Point
King River   *Arria Bay*   Cuthbert Point   *Madarrgaldi Bay*   Hall Point
Braithwaite Point

Crocodiles and Box Jellyfish
Saltwater crocodiles inhabit coastal waterways
especially river estuaries. Swimming is not recommended.
Highly venemous box jellyfish infest these waters between
October and May. Swimming is not recommended.

Northwest Crocodile Island
Crocodile Islands

Goomadeer Point   *Rolling Bay*
Garrabu   Hawkesbury Point   *Mooroongga Island*   Warnga Point
Jungle Creek   *Nungbalgarri Creek*   Entrance Island   False Point   Cape Stewart   *Darbada Island*   *Crocodile Island*   *Crocodile Islands*   Galiwinku   *Elcho Island*
Skirmish Point

12°   Maningrida   *Boucat Bay*   Ji-marda   *Milingimbi Island*   Milingimbi   *Yabooma Island*   Jigaimara Point   Wormmi Point   *Napier Peninsula*
Bat I.   *Castlereagh Bay*   *Howard Island*   *Hutchinson Strait*   *coastal flats*   *Buckingham Bay*
Mamadawerre   *Liverpool River*   Point Guy
133   Marlwon   *Cadell River*   *Blyth*   33   43   20   *Glyde Inlet*   *Banyan Island*
Gudjekbin   Kikiyown   Marrkolidjban   *Nei= ngmut*   *Muralidbar*   49   Nangalala   *Glyde R.*   *Woolen River*
18   Nabarlek   *Goomadeer*   *Manggabor*   28   25   9   Ramingining   *Buckingham R.*
Cooper Ck   Mumeka   Maningrida Turn-off
Myra Falls   *River*   *Arafura Swamp*   **ARNHEM LAND**
ARNHEM LAND ABORIGINAL LAND TRUST
Manmoyi   *Gulbuwangay River*   Lake Evella
12°30'   *Mann River*   *Imimbar Creek*   *Creek*   24   24
Gamargawan   110   *Goyder River*   Flat Rock Creek (Dhingara)
Liverpool River   *Saddlers Creek*   30   Donydji
Malgawa   *Shadforth Creek*   *Blyth*   Dhunganda   31   14   3   *Maidjunga River*
13°   No camping at Goyder River Crossing   24   Djapingapu   Rocky Bottom Creek

20'   30'   **134°**   10'   20'   30'   40'   50'   **135°**   10'   20'   30'   40'

50' **136º** 10' 20' 30' 40' 50' **137º** 10' 20' 30' 40' 50' **138º** 10' 20'

10º

10'

20'

30'

40'

50'

11º

Cape Wessel

Rimbija Island   Low Point

Mort Point

Auster Point

10'

Jensen Bay

Gedge Point   Sphinx Head

Marchinbar
Island

Red Point

Lagoon Bay   20'
Nip Point

Hopeful Bay

Guluwuru
Island   *Cumberland Strait*

Gugari Rip   30'

Stevens Island

Burgunngura Island

W E S S E L

Drysdale
Island   *I S L A N D S*

Raragala   Truant Island   40'
Island

Jirrgari Island

Stretton Strait   *Brown Strait*   Bumaga Island

Cunningham Island   Wigram Island

Warnawi Island   Cotton   Bromby   50'
Island   Islands

Malay Road

Cadell Strait   Alger Island   Astell Island   Cape Wilberforce

T H E   E N G L I S H   C O M P A N Y S   I S L A N D S   Pobassoo
Bosanquet   Island
Point Napier   Island
Inglis
Island   *Nalwrung Straits*   **12º**

Flinders
Point

Flinders   Mata Mata   Mt Bonner   Gove Peninsula   Bremer Island   10'
Peninsula   •72 m
Probable
Island   Godijboi
Point   Cape Wirawawoi
Mallison I.   Dundas   Nhulunbuy
Point   12
Ulundurwi   Peter John R   10   6 Yirrkala
Bay   Everett Island   *Melville*   19   Gove
Bay   Mine   20'
Hardy Island   Laram R   14
Dalywoi Bay
A R N H E M   Giddy R   Cape Arnhem
B A Y   Tower   14
Ramungir   Cato   14   Giddy River
Bay   Dhalinybuy   6   Crossing

Gapuwiyak   River   25   30'
(Lake Evella)
Gwapilina Point
Baralminar R   Port Bradshaw
Binanangoi Point
Habgood R   11
Gapuwiyak   Road   19   Buymarr
Turn-off   40'
Snowy's Rock   Tower   Wanyanmera Point
Memorial
Central   6   Grays
FREDERICK   43   Arnhem   Garrthalala   *Bay*
HILLS   23   Point Alexander
Wyonga River   Birany   *Caledon*
Durabudboi River   Birany   *Bay*   50'
Mt Caledon
105 m

Cape Grey   **13º**

50' **136º** 10' 20' 30' 40' 50' **137º** 10' 20' 30' 40' 50' **138º** 10' 20'

20'   30'   40'   50'   **129⁰**   10'   20'   30'   40'   50'   **130⁰**   10'   20'   30'   40'

10⁰

NORTH

10km   0   10   20   30   40km

© Copyright Westprint Maps Pty Ltd 2022

11⁰

Cape Van Diemen

The Narrows

Purumpenelli Point

Shark Bay

Snake Bay

Brace Point

Deception Point

Pirlangimpi
(Garden Point)

Milikapiti
(Snake Bay)

Minkaruwala Creek

Rocky Point

Apsley Strait

Wurankuwu

**TIWI ABORIGINAL
LAND TRUST**

Cape Helvetius

Gordon
Bay

*BATHURST
ISLAND*

Paru

Point Fawcett

Nguiu

Shoal
Bay

Mitchell
Point

12⁰

BEAGLE GULF

TIMOR SEA

Wagait
Beach

Gilruth Point

13

Tapa Bay

Point Margaret

Mandorah

15

Ida Bay

Cox
Peninsula

15

Indian
Island

Belyuen

Grose I

13

Beer Eetar I

Port
Patterson

Dum In Mirrie I

17

Paterson Point

19

Rankin Point

Crab Claw
Island
Resort

Dundee Lodge

Dundee
Downs
Bush Resort

13

Road

Dundee Beach

28

Fog

Bay

23

Five Mile Beach

14

Sand Palms
Tavern

Fog Bay

Finniss
River

Point Blaze

Finniss

River

**DELISSAVILLE/WAGAIT/LARRAKIA
ABORIGINAL LAND TRUST**

20'   30'   **129⁰**   10'   20'   ◣112◢   30'   40'   50'   **130⁰**   10'   20'   30'   40'

Coordinate labels (top): 50' 131° 10' 20' 30' 40' 50' 132° 10' 20' 30' 40' 50' 133° 10' 20'

Coordinate labels (right): 10° 10' 20' 30' 40' 50' 11° 10' 20' 30' 40' 50' 12° 10' 20' 30' 40' 50' 13°

Coordinate labels (bottom): 50' 131° 10' 20' 30' 40' 50' 132° 10' 20' 30' 40' 50' 133° 10' 20'

Garig Gunak Barlu Marine Park

Cape Croker
Oxley Island
Somerville Bay
Darmarl Point
Croker Island
Lawson Island
McCluer Island
Ngardimardi (Smith Point)
Garig Gunak Barlu Camps 1&2
Danger Point
Palm Bay
Minjilang
Mission Bay
Vashton Head
Ranger
Gul Gul
Bowen Strait
Adjamarragu
Grant Island
Araru Point
Trippang Bay
Popham Bay
Port Essington
Raffles Bay
Darch Island
Seven Spirit Wilderness Resort
Port Bremer
Djmngan Point
Ardigbiyi Point
COBOURG PENINSULA
40
Cape Don Lighthouse and Cape Don Experience (fishing lodge)
Barrow Bay
Garig Gunak Barlu National Park
Point David (Inngirnatj)
Cape Cockburn
De Courcy Head
Victoria Settlement
Valencia Island
Malay Bay
Shamrock Bay
10
Oenpelli
Malay Bay
Aiton Bay
Wurgurlu Bay
86
Guialung Point
Mountnorris Bay
Gningarg Point
Soldier Point
Napier Bay
Garig Gunak Barlu Marine Park
Warigili Point
Sir George Hope Islands
Morse Island
Brogden Point
MELVILLE ISLAND
Radford Point
Lethbridge Bay
Brenton Bay
Smoky Point
Point Jahleel
Yunanti Bay
Jessie (Alu) River
Tiwipu River
Tinganoo Bay
Cobham Bay
Cape Keith
Webb Point
Greenhill Island
Murgenella Road
Murgenella (Ranger Station)
Endyalgout Island
Salt Water Ck
Murgenella Creek
Macquarie Strait
Aurari Bay
Permit required 97
Pickertaramoor
Wellington Range
116
Cape Gambier
CLARENCE STRAIT
VAN DIEMEN GULF
Bill Shoal
Victoria Shoal
Aralaij Beach
Taylor Patches
Cooper Creek
N.W. Vernon I
East Vernon I
Cape Hotham
Draytons Reef
Gardanggarl (Field Island)
Gularri (Pt Farewell)
Cairncurry Plain
Mangardubu
S.W. Vernon I
Vernon Islands Cons Res
Point Stephens
Elizabeth Reef
Waldak Irrmbal (West Alligator Head)
Djidbordu (Barron I)
Birraduk Creek
Fright Point
Djukbinj National Park
Adam Bay
Finke Bay
KAKADU ABORIGINAL LAND TRUST
Cooper Ck
Gunn Point
Leaders Creek Fishing Camp
Chambers Bay
(Day use area, no camping)
Stuart Point
Carmor Plain
Culaly Plain
Injaluk Art Centre
Nabarlek
Shoal Bay
15
Melacca Swamp Cons Res
Stuart's Tree Memorial
Stuart's Tree Fishing Camp
East Alligator River
22
18
Lee Point
Mary River National Park
Carmor Plains Wildlife Reserve
Gunbalanya (Oenpelli)
Ck
Fannie Bay
Casuarina Coastal Res
Lake Finniss
Woolner
Swim Creek
Swim Ck
Track closed during wet season
Kakadu National Park
Ubirr
Cahills Crossing
Myra Falls
DARWIN
Port Darwin
24
9
9
30
56
Munmarlary
Border Store
Marnanj (Magela Plain)
Tin Camp Ck
Middle Arm
Black Jungle Lambells Lagoon Cons Res
Alligator Head
Shady Camp
14
16
Four Mile Hole
Wildman River
ALLIGATOR RIVER
Magela
Mt Howship 378 m
10
Fogg Dam CR
Adelaide River Experience
Djukbinj NP
Opium Creek
15
Point Stuart Wilderness Lodge
23
Jabiluka Mine Lease
Mudginberri
25
36
Middle Point
Marrakai
Wildman Wilderness Lodge
8
Two Mile Hole
25
Kakadu Resort
Mamukala Wetlands
HWY
29
Ranger Mine Lease
Jabiru
12
Widow on the Wetlands
19
Wildman Ranger Station
17
Bowali Visitor Centre
Peninsula
18
Adelaide River Cruises
11
9
Twin Sisters Lagoon
10
Nourlangie Ck
Anlarrh
Illigadjar Floodplain Walk
Southport
18
Corroboree Billabong
4
35
36
20
Berry Springs Territory Wildlife Park
Rockhole
Hardies Lagoon
Ceuzens Lookout
16
Park Entrance Station
8
5
Red Lily Billabong
Murella Park
Tumbling Waters
11
9
Corroboree Park Tavern
23
Bucket Billabong Gurdurunguranjduju (Alligator Billabong)
19
Nourlangie Rock
Koongarra Mineral Lease
STUART
18
Toms Gully Mine
Mary River Nat Park
ARNHEM
252
39
Yellow Water
21
47
26
50
Rustlers Roost Mine
Jim Road
Cooinda
9
Sandy Billabong
Manton Dam Rec Area
Rum Jungle
Marrakai Crossing
Mary River Wilderness Retreat
Annaburroo
21
45
Jim Jim Billabong
27
111
Lake Bennett Resort
Owens Lagoon
Mary River National Park
MT BUNDY MILITARY TRAINING AREA
32
Kub-O-Wer Hill 570 m
Walangurrminy
28
6
5
Coomalie WWII Airstrip
Marangarrayu
Jim Jim Road
Manton Dam
Darwin River Dam
Owens Lagoon

NORTH

10km 0 10 20 30 40km

© Copyright Westprint Maps Pty Ltd 2022

GULF OF CARPENTARIA

Boyd Point
Pera Head
Thud Point
North Camp
False Pera Head
Weipa Mining Lease
Worbody Point
Aurukun
Wallaby Island Long Island
Sydney Island

ARAKUN

Merluna
Station stay

MANGKUMA
Batavia Goldfield
Chuula Outstation
Wenlock

Gold was discovered in 1892. Although it was not a large or rich field but mining continued for almost 60 years. Many relics still exist.

Wolverton
Old Pratt Tin Mine

Horsetailer Waterhole
Goose Swamp
Crescent Lagoon
Old Archer Crossing
10 Mile Junction
Archer River Roadhouse
Governors Waterhole
Bunda Swamp
Langi Lagoon
Jerry Lagoon

Oyala Thumotang National Park

Vardons Lagoon
Chong Swamp
Mango Lagoon
Rokeby

Birthday Mtn 441 m
WATHADA
Blue Mtns
Geikie Range
117

Whistlers Lagoon
Lake Archer
Kendall River
Running
Tea Tree Lagoon
Meripah
Merepah Lagoon

Quarantine Station
TOOLKA

Peret Outstation
Wathanhiin
Stoney Crossing

Kenchering Camp

Oyala Thumotang National Park
Formerly known as Mungkan Kandju National Park, this large wilderness park features open eucalypt woodlands, melaleuca swamps and a variety of rainforest types.

Oyala Thumotang National Park

Crystal Vale
Holroyd River
Bally Junction
Coen
The Bend

Kuchendoopen Outstation
Kulinchin Outstation

Old gold mining town site
Ebagoola

Strathburn

Deep Lagoon
Strathgordon
PORMPURAAW
Strathgordon
Strathgordon
Strathgordon Road
Astrea
Boomerang Plain
Strathmay
Strathhaven

Pormpuraaw
Musgrave Station
Chapman River

Wallaby Island
Mitchell River
Sth Mitchell
The Landing
KOWANYAMA
Numerous tracks in this area

Mitchell - Alice Rivers National Park

Aerodrome Plain
Oriners
Sefton

Old Alice Queen Mine
Imooya

Kowanyama

Rutland Plains

Dixie Road subject to innundation after rain

Mosquito Waterhole
Flying Fox Swamp

Koolatah
Drumduff Road

Kangaroo Lagoon

20' 30' 40' 50' **144°** 10' 20' 30' 40' 50' **145°** 10' 20' 30' 40' 50'

13°

Cleveland Hill
326 m
Old Lockhart River
Second Red Rocky Point
Cat Reef

Round Point

First Red Rocky Point

Night Island

Hangklip Peak
375 m
Diamond
Reign Reefs

Table Mtn
461 m

S O U T H   P A C I F I C

O C E A N

Crocodiles and Box Jellyfish
Saltwater crocodiles inhabit coastal waterways
especially river estuaries. Swimming is not recommended.
Highly venemous box jellyfish infest these waters between
October and May. Swimming is not recommended.

Friendly Point

Blanchard
Reef
Sand Bank No 8
**Sandbanks
Nat Park**
Sand Bank -
No 7
First Three Mile Opening

Cape Sidmouth

Morris
Island
Reef
Ogilvie
Reef

KULLA
KULLA
Campbell
Point

C O R A L   S E A

McIlraith
Range
Noddy
Reef

14°

Lytton
Reef

Creech
Reef

Fife Island
Hay Island
**Claremont
Isles NP**
Colmer
Point
Wilkie I.
Magpie
Reef

G R E A T

Great Barrier Reef

Marine Park

Kulla
(McIlwraith Range)
National Park

Roberts
Point
Hannah I.
**Claremont
Isles NP**
Silver Plains
Fish Habitat
Area
Pelican I.
Burkitt I.
Hedge
Reef
Rooda
Reef
Wilson
Reef
Corbett
Reef

B A R R I E R

Silver Plains
Claremont Point
Grub
Reef
Tydeman
Reef

Port
Port Stewart
Princess Charlotte
Bay Fish Habitat Area
Evanson Point
Clack Islands
**Flinders Group
National Park**
King Island
Pipon Island

Stewart Rd
Fish Camp
Waterhole
Stanley Island
Nares Point
Flinders Island
Cape Melville
Mahina Monument
(1899 Cyclone Memorial)
Sand Bank
No 1 Reef

Cooktown
In 1770 Captain James Cook beached his
ship, the Endeavour, in a sheltered cove to
make repairs to damage from a coral reef.
Cooktown and the Endeavour River take
their names from this event.

Margaret Lagoon
KULLA
Heming Point
Blackwood Island
Pullen Point
Bathurst Head
Denham I.
**Melville
Range**
North Bay Point
South
Warden
Reef

Binyo
Timber
Reserve
LAMA LAMA
Cliff Islands
National Park
Princess
Charlotte
Bay Fish
Habitat
Area
Ninian
Bay
Barrow Point
Munro Reef
Stapleton I.

Yarraden
Lily Vale
Running
Creek
**Lama Lama
National Park**
**Cape Melville
National Park**
Cape Bowen
Combe I.
Ingram I.
Berwick I.
**Howick Group
National Park**
Jewell
Reef
Two Mile Opening

Developmental
Aloszville
Marina Plains
Old Kalpowar
WAKOOKA
Wakooka
Newton I.
Howick Island
Red Point
Cole Islands
Hampton I.
Crescent
Reef
Waining
Reef
Hicks Reef
Hilder
Reef

New
Bamboo
Violet
Vale
Lotus Bird
Lodge
Bizant
KALPOWAR
Murdoch Point
Day
Reef
Carter Reef
Yonge
Reef

Musgrave
Roadhouse
Boggy
Lagoon
**Rinyirru (Lakefield)
National Park**
Black Gun
Waterhole
NGULUN
Lizard Island
Resort
Palfrey I.
**Lizard Island
National Park**
Nymph I.
South Island
Eagle Islet
Pethebridge
Islets
Turtle Group
Nat Park
Eyrie Reef
Rocky Islets
**Three Islands Group
National Park**
Ribbon Reef

Glen Garland
Breeza Plains
Outstation
Barramundi
Waterhole
Beattie
KALPOWAR
Jeanne
River
Martin Reef

Artemis
Kalpowar
Lakefield
Pandanus Park
War Veterans
Retreat
Jack
Lakes
**Muundhi (Jack River)
National Park**
Munburra
Resources
Reserve
Lookout Point
Flattery
Harbour

Mary Valley
Kennedy
Lake
Road
Starcke
NP
Cape Flattery
Silica Mining Lease
Cape Flattery
Helsdon
Reef

New Dixie
**Alwal
National
Park**
OLKOLA
Hann River
Roadhouse
Kalinga
Koolburra
Peninsula Developmental
New Laura
Ranger
Twelve
Mile Hut
**Rinyirru (Lakefield)
National Park**
BALNGGARRAWARRA
Brown
Lake Coen
Couch Grass
Hut
Battle
Camp
**Melsonby
(Gaarraay)
NP**
DARRBA
Mount
Webb NP
Starcke
Glenrock
Parkers Hut
Elderslie
**Three Islands Group
National Park**
Low
Wooded
Island
Three Islands
Mackay
Reefs

Killarney
Alice Queen
Old Peninsula
King Mine
One Mile Ck
The Maytown Road
south from Jowalbinna was cut by hand in the
1870s and is believed to be the only road in
Queensland that has not been upgraded by
an engine-powered earth-moving machine.
Six Mile
Waterhole
Old
Laura
Battle
Lake
Emma
Sandy
Camp
Rd
Isabella
Falls
HOPE
VALE
Cape Bedford
South Cape Bedford
Elim
Hope Vale
Pullen
Reefs

Kimba
Kimba
Palmerville Rd
Fairview
Olive Vale
Laura
Deighton
The Battle Camp track to Laura and
Maytown was cut for miners travelling from
Cooktown. Attacks from Aborigines
particularly on Chinese, made the
journey very hazardous.
Endeavor
Falls
Marton
Endeavour River NP
Nob Point
Indian Head
Boulder
Reef
Williamson
Reefs
Egret Reef

The Desert
Pinnacles
Palmerville
AGAYRRA-
TIMARA
Split Rock
Art Site
Old Kennedy
Creek Mine
Crocodile
Cooktown
Mount Cook NP
Mt Cook 431 m
Monkhouse Point
Walker Bay
Grave Point
**Annan River
(Yuku Baja-Muliku)
Nat Park**
Archer Point
Trevethan
Falls
Walsh Bay
Annan River (Yuku Baja-Muliku) NP

Fairlight
Jowalbinna
Maytown Road
can be slow and
difficult going
Barrons Ra
Black Mtn Lookout
Black Mtn NP
Helenvale
Lions Den Hotel
Home Rule
Lodge
Obree Point
**Nat Park
Hope Islands**
Cairns
Reef

King Junction
Strathleven
Logan Jack
Memorial
Palmer Gold
Mining Area
**Palmer Goldfield
Resources Reserve**
WULBURJUBUR
Honey
Dam
Lakeland
WUNBUWARRA
Rossville
Cedar Bay
Cedar Bay NP
Cedar Bay
Rattlesnake Point (North Head)
Mt Finnigan
1148 m
Mt Boolbun
North
921 m
Wujal Wujal
Ayton
Bloomfield Track
Weary Bay
Cowie Point

20' 30' 40' **144°** 10' 20' 30' 40' **145°** 10' 20' 30' 40' 50'

Boab tree

Broome, Western Australia

Wave Rock Formation Near Hayden, Western Australia

Kata Tjuta, The Olgas

Island In Whitsundays, Queensland

Simpsons Gap, MacDonnell Ranges

Barron Falls, Queensland

Outback Emus, New South Wales

Humpback at Hervey Bay, Queensland

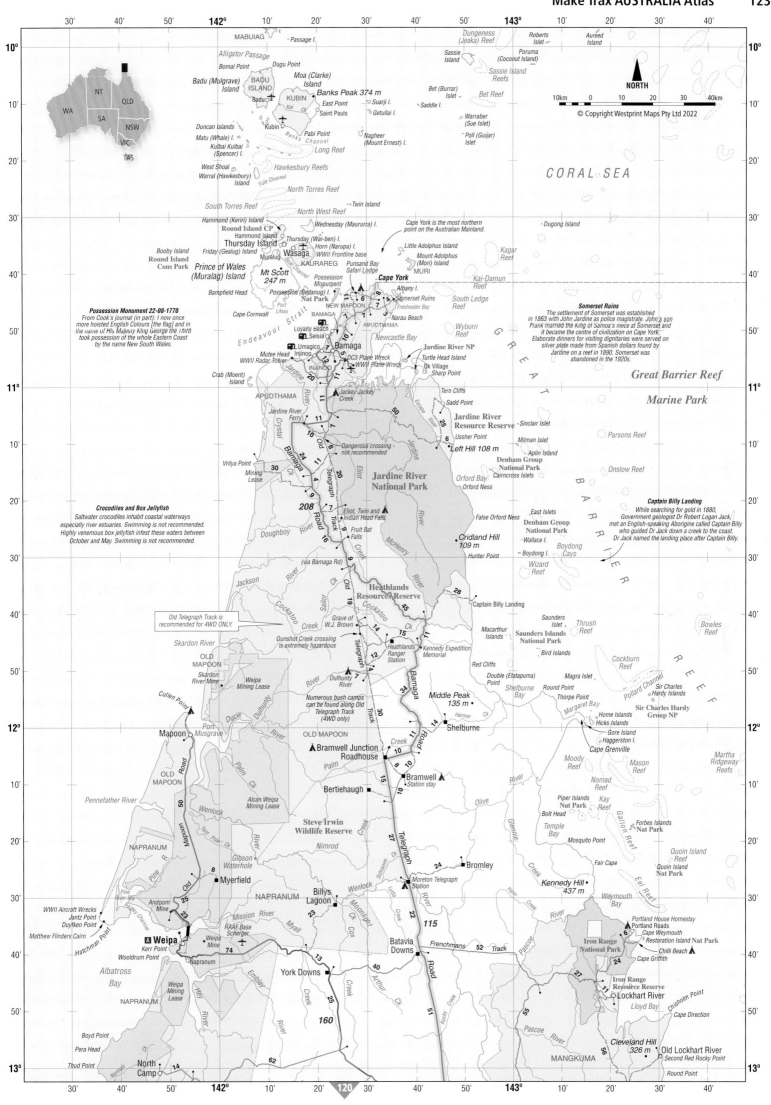

NORTH

10km 0 10 20 30 40km

© Copyright Westprint Maps Pty Ltd 2022

NT
QLD
WA
SA
NSW
VIC
TAS

B A S S   S T R A I T

King Island (inset)

Cape Wickham
Cape Farewell
Phoques Bay
Egg Lagoon
New Year Island
Christmas Island
Whistler Point
Lavinia Point
Yambacoona
Lavinia State Reserve
Reekara
KING ISLAND
Loorana
Cowper Point
Sea Elephant Bay
Naracoopa
Currie
Pegarah
Fraser Bluff
Lymwood
Yarrah Creek
Fitzmaurice Bay
Bold Head
Cataraqui Point
Grassy
Surprise Bay
Seal Bay
Stokes Point

Main map

Three Hummock Island State Reserve
Cape Keraudren
Coulomb Bay
Cape Rochon
Three Hummock Island
Cape Adamson
Cuvier Bay
Hunter Island Conservation Area
Hunter Island
Walker Island
Trefoil Island
Woolnorth Point
Ransonnet Bay
Cape Grim
Kangaroo Island
Robbins Island
Guyton Point
Bluff Point
Wind Farm
Cape Elie
North Point
Bluff Point
Montagu
Stanley
The Nut
Circular Head
A scenic coastal area with Aboriginal history
Smithton
Sawyer Bay
Crayfish Creek
Rocky Cape
Ann Bay
Christmas Hills
HWY
Forest
Rocky Cape National Park
Marrawah
Redpa
67
Irishtown
Rocky Cape
Sisters Beach
Boat Harbour
West Point
BASS
A2
Duck River
Mawbanna
75
Table Cape
Mawson Bay
West Point State Reserve
Roger River
Edith Creek
Lileah
Sisters Creek
Myalla
Wynyard
A2
Bluff Hill Point
Arthur River
Trowutta
Detention Falls Cons Area
Calder
Somerset
Burnie
Blythe River Cons Area
Arthur River
Dip Falls
Big Tree
Elliott
Sulphur Creek
Tarkine Forest Drive
Yolla
Stowport
Penguin
57
Couta Rocks
Frankland River
Rapid River
Henrietta
Ridgley
Riana
North Motton
Ulverstone
Temma
Horton River
Donaldson River Nature Recreation Area
Hellyer Gorge State Reserve
A10
68
Hampshire
South Riana
Preston
Sprent
Richardson Point
Hazard Bay
Arthur River
Savage River National Park
Parawee
Leven Canyon Regional Res
Nietta
Wilmot
Lake Paloona
Western River
Savage River Reg Res
Guildford
Black Bluff NCR
Gowrie Park
Arthur-Pieman Conservation Area
Explorer River
Waratah
44
Talbots Lagoon
Lake Lea
Moina
Mount Roland Res
Mt Norfolk 759 m
Sandy Cape
Luina
MURCHISON
Lake Cethana
Kenneth Bay
Savage River
Meredith Range Regional Reserve
Hatfield
43
Reynolds Falls NCR
Cradle Valley
Dove Lake
Lake Rowallan
Lagoon R
Pieman River State Reserve
Savage River
Cradle Mtn 1545 m
Lake Mackintosh
Granite Tor Cons Area
Lake Will
Lake Parangana
Conical Rocks Point
Corinna
Whyte River
Meredith Range Regional Reserve
Cradle Mountain-Lake St Clair National Park
Tikkawoppa Plateau Regional Reserve
Pieman R
Rosebery
Tullah
Lake Murchison
Murchison River
Mersey River
Bernafai Ridge Conservation Area
38
Lake Pieman
Montezuma Falls
S O U T H E R N   O C E A N
Mount Heemskirk Regional Reserve
Lake Plimsoll
Mt Ossa 1617 m
(Part of the Tasmanian Wilderness World Heritage Area)
Walls of Jerusalem National Park
Zeehan
A10
54
Eldon River
Trial Harbour
31
River
Lake Margaret
Mount Dundas Regional Res
B27
48
Henty River
Lake Burbury
Mt Olympus 1449 m
Lake St Clair
Please Note:
Many features on this map have been derived from Australian Government digital data and have not been thoroughly checked in the field by Westprint Maps.
Henty Dunes
Queenstown
Gormanston
LYELL
Macquarie Heads
Strahan
44
Crotty Dam
Crotty Cons Area
Derwent Bridge
Regatta Point
King River
Darwin Dam
88
A10
HWY
Cape Sorell
Macquarie Harbour
West Coast Range Res
Franklin River
Lake Burbury
Loddon River
Lake King

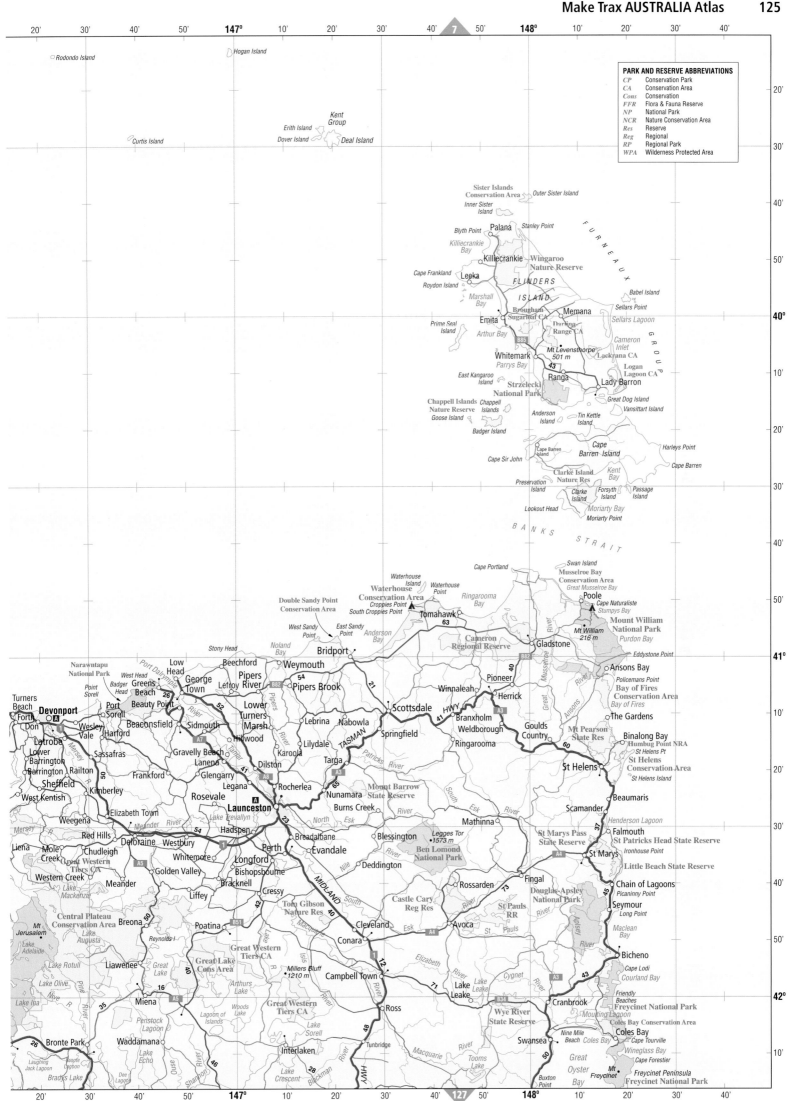

PARK AND RESERVE ABBREVIATIONS
CP   Conservation Park
CA   Conservation Area
Cons   Conservation
FFR   Flora & Fauna Reserve
NP   National Park
NCR   Nature Conservation Area
Res   Reserve
Reg   Regional
RP   Regional Park
WPA   Wilderness Protected Area

124

Arthur-Pieman Conservation Area
Kenneth Bay
Sandy Cape
Mt Norfolk
759 m

Savage River National Park
Parawee
Savage River Reg Res
Waratah
Luina
Savage River
Guildford

Western River
Explorer River
Savage River
Whyte River
Pieman River
Hatfield River

Preston
Lake Paloona
Lower Barrington
Barrington
Sassafras
Railton
50
Kimberley
Sheffield
West Kentish
Elizabeth Town
Leven Canyon Regional Res
Nietta
Wilmot
Leven River
Black Bluff NCR
Moina
Gowrie Park
Weegena
Deloraine
A5
Mersey River
Lake Cethana
Mount Roland Res
Liena
Mole Creek
Great Western Tiers CA
Chudleigh
Meander
Mole Creek Karst NP
Western Creek
Central Plateau Conservation Area
Breona

MURCHISON HWY
43

Pieman River State Reserve
Conical Rocks Point
Tikkawoppa Plateau Regional Reserve
Bernafai Ridge Conservation Area
Corinna

Meredith Range Regional Reserve

Reynolds Falls NCR

Cradle Valley
Dove Lake
Cradle Mtn 1545 m
Lake Will
Lake Mackintosh

Rosebery
Tullah
Granite Tor Cons Area
Lake Parangana
Lake Mackenzie

Cradle Mountain-Lake St Clair National Park
Mt Ossa 1617 m
(Part of the Tasmanian Wilderness World Heritage Area)

Walls of Jerusalem National Park
Mt Jerusalem
Lake Adelaide
Lake Rotuli
Liawenee
Lake Augusta

Montezuma Falls
38

Lake Pieman
Lake Plimsoll
Lake Murchison
Murchison River
Eldon River

Mount Heemskirk Regional Reserve
Zeehan
A10
31
54
Lake Margaret

Trial Harbour

Mount Dundas Regional Res
B27
48
Henty River

Lake Burbury
Mt Olympus 1449 m
Lake Ina
Miena
35

Please Note:
Many features on this map have been derived from Australian Government digital data and have not been thoroughly checked in the field by Westprint Maps.

Henty Dunes
Gormanston
Lake St Clair
Lake Echo

Queenstown
Crotty Dam
Crotty Cons Area
LYELL
88
Derwent Bridge
26
Bronte Park
Lake King William
Bronte Lagoon
Brady's Lake

Strahan
44
King River
Darwin Dam
Lake Burbury
HWY A10
Laughing Jack Lagoon
Dee Lagoon

Macquarie Heads
Regatta Point
Cape Sorell

Frenchmans Cap 1443 m
Franklin River
Loddon River
Tarraleah

West Coast Range Res
Sloop Point

Macquarie Harbour
Gould Point
Sarah Island Convict Ruins
Rum Point
Heritage Landing Nature Walk

Franklin-Gordon Wild Rivers National Park
(Part of the Tasmanian Wilderness World Heritage Area)

78
A10
Wayatinah
Lake Catagunya

Birthday Bay
Varna Bay

Birch Inlet
Spero River
Jane River
Gordon River
Maxwell River

Lake Curly
Mount Field National Park
Lake Repulse

Hibbs Bay
Point Hibbs
Endeavour Bay
Wanderer River

Mt Lewis 793 m
Denison River
Lake Gordon
Gordon Dam
Strathgordon
Lake Fenton
National Park Tyenna
Maydena
Styx River

High Rocky Point
Southwest Conservation Area
Olga River
Serpentine Dam
B61
62

43°

Low Rocky Point
Elliott Bay
Lewis River
Giblin River
Lake Pedder
Mt Anne 1425 m
Lake Judd
Mt Weld 1338 m

Nye Bay
Elliot Point
Davey River
Crossing River
Scotts Peak Dam
Edgar Dam
Gallagher Plateau

Mulcahy Bay
Brier Holme Head
Mt Hean 747 m
Mt Orion 1120 m
Huon River
Lake Picton

Svenor Point
Wreck Bay
Southwest National Park
(Part of the Tasmanian Wilderness World Heritage Area)
Lake Jupiter
Federation Peak 1224 m
Lake Geeves
Pine Lake

Davey Head
Port Davey
Bathurst Harbour
Old River
New River

Point St Vincent
Hilliard Head
Stephens Bay
Mutton Bird Island
Southwest Conservation Area
New River Lagoon
Oval Lake
Prion Bay

Window Pane Bay
Cox Bight
South West Cape
Telopea Point
Cox Bluff
De Witt Island
Flat Witch I.
Maatsuyker Island
Maatsuyker Group
Havelock Bluff
Point Vivian
Shoemaker Point

SOUTHERN   OCEAN

WA
NT
QLD
SA
NSW
VIC
TAS

NORTH

10km 0   10   20   30   40km

PARK AND RESERVE ABBREVIATIONS

CP	Conservation Park
CA	Conservation Area
Cons	Conservation
FFR	Flora & Fauna Reserve
NP	National Park
NCR	Nature Conservation Area
Res	Reserve
Reg	Regional
RP	Regional Park
WPA	Wilderness Protected Area

TASMAN SEA

Gravelly Beach, Frankford, Lanena, Glengarry, Legana, Rosevale, Dilston, Rocherlea, Targa, Nunamara, Launceston, Hadspen, Breadalbane, Perth, Evandale, Westbury, Whitemore, Longford, Bishopsbourne, Bracknell, Golden Valley, Liffey, Cressy, Deddington, Blessingtn, Mathinna, Burns Creek, Mount Barrow State Reserve, Legges Tor 1573 m, Ben Lomond National Park, Poatina, Tom Gibson Nature Res, Rossarden, Fingal, Castle Cary Reg Res, Avoca, St Pauls RR, Douglas-Apsley National Park, Cleveland, Conara, Ross, Campbell Town, Lake Leake, Great Western Tiers CA, Great Lake Cons Area, Waddamana, Interlaken, Lake Sorell, Lake Crescent, Tunbridge, Oatlands, York Plains, Parattah, Swansea, Coles Bay, Freycinet National Park, Freycinet Peninsula, Bicheno, Cranbrook, St Helens, Beaumaris, Scamander, St Marys, Falmouth, Chain of Lagoons, Seymour, Osterley, Bothwell, Jericho, Melton Mowbray, Tunnack, Woodsdale, Triabunna, Hamilton, Ellendale, Westerway, Kempton, Colebrook, Levendale, Louisville, Orford, Maria Island National Park, Buckland, Runnymede, Campania, Nugent, Bushy Park, Plenty, New Norfolk, Lachlan, Gretna, Rosegarland, Brighton, Bridgewater, Old Beach, Richmond, Sorell, Forcett, Copping, Dodges Ferry, Dunalley, Murdunna, Eaglehawk Neck, Tasman National Park, Glenorchy, HOBART, Fern Tree, Taroona, Kingston, Seven Mile Beach, Lauderdale, Primrose Sands, Koonya, Port Arthur, Judbury, Ranelagh, Longley, Grove, Huonville, Margate, South Arm, Nubeena, Franklin, Cradoc, Snug, Kettering, Woodbridge, Port Huon, Geeveston, Cygnet, Middleton, Verona Sands, Cairns Bay, Hartz Mountains NP, Dover, Strathblane, Alonnah, Adventure Bay, South Bruny National Park, Ida Bay, Southport, Catamaran, Cockle Creek

OUTBACK TRACKS AND TRIPS

The suggested 4WD tracks and trips listed below are all clearly highlighted and labelled on the atlas maps. To locate a track, simply refer to the page numbers shown.

The beauty of the Simpson Desert changes every day. The life-cycle of some plants is measured in days, perennial bushes in years and trees more than 100 years.
Photo by John Deckert, Westprint Maps.

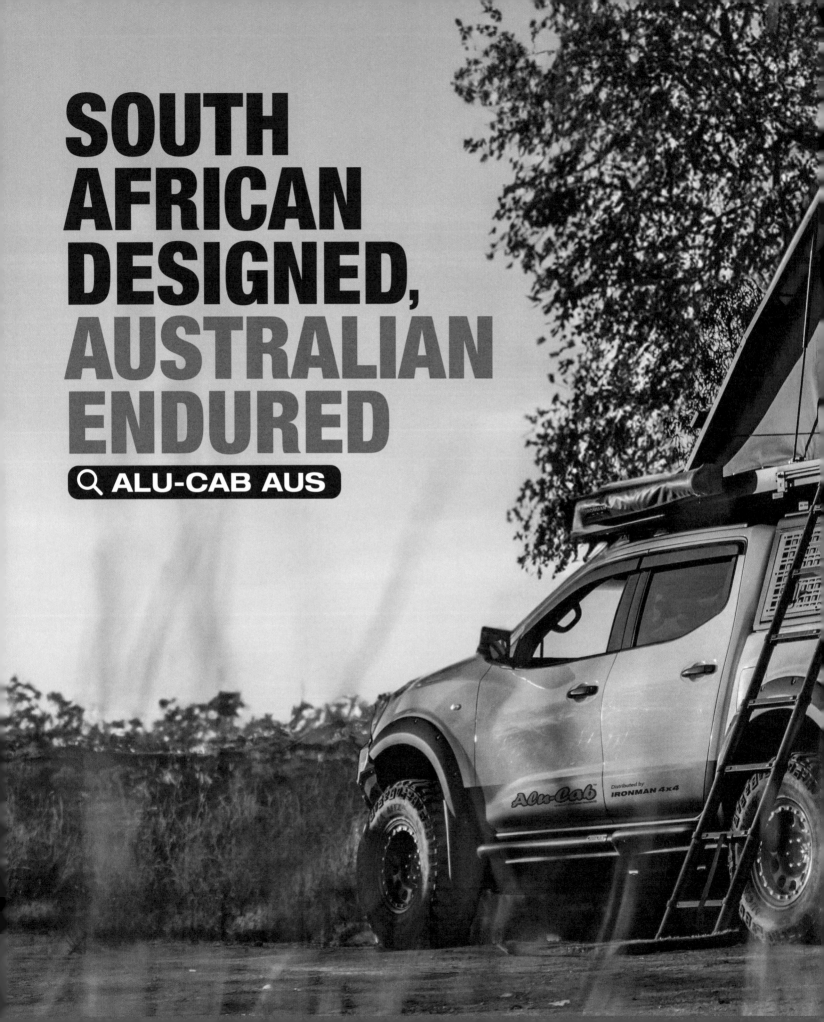

SOUTH AFRICAN DESIGNED, AUSTRALIAN ENDURED

🔍 **ALU-CAB AUS**